THE AMBASSADOR PREPARES FOR WAR

INTERNATIONAL SCHOLARS FORUM

A SERIES OF BOOKS BY AMERICAN SCHOLARS

7

THE AMBASSADOR PREPARES FOR WAR

The Dutch Embassy

of

Arnauld de Pomponne

1669–1671

by

HERBERT H. ROWEN

Department of History

State University of Iowa

Springer-Science+Business Media, B.V.

1957

ISBN 978-94-017-4587-1 ISBN 978-94-017-4778-3 (eBook)
DOI 10.1007/978-94-017-4778-3

Originally published by Martinus Nijhoff, The Hague, Netherlands in 1957.
Softcover reprint of the hardcover 1st edition 1957

In memory of my father

PREFACE

The scope of this study is narrow—the activities of a single ambassador for little more than two years. The problem it treats is wide and universal—the origins of a great war.

There can be no adequate history of the relations between states which does not take into account the knowledge, judgment and decisions of individual statesmen. Diplomatic history, though only a part, is a necessary part of the history of international relations. Within a more or less closely circumscribed range of possibilities, men in power choose between alternative policies, with results they may or may not have anticipated. The historian therefore can and should describe the past, present and future, as it were, of the historical persons whom he studies: the past which provides them with opportunities and limitations, both objective and subjective; the present in which they act; the future in which the consequences of their actions appear, for the most part beyond their control.

This is a study of the part played by a great diplomat—the perfect ambassador, his own age called him—in the formation of policy. My task has been a dual one. First, I have observed Arnauld de Pomponne at work. Second, I have attempted to evaluate the French plans for war against the Dutch republic, with particular attention to Pomponne's contribution to them.

I have not attempted to write either a general history of the diplomacy of the years before the Dutch War of 1672 or an account of the United Netherlands in the twilight years of De Witt's administration, though I have something to say about each.

Among all those who have read or listened to parts of this work at various stages of its preparation, I owe a special debt of gratitude to three: my wife, Mildred Ringel Rowen; my *maître* in history, Prof. Garrett Mattingly of Columbia University; and Prof. Pieter Geyl of the University of Utrecht. The *Commission des archives étrangères* of the French foreign ministry and the Bibliothèque de l'Arsenal in Paris graciously permitted the microfilming of manuscripts in their collections; I am particularly thankful to John Woodall for his aid in selecting these documents. I wish to express my gratitude to Dean Walter F. Loehwing for the assistance given me by the Graduate College of the State University of Iowa in defraying the costs of publishing this work. Parts of this work which previously appeared in the American Historical Review and the Journal of Modern History (my article, "John de Witt and the Triple Alliance," copyright 1954 by the University of Chicago) are reproduced with their permission.

A NOTE ON NAMES

Usage has been the main principle in the choice among various forms of names. Where standard English forms, e.g., The Hague and Flushing, exist, these are used. Otherwise, the modern Dutch form is employed, e.g., Nijmegen, not Nymwegen.

Political nomenclature in the later seventeenth century had certain accepted forms differing from both earlier and later usage.

The Dutch republic was usually called "Holland" by foreigners, but not by its citizens. I have employed the forms "the Netherlands" (conforming to the modern Dutch "Nederland"), "the United Netherlands," and "the United Provinces." The "States General" (in full, "The States General of the United Provinces of the Low Countries") is the accepted name for the government of the Union. Because the separate political rôle of the province of Holland is of essential significance, the name "Holland" is restricted to the province and never used for the whole country except within quotations, where context ordinarily makes the meaning clear. Similarly, the name "States of Holland" refers to the provincial assembly.

The term "the Low Countries" was normally employed by the English (and its equivalent, "les Pays Bas," by the French) for the southern provinces under Spanish sovereignty. This territory is also called the "Spanish Netherlands." The adjective "Belgian," though a modern usage, is occasionally employed for this area.

"Flanders" refers to the province in the "Low Countries," or sometimes, in quotations, to the whole of the Spanish Netherlands. "French Flanders" is the name for the French-held portion of historic Flanders, or for the entire French-held territory ceded by Spain to France along the southern border of the Low Countries.

No distinction is made between "England" and "Great Britain." The "empire" is used for the territory of the Holy Roman Empire, the "emperor" for its titular sovereign and reigning head of the House of Austria.

Iowa City, Iowa H. H. R.
September 8, 1955.

TABLE OF CONTENTS

Preface vii

Introduction: THE WAR OF 1672 — MASTERPIECE OF DIPLOMACY? 1

I POMPONNE, MAN AND STATESMAN. 4

II THE TRIPLE ALLIANCE 18
1667–1669

III PURPOSES AND PLANS 30
February, 1669

IV DUTCHMEN AND THEIR POLITICS 41
February, 1669 – May, 1670

V POSITIONS EXPLORED AND DEFINED 58
February–May, 1669

VI "CANTONMENT" — DE WITT'S SOLUTION 76
June, 1669 – May, 1670

VII SPAIN, SWEDEN AND SUBSIDIES 94
February, 1669 – May, 1670

VIII ALLIES TO THE EAST? 107
February, 1669 – May, 1670

IX THE DOVER TREATY 122
May–June, 1670

X UNEASY CALM 133
June–August, 1670

XI STORM OVER LORRAINE 143
September, 1670 – January, 1671

XII WHO WILL BELL THE CAT?. 158
January–April, 1671

XIII MISSION COMPLETED 177
April–July, 1671

XIV TARIFFS—THE LESSER "WAR" 185
1667–1671

Conclusion: POMPONNE, LIONNE AND LOUIS XIV . 197

Bibliographical Note 204

Index 207

ABBREVIATIONS

Arch. étr., Holl. : Archives du ministère des affaires étrangères, Paris, Correspondance de Hollande.

Bib. Ars. : Bibliothèque de l'Arsenal, Paris.

THE WAR OF 1672–MASTERPIECE OF DIPLOMACY?

In April 1672, Louis XIV invaded the United Netherlands. He was confident of swift triumph. Lionne, his foreign minister, had bought over the republic's allies and frightened her friends into neutrality. Louvois, his minister of war, had built up a huge army and a vast supply system to support it. Through the spring and summer of 1672, the king's troops swarmed over the land. One more thrust to The Hague, to Amsterdam, and all was won!

Final victory evaded the French armies. Soon it was they who fought almost without allies, while the Dutch, incredibly surviving, were befriended on every side. Only by abandoning his original war aims could Louis XIV persuade the Dutch, six years later, to accept an end to the fighting.

Something had gone wrong. The French armies had won battles and campaigns but not the war. Why?

Part of the answer lies in the mishaps and mistakes of the war itself. Even more is explained by the way in which Louis XIV decided upon the war and the plans he made for fighting it.

Most accounts of the origins of the Dutch War treat the French diplomatic preparations as a masterpiece of their kind.[1] One exception

[1] More than a century ago, François Mignet, receiving the direction of the archives of the Quai d'Orsay as his, the scholar's, share of the spoils of the 1830 revolution, turned his attention to this problem. The four volumes of his *Négociations relatives à la succession d'Espagne* (Paris, 1835–42), in the *Collection de documents inédits sur l'histoire de France*, spell out the story by means of selected diplomatic dispatches from the years 1659 to 1679. But the secondary works, almost exclusively eighteenth-century historical collections and writings, upon which Mignet drew for the narrative background of his tale, are now hopelessly outdated and limited. Virtually all the important specialized studies in this period come after Mignet, indeed build upon his work, so that his synthetic conclusions require considerable amplification and reinterpretation.

In his *Het voorspel van den oorlog van 1672: De economisch-politieke betrekkingen tusschen Frankrijk en Nederland in de jaren 1660–1672* (Haarlem, 1926), the modern Dutch historian Simon Elzinga brought valuable materials out of the dust of the archives into the light of print; but we cannot trust his explanations because a systematic bias in favor of the economic factor leads him to exaggerate and distort its rôle. (See the reviews by Pieter Geyl, in *History*, new ser., XIII [1928], 162–63, and Nicolaas Japikse, is Georges Pagès' study of the relations between Louis XIV and Frederick William II, the "Great Elector" of Brandenburg.[1] Where others praise the brilliance of the plans of Hugues de Lionne, the French foreign minister until 1671, Pagès berates him for inconsistency and ineptness. The admirers of Lionne emphasize his skill in stripping from the Dutch their partners in the Triple Alliance of 1668, so that at the beginning of the war, England and Sweden were leagued with France, not the United Provinces. Pagès, however, sees beyond 1672 to the failure of the French war plans, though he does not examine in detail just where they were at fault.

One purpose of this study is to answer in part the question, "How well-laid in fact were the French plans for the war of 1672?"

The formation of the French war plans can be studied only indirectly. No records were kept of the debates in Louis XIV's council of ministers, the *Conseil d'en haut*, and the strictest secrecy as to its proceedings was effectively maintained. Diplomatic correspondence and reminiscences therefore bring us as close to the object of our inquiry as we can come.

Important as were events elsewhere, especially at London and Vienna, it was upon the reports of Arnauld de Pomponne, French ambassador at The Hague from 1669 until 1671, that Louis XIV and Lionne depended most of all. It is in their dispatches to Pomponne that their policy-making can be examined most precisely and profoundly.

We are fortunate in possessing as well Pomponne's own relation of his embassy at The Hague. This is a considered account written after Pomponne had served throught the war as Lionne's successor in the foreign ministry.[2] The veils about mysteries of state were drawn aside for Pomponne, so that he was able to judge his own rôle at The Hague with a fuller knowledge of the elements of policy than one only an ambassador could possess.

Pomponne's own character and personality, his standards of judgment and view of the world and its ways, entered into his reports and opinions. Previous historians, unfortunately, have given us no clear picture of Pomponne, the man or the statesman. He is at most a dimly glimpsed wraith in the usual accounts of his time. Of all the great

in *Bijdragen voor Vaderlandsche Geschiedenis en Oudheidkunde*, IV [1928], 302–06). Keith Feiling has turned his brilliant analysis upon the whole period of diplomatic history from 1660 to 1672, with remarkable success, but his attention was focused on Britain and he did not draw heavily upon the French diplomatic archives (*British Foreign Policy: 1660–1672* [London, 1930]).

[1] *Le Grand Électeur et Louis XIV* (Paris, 1905).

[2] *La relation de mon ambassade en Hollande (1669–1671)*, ed. Herbert H. Rowen ("Werken uitgegeven door het Historisch Genootschap te Utrecht," 4th ser., no. 2) (Utrecht, 1955).

ministers of Louis XIV, he is probably the least well understood,[1] although a modern British historian has called him the "greatest of French envoys."[2]

The problem of comprehending Pomponne resolves itself for our purposes into two questions: First, why did fellow-diplomats and contemporary publicists agree that he was fundamentally a moderate man,[3] even though he served the king of France as foreign minister during the Dutch War and the War of the League of Augsburg, when most of them thought French policy most immoderately aggressive? Was he no more than the honest man of Sir Henry Wotton's quip, sent abroad to lie for the good of his country? The second problem, more frequently noted, is this: Why should Louis XIV, the cruel oppressor of Jansenism, have placed Pomponne, a member of the outstanding Jansenist family in France, in his highest councils? To this we might add another question: How could any honest Arnauld serve Louis XIV?[4]

Before we study Pomponne's Dutch mission in detail, we can find some answer to these general questions about his character by a brief examination of his ideas and conduct throughout his career.

[1] Georges Livet correctly remarks ("Louis XIV et les provinces conquises: État des questions et remarques de méthode," *XVIIe siècle*, II [1952], 484) that the edition by J. Mavidal of Pomponne's *Mémoires* (Paris, 1861) "contributes little" to the understanding of Pomponne, and that the materials on Pomponne published by Louis Delavaud, especially *Le marquis de Pomponne, ministre et secrétaire d'État aux affaires étrangères* (Paris, 1911) "give only a brief glimpse of the man and his work." The article by Henri Courteault in the *Dictionnaire de biographie française* (III [1939], cols. 890–97), is merely a summary of published materials. Pierre Varin writes in some detail about Pomponne in *La vérité sur les Arnauld* (Paris, 1847) (II, 41–179), but this author was an *érudit*, not a historian; his book bristles with hostility to the Arnauld family and, except for its archival materials, is little more than a piece of anti-Jansenist propaganda two centuries later. The portrait of Pomponne by the duke of Saint-Simon (*Mémoires*, ed. A. de Boislisle Paris, [1881–1928], VI, 337–50) is a masterpiece of characterization, but though the great memorialist here is in a favorable mood rare for him, his judgment must still be weighed in the light of the total evidence.

[2] Feiling, p. 193.

[3] For instance, Bishop Gilbert Burnet's contemporary description of him as a man of "great probity", in his *History of My Own Time* (ed. Osmund Airy [Oxford, 1897], I, 548).

[4] Cf. Charles Beard, *Port-Royal: A Contribution to the History of Religion and Literature in France* (London, 1861), I, 20; Saint-Simon, VI, 340.

CHAPTER I

POMPONNE, MAN AND STATESMAN

Simon Nicolas Arnauld, known to history as the marquis de Pomponne,[1] followed only one career, that of a government servant. For him, as for many others, it was the pathway to riches, influence and enhanced dignity. But he was not the slave of the career he had chosen, he would not sacrifice all things on the altar of success. The interplay of these two factors—a deep devotion to his career, and independence of it—helped to define his character as a man and as a statesman.

Government service seemed his fated career from the date of his birth in 1618. His forebears on both sides included noted royal servants. His own father, Robert Arnauld, seigneur d'Andilly, was high in Richelieu's councils, and some thought that he might even become the great cardinal's foreign minister. His adoption of Jansenism shattered his mundane career. Quitting the world of affairs himself, Andilly transferred his ambitions to Simon, and the sternness he showed all his children took for this favored son the compulsion to make good these aspirations.[2]

Pomponne's career in the government began under the sponsorship of Michel le Tellier, the minister of war.[3] From 1642 until 1647 he was an intendant at Casale, learning the tasks of government administration in the field and performing a number of diplomatic missions to Italian courts. In 1644 he was named for the first time a *conseiller d'État*—a post he always prized because it provided "pleasant occupation and wide knowledge of affairs."[4] Two years later he visited Rome;

[1] For convenience, we shall hereafter refer to Simon Arnauld as Pomponne, though he adopted the title of this estate only in 1660. Known in his youth as M. de Briottes, he later used his father's title, being known as M. d'Andilly *fils*. It is anachronistic to call him the marquis de Pomponne before 1682.

[2] C. A. Sainte-Beuve, *Port-Royal*, ed. R. L. Doyon and C. Marchesné (Paris, 1926–32), V, 98.

[3] Though Pomponne proved to be one of the most important of Le Tellier's protégés, Louis André, in his valuable study of Le Tellier as minister of war (*Michel le Tellier et l'organisation de l'armée monarchique* [Montpellier, 1906], does not discuss Pomponne's relationship to him.

[4] Pomponne to Feuquières, March 31, 1678, *Lettres inédites des Feuquières* (Paris,

the relaxed quality of its life drew from him only a scornful comparison with its ancient grandeur.[1] He did not believe in *dolce far niente.*

A year after returning to Paris in 1647, Pomponne was confronted by the great crisis of the Fronde. Le Tellier sent him to various royal armies as their intendant, in charge of all aspects of their activity but the purely military. The temporary disgrace of Le Tellier in 1651 led to the collapse of Pomponne's mission in Catalonia. By 1654, Pomponne again went on diplomatic mission, this time to the court of Mantua, where, on June 3, 1655, he was able to conclude a treaty of alliance with duke Charles III which saved Casale for France.[2]

The triumph of the royal party turned to Pomponne's disadvantage. The queen-mother, Anne of Austria, whose power it effectively restored, was a bitter foe of the Jansenists, to her a "new sect" of near-heretics. Considering Pomponne only as an Arnauld and hence as a Jansenist, she consistently rebuffed Mazarin's proposals to appoint him to various high posts. "You know why as well as I," the cardinal-minister wrote to Pomponne, reassuring him of his own esteem and affection.[3] The lesson was not lost on Pomponne. Recondite points of theology did not interest him, and he did not wish to sacrifice his career to a particular interpretation of the doctrine of grace. He remained loyal to his family and friends, but as persons—not as theological standard-bearers.

In May, 1660, Pomponne married Catherine Ladvocat, cousin of Nicolas Fouquet, the powerful superintendant of finances. Pomponne seemed destined for some new high post in government, for Fouquet's support outweighed Anne's opposition. In 1661 Pomponne's councilorship of state was renewed; his good favor at court was clear.

Fouquet's arrest at Nantes late in August was a "thunderbolt shattering all his hopes."[4] Pomponne was not arrested, however, though Fouquet had maintained contact with the leaders of Port-Royal through him; he was merely relegated by *lettre de cachet* (February 2, 1662) to

1845–46), IV, 193. Cf. the astute observation by Richard Pares (*King George III and the Politicians* [Oxford, 1953], p. 30) that historians too infrequently "have recognized the fact that men were in politics not only for party and for profit, but most of all for the due exercise of the talents God gave them, and for fun."

[1] Briottes (Pomponne) to Andilly, Sept. 30, 1646, Varin, II, 5.

[2] *Recueil des instructions données aux ambassadeurs et ministres de France: Savoie-Sardaigne*, II, ed. Horric de Beaucaire (Paris, 1899), 137, 173–80.

[3] Mazarin to Pomponne, July 16, 1659, *Mémoires de M. de Coulanges...*, ed. L. J. N. de Monmerqué (Paris, 1820), pp. 372–73; Mazarin to Fabert, Aug. 25, 1659, *ibid.*, pp. 373–74; Abraham de Wicquefort, *Histoire des Provinces Unies des Païs-Bas...*, ed. E. Lenting and C. A. Chais van Buren (Amsterdam, 1861–74), III, 33.

[4] Abbé Antoine Arnauld, *Mémoires*, in C. B. Petitot, *Collection de mémoires relatifs à l'histoire de France, depuis l'avènement de Henri IV jusqu'à la paix de Paris conclue en 1763* (Paris, 1820–29), XXXIV, 316–17.

Verdun, where his cousin, marshal Feuquières, was governor.[1] He took up residence at the abbey of Saint-Nicolas. When friends visited him later in the year they found him "much older and sadder." He "did not see when it would end, and was bored to madness."[2]

Though his friends stood by him in this time of difficulty,[3] those whose support now mattered most were Le Tellier, his first sponsor, and Claude le Peletier, *président à mortier* of the parlement of Paris. Le Peletier took the initiative in seeking relaxation of Pomponne's exile, while Le Tellier, closer to the king and better able to judge the royal intentions at a given moment, was more prudent. "We must await the end of the Fouquet business," was Le Tellier's judgment to Le Peletier.[4] It took their combined efforts, powerfully reinforced by the support of Turenne, the greatest of Louis' soldiers, to win permission early in 1663 for Pomponne to come closer to Paris, at La Ferté-sous-Jouarre, only 36 miles to the east.[5] Even after Pomponne was permitted to reside at his beloved name estate of Pomponne, at Lagny on the outskirts of Paris, in the mid-year of 1664, he was bedeviled by lack of things to do, "thinking no longer of anything but passing easily this time of disgrace."[6]

After Fouquet was condemned to perpetual imprisonment in December, 1664, Louis XIV relaxed his wariness regarding the friends of the fallen minister. Less than two months later, on February 2, 1665, the king authorized Pomponne to return to Paris.[7] Pomponne first visited Lionne, the foreign minister and his personal friend. Then, a week later, he saw the king and all the ministers. Though the king had just admitted, almost grudgingly, that Pomponne was loyal, intelligent and worthy of confidence, the royal look, Pomponne remarked, was "neither good nor bad, which is sufficient for one back from exile."[8]

By November, the king was less reserved. When Lionne, with Le Tellier's support, put forward Pomponne's name for ambassador to

[1] Petitot, "Notice sur Port-Royal," in *ibid.*, XXXIII, 160; Arnauld, p. 318; Thomas Pierre du Fossé, *Mémoires pour servir à l'histoire de Port-Royal* (Utrecht, 1739), p. 174.

[2] Abbé Matthieu Feydeau, quoted in Sainte-Beuve, V, 19, note.

[3] François Ravaisson-Mollien, ed., *Archives de la Bastille* (Paris, 1866–1904), II, *passim*; Ph. Tamizey de Larroque, ed., *Lettres de Jean Chapelain, de l'Académie Française* (Paris, 1880–88), II, 202–03; Beard, II, 56.

[4] Le Peletier to Pomponne, March 31, June 10, 1662, Ravaisson, II, 27, 44.

[5] *Ibid.*, II, 113–14, 123 note 1; Pomponne to Le Tellier, March 14, 1663, to Turenne, *ca.* March, 1663, *ibid.*, II, 122–23; Camille Georges Picavet, *Les dernières années de Turenne (1660-1675)* (Paris, 1914), p. 52.

[6] Arnauld, p. 340.

[7] Louis XIV to Pomponne, Feb. 2, 1665, Ravaisson, II, 398; Arnauld, p. 318; Coulanges, p. 384, note 3.

[8] *Ibid.*, pp. 385–88.

Sweden, Louis assented.[1] But, much as Pomponne wanted the post, he accepted only after he was assured that he would not have to finance it out of his own pocket. Because the king wanted the service "not of my wealth, but of my head," he was permitted to spend no more at Stockholm than he received.[2] In Sweden, Pomponne's expectation that diplomatic activity would exorcise his private demon of idleness proved vain. With Sweden isolated from the continent for months by the freezing over of the Belt and the Sound, his negotiations were slow and intermittent. The Baltic land was now "a country which only letters from family and friends make bearable," he wrote his father. "You can imagine what boredom I suffer."[3]

Escape from boredom was not the only benefit he sought, sometimes futilely, in an official career. He also wished to aid the advancement of his family. But he complained that his own success had not benefited his children. "Perhaps the star will change," he wrote, "and bestow its kind gifts upon our children."[4] The "star"—or rather the "Sun", to use Louis' own emblem—did begin to shine more brightly on the Arnaulds, and on the Jansenists generally. After the election of Cardinal Rospigliosi as Pope Clement IX in June 1667, Lionne and the papal nuncio, Bargellini, worked out a formula for settling the controversy between the Catholic authorities and the Jansenists.[5] The "Peace of the Church," as it was known, was vigorously supported by the ministers of Louis XIV, especially Lionne and Le Tellier, Pomponne's sponsors within the government.[6] Louis was pleased with the "Peace" and sternly rebuffed Father Annat, his Jesuit confessor, who charged it led to the ruin of religion and the State.[7]

Pomponne meanwhile won a reputation as a skillful diplomat at Stockholm.[8] In France, the king was impressed by the literary elegance of Pomponne's dispatches as well as by his abilities as an observer and judge of men and events.[9] It was a propitious moment for taking

[1] Arnauld, pp. 318–19.

[2] Pomponne to Andilly, Dec. 18, 1665, Coulanges, pp. 392–94; Arnauld, pp. 319–20.

[3] Feb. 12, 1667, Coulanges, pp. 416–17. Chapelain spoke of ennui as "the bitterness of his embassy." Chapelain to Heinsius, Feb. 8, 1668, Chapelain, II, 551.

[4] Pomponne to marquis Isaac de Feuquières, Sept. 4, 1667, Feuquières, II, 30.

[5] Nigel Abercrombie, *The Origins of Jansenism* (Oxford, 1936), p. 272.

[6] Charles Gérin, *Louis XIV et le Saint-Siège* (Paris, 1894), II, 11, 303; Augustin Gazier, *Histoire générale du mouvement janséniste depuis ses origines jusqu'à nos jours* (Paris, 1923–24), I, 182.

[7] *Ibid.*, I, 184.

[8] Pieter de Groot to John de Witt, July 14, 1668, *Brieven geschreven ende gewisselt tusschen den Heer Johan de Witt... ende de Gevolmaghtigden van den Staedt der Vereenighde Nederlanden* (The Hague, 1723–24), IV, 576. Hereafter cited as De Witt, *Brieven*.

[9] Chapelain to Heinsius, Feb. 8, 1668, Chapelain, II, 551; Varin, II, 50.

the king's notice. Godefroi count d'Estrades, the French ambassador at The Hague, had failed to prevent the conclusion of the Triple Alliance, and it was decided to replace him with Pomponne. In July, the king recalled Pomponne from Sweden. Two months later the diplomat arrived at Saint-Germain, where the king and the ministers received with great satisfaction his report on his "thorny embassy." This time there was no question of royal reticence. The king received Pomponne "most graciously," especially charming him "when he doffed the majesty and the proud, haughty air he wore in public." He also impressed Pomponne with his command of the details of his various diplomatic undertakings.[1]

The king's good favor was given meanwhile to Pomponne not only as a royal servant, but also as an Arnauld. That name now became one of high repute and honor at court. Louis was particularly delighted by the part played by Antoine Arnauld, Pomponne's uncle, in the conversion of marshal Turenne to Catholicism. To win the greatest soldier of the realm and its leading Huguenot for the king's own faith was like a victory on the battlefield. Louis personally instructed Pomponne to bring Antoine to court. No longer would *le grand* Arnauld have to stay in hiding from the king's police, as he had done for a quarter of a century.[2] The momentous day when his uncle was received by the king was linked with Pomponne's own career. That same evening Le Tellier told him that his appointment to The Hague would be made public the next day.[3]

On October 25, 1668, Pomponne received his official appointment as ambassador to the States General, but did not leave for his new post till the following February. He remained at The Hague until July two years later, returning to France only twice on short visits to confer with the king during royal tours of inspection of the conquered provinces in the Low Countries. During his stay in the Netherlands, his reports and counsel were an important element in the final crystallization of the French decision to wage war upon the Dutch republic, and the elaboration of the plans for its conduct. The king's satisfaction with his reports and endeavors was confirmed by his grant to Pomponne of the position in the council of State he requested in anticipation of the time when he would retire from his active career. Colbert, who

[1] Arnauld, p. 330.

[2] Du Fossé, p. 315; *Journal d'Olivier Lefèvre d'Ormesson, et extraits des mémoires d'André Lefèvre d'Ormesson*, ed. A. Chéruel (Paris, 1860–61), II, 558; marquis de Saint-Maurice, *Lettres sur la cour de Louis XIV, 1667–1670*, ed. J. Lemoine (Paris, 1910), pp. 239–40; Gazier, I, 184.

[3] Ormesson, II, 558.

corresponded directly with Pomponne concerning matters of trade and navy, supported Pomponne's request, as did his personal friend Lionne. It was Colbert who first informed Pomponne of the appointment.[1]

During his second visit to Flanders (May-June, 1671), Pomponne was informed that he must go to Stockholm again in an effort to draw the Swedes out of the Triple Alliance. He found the situation there much as he had anticipated: they were difficult to negotiate with, thinking only of getting pay, not of deserving it.[2] Other difficulties arose from the uncertainties in French policy-making. At one point, having pressed for a quick reply to his proposals, he was thrown off balance by orders from France to delay concluding an alliance: the French court had not yet decided whether it would be better to purchase the assistance of the dukes of Brunswick-Lüneburg or of the king of Sweden. Now he had to dillydally—but without seeming to! Only the "natural slowness" of the Swedes saved him from "great embarrassment," for he feared lest they realize that they were not required and at once take up his prior offers.[3] Pomponne was annoyed, too, that his negotiation had been undercut in this fashion. He wrote to Lionne early in September that he wished very much he had not come to Stockholm.[4] He began to look forward to another period of boredom "in a languishing negotiation, with little repute."[5]

Lionne was no longer alive when Pomponne wrote this complaint. When Pomponne heard the news of Lionne's death on the first day of September, he sincerely mourned a friend who "had always supported him." A report in the *Gazette de Hollande* that he might succeed Lionne did not arouse his hopes: "being so far away from court, where I expected no other recommendation than that of my services, I scarcely believed myself to be in a position to seek the office of secretary of state."[6] At first the "informed" public thought that Colbert de Croissy, brother of Jean Baptiste Colbert, was the leading candidate, with archbishop Bonzy of Toulouse, former ambassador to Spain and Poland, close behind him.[7] But the public, informed or otherwise, cast

[1] Lionne to Pomponne, Nov. 22, 1669, Bibliothèque de l'Arsenal, Paris, MS 4712, fo. 143; Colbert to Pomponne, Nov. 25, 1669, *ibid.*, MS 4586, fo. 73; Louis XIV to Pomponne, Nov. 29, 1669, *ibid.*, MS 4712, fo. 148; Pomponne to Lionne, Nov. 28, 1669, Archives du ministère des affaires étrangères, Paris, Correspondance de Hollande, vol. 89, fo. 431.

[2] Pomponne, "Ambassade extraordinaire de Suède 1671," Bib. Ars., MS 4715, fo. 145.

[3] *Ibid.*, fos. 151–53.

[4] Pagès, p. 265, note 3.

[5] Pomponne, "Ambassade de Suède 1671," fo. 153.

[6] *Ibid.*, fo. 154.

[7] Ormesson, II, 613; De Groot to De Witt, Sept. 4, 1671, *Lettres de Pierre de Groot à Abraham de Wicquefort (1668–1674)*, ed. F. Krämer ("Werken uitgegeven door het His-

no ballots in France in 1671, and Louis XIV decided this new and important appointment without consultation. He selected Pomponne because he had "performed well" in his diplomatic posts,[1] and made arrangements by which Pomponne could purchase the office of secretary of state from Berni, Lionne's son.[2] Thankful as he was to the king, Pomponne was aware that things might not always go as well.

> Thus [he wrote later], I saw myself suddenly elevated to one of of the most important posts in the state, without being obligated to anything except the single action of the king, and having undergone none of the difficulties and anxieties always attached to claims and solicitations at court. All the same, I may say that I did not misunderstand fortune because she presented herself to me in a pleasant aspect; that, not allowing myself to be overwhelmed by her favors, I kept always in mind her native inconstancy; and that, when she seemed to be thrusting more gifts upon me than I could bear, I did not forget that a wise man can place no confident reliance upon them.[3]

While Louvois, the son of his old friend Le Tellier, performed, not unskillfully,[4] the duties of his office until his return, Pomponne had to stay on at Stockholm. By early December, he completed a treaty of alliance, with only the exact amount of the French subsidies left open. "That very night, only a few hours after the (Swedish) deputies had left," Pomponne sailed from Stockholm.[5] After reaching Hamburg, he hastened home over bad roads, through wintry weather, arriving at Saint-Germain on January 12, 1672. The king talked over the state of affairs with him in private conference the very same evening, the next day he entered the *Conseil d'en haut* as a minister, and three days later he took his oath as secretary of state for foreign affairs. The king accepted his proposals for maintenance of the re-established Swedish

torisch Genootschap te Utrecht," 3rd ser., no. 5) (The Hague, 1894), pp. 43–44; *The Despatches of William Perwich, English Agent in Paris, 1669–1677*, ed. M. B. Curran ("Camden Series," 3rd ser., no. 5) (London, 1903), pp. 165–66.

[1] Charles Dreyss, ed., *Mémoires de Louis XIV pour l'instruction du Dauphin* (Paris, 1860), II, 520–21. Cf. De Groot to Wicquefort, Sept. 13, 1671: "It is a good reward for six years in the embassies." De Groot, p. 54.

[2] Louis XIV to Pomponne, Sept. 5, 1671, Coulanges, pp. 434–35; Pomponne, "Relation de Suède 1671," fo. 154; Arnauld, p. 355.

[3] Pomponne, "Relation de Suède 1671," fo. 154. Cf. a similar statement by his brother, in Arnauld, p. 339.

[4] Ezéchiel Spanheim, *Relation de la Cour de France en 1690*, ed. Émile Bourgeois (Paris and Lyons, 1900), pp. 330–31, reporting the recollections of diplomats then at the French court.

[5] Pomponne, "Relation de Suède 1671," fos. 154–61. Lavisse (*Histoire de France depuis les origines jusqu'à la Révolution française*, VII[2] [Paris, 1906], 305), apparently relying on an unclear passage in Mignet (III, 330), thought that Pomponne remained in Sweden at his own request.

alliance, and he could feel, as he began his new tasks, that he had fulfilled his assigment at Stockholm.[1]

Apart from the conclusion of the Swedish business, there was little major diplomatic activity to hold his attention.[2] In April the war against the Dutch began. The start of the campaigning placed the chief burden of activity upon Louvois, now war minister. Louvois wished to run the war against the United Provinces in his own way, as his own affair, and inevitably came into conflict with Pomponne. The first clash occurred in late June of 1672, when the States General, with their eastern defenses in almost complete collapse, sent a delegation to Louis' camp to offer advantageous terms for peace.

Pomponne argued for accepting the Dutch offer: its terms would end the war with a glorious victory for France; the menace of a combination of powers against France would be smashed even before it was formed. But Louvois, in his ignorance of the Dutch spirit, thought that the envoys from The Hague would sign anything. He persuaded Louis to demand conditions that would have destroyed the effective independence of the United Provinces. The States General, preferring to fight in such a case, rejected these terms. Afterward the king seems to gave realized that Louvois, by playing on his love of glory, had led him into needless difficulties.[3] Pomponne himself has left no explicit defense of his position at this time, but we may well imagine his attitude from his brother's savage criticism of Louis' decision:

> Everyone pays M. de Pomponne the honor of believing that he favored peace. But the contrary view prevailed, however, and we must believe rightly so, for the king allowed himself to be

[1] Pomponne, "Relation de Suède 1671," fo. 161; Pagès, p. 267.

[2] Pomponne's career at this point briefly crossed that of the great thinker Leibniz. The French minister was asked to bring before the king a plan drawn up by the young mathematician-philosopher for the court of J. P. von Schönborn, elector of Mainz. Pomponne never learned specifically that it provided for a French attack upon Egypt rather than the Dutch republic, but the first clear indication of its nature drew from him the blunt comment, "I have nothing to say about the plans for a holy war, but you know that they have ceased to be in fashion since St. Louis." G. Guhrauer, *Kurmainz in der Epoche von 1672* (Hamburg, 1839), I, 294; Paul Ritter, *Leibniz Aegyptischer Plan* (Darmstadt, 1930). The proposal for a new crusade was indeed more academic and lifeless than a pure intellectual exercise would have been, for it disregarded the difficulties in the way of conquest of distant, defended lands, demonstrated only a few years before in the failure of the French expedition against Gigeri (Djijelli) in Algeria. If it had not been for the merited fame of Leibniz in the realm of thought, his plan would have stayed buried and deservedly forgotten.

[3] Mignet, IV, 22, 31–37; Camille Rousset, *Histoire de Louvois et de son administration politique et militaire* (Paris, 1862–63), I, 376–79; Burnet, I, 576-77; H. C. Foxcroft, ed., *A Supplement to Burnet's History of My Own Time . . .* (Oxford, 1902), p. 185; (Charles Auguste marquis de la Fare), *Mémoires et réflexions sur les principaux évenemens du Règne de Louis XIV . . .* (new ed., Amsterdam, 1755), pp. 86–87; Antoine marquis de Feuquières, *Mémoires historiques et militaires . . .* (Amsterdam, 1735), I, 111–13.

> won over to it. Indeed, there is the greatest of pleasures for a prince in love with glory in seeing himself at the head of a victorious army, able to carry his conquests where he pleases. If England had not failed him, if some slight impatience to see Versailles again had not slackened the ardor of his troops by depriving them of his presence, he might have carried out his great decision. It must also be granted that he rose to greater fame because the war continued. Otherwise, no one would have believed that he would be able by his forces alone not only to resist all the powers of the empire, Spain and the United Provinces, but even to make considerable gains over them each year. To be sure, these are weighty reasons for approving the resolutions that were taken then. But, on the other hand, if we consider how much blood and how many millions this glory cost us, there may be a few to hold it bought most dearly...[1]

Meanwhile, at The Hague, John de Witt resigned his office, and the government fell into the eager grip of William III. Then, on August 20, a mob lynched the fallen grand pensionary and his brother Cornelius. To Pomponne, De Witt's murder was always a "black deed," a "tragic *(funeste)* death," and he honored the grand pensionary as "the first man of his republic and one of the most capable ministers of his time."[2]

Once the French armies proved incapable of transforming their early triumphs into total victory, diplomatic activity again became important. To prevent the German princes from uniting against Louis, Pomponne plied them with his usual persuasive arguments, although Turenne's repeated victories in Alsace and the Rhineland until his death in 1675 were perhaps reasons of greater cogency.[3] Louvois, now openly the rival of the man whose governmental career his father had sponsored and supported, and whose aid he himself had "beseeched most humbly" in 1669,[4] interfered where he could. He persuaded the king to re-establish Roman Catholicism in the conquered provinces, at the very time when Pomponne warned that the Protestant powers would turn against France if the war took on a religious character.[5] One minor negotiation which Louvois conducted was kept secret from Pomponne.[6] More important was Louvois' opposition to Pomponne's efforts to prevent the war in Germany from spreading. Pomponne urged the French representatives at the peace conference which opened at Cologne in

[1] Arnauld, pp. 346–48.
[2] Pomponne, *Mémoires*, II, 488, 492, 494.
[3] Bertrand Auerbach, *La diplomatie française et la cour de Saxe* (*1648–1680*) (Paris, 1887), p. 373.
[4] Louvois to Pomponne, May 14, 1669, Bib. Ars., MS 4586, fo. 27.
[5] Pomponne to duke d'Estrées, Aug. 12, 1672, Gérin, II, 482–83.
[6] *Ibid.*, II, 491–92, note 4.

1673 to seek an end to the war, but Louvois assured them that even if all Europe joined together against France, there would be no danger. French and imperial intransigeance combined to make the conference a failure.[1] Yet Pomponne continued to hope for peace, believing that sometimes it comes when most talk is of war.[2]

By October, 1673, public pressure for peace was strong. Colbert, already aghast at the failure of his great handiwork of the economic reorganization of France, looked forward to the end of hostilities. As for Louvois, however, a British agent at Versailles found him "very merry" at the prospect that the war would go on.[3] Observers began to notice a decline in Pomponne's favor. "Gentle" with those having business with him, he was blamed by the king for lacking the vigor of his fellow-ministers.[4] By 1674, Lionne's elaborate structure of alliances had proved useless; many of the erstwhile friends of France were in the camp of her foes. Louis began to understand why Pomponne distrusted a complex system of alliances, but from this attitude he drew Louvois' conclusion, not Pomponne's. Authority in himself alone, Louis then wrote, "is an advantage I have against my enemies during this entire war."[5] In the debates in the *Conseil d'en haut*, as Louvois' arrogant policy won increasing support from the king, Pomponne's arguments on behalf of conciliation and moderation fell on ever less sympathetic ears.[6]

After 1676, Pomponne's diplomatic activity centered on the negotiations between the belligerents at Nijmegen. Though Louis' armies continued to win most of the victories on the battlefields, Pomponne directed the efforts of the French negotiators essentially toward the goals of ending the war and breaking up the coalition against France. He drew upon his deep knowledge of the Dutch to win them away from the grand alliance. First, he sacrificed Colbert's high tariff of 1667,[7] then he played upon the fears of the Dutch republicans that the stad-

[1] Lavisse, p. 379; cf. J. B. H. R. Capefigue, *Louis XIV, son gouvernement et ses relations diplomatiques avec l'Europe* (Paris, 1837–38), II, 1, 270–71, and Jacques Droz, *Histoire diplomatique de 1648 à 1919* (Paris, 1952), p. 34.

[2] Mme. de Sévigné to Mme. de Grignan, reporting a remark by Pomponne to Hacqueville, Nov. 2, 1673, Sévigné, *Lettres*, ed. G. Gailly, I, (Paris, 1953), 624.

[3] Perwich to Arlington, Oct. 18, 29, to Williamson, Oct. 18, Nov. 3, 1673, Perwich, 267, 269–72.

[4] Primi Visconti, *Mémoires sur la cour de Louis XIV*, ed. trans. Jean Lemoine (Paris, 1908), pp. 34–35.

[5] Louis XIV, "Fragment sur la campagne de 1674," *Oeuvres de Louis XIV* (Paris, 1806), III, 453–56. For a critique of French policy toward Germany in this period, see Auerbach, pp. 397–98.

[6] Rousset, III, 85, 103.

[7] Charles W. Cole, *Colbert and a Century of French Mercantilism* (New York, 1939), I, 449–50.

holder William III was trying to make himself a dynastic monarch—it was almost as if he were negotiating with the ghost of John de Witt.[1]

Though Franche-Comté was almost the only large and important French gain,[2] Louis' adulators proclaimed that he had reached "the summit of human glory," and bestowed upon him the appelation of "*le Grand.*" Despite Pomponne's successful direction of the negotiations at Nijmegen, he was dismissed from office in November, 1679, not long after the treaties of peace were all at last signed. Louis wished more substantial glory than Nijmegen; in his own words, "A lofty heart is difficult to make content and cannot be fully satisfied except by glory."[3] He complained, too, that Pomponne "lacked the grandeur and force one should have in executing the orders of a king of France who is not unfortunate." He felt that his foreign minister's "complaisance and goodness," combined with "weakness, stubbornness and lack of assiduity," had cost him dearly at Nijmegen.[4] Also contributing to Pomponne's downfall was the rivalry of Colbert and Louvois with him. Both had desired his office, but Colbert furnished the occasion for his dismissal on the grounds that he had gone off to his name estate at Pomponne instead of bringing to the king eagerly awaited dispatches on the projected marriage of the duke of Orléans. Colbert's brother, Croissy, was appointed in Pomponne's place.[5]

Pomponne's dismissal turned out to be a disgrace with a difference. Despite his criticism, the king recognized that Pomponne had never been disloyal and paid him unusual personal honor for one turned out of office. He was not exiled, and retained the title of minister of state and his pension of 20,000 francs. But it was still a disgrace and a blow to Pomponne; he lost his influence over policy, his post of activity, his opportunity to aid his own.

Pomponne and his family went off to his name estate to live. By February of 1680, the king's ire against him evaporated. In a personal audience with him, the king promised to aid his family,[6] and Pomponne made three more visits to court by mid-March.[7] It was not very long before the king made good his promise. In 1682, he elevated the estate of Pomponne to a marquisate, and in subsequent years granted

[1] Capefigue, II, 71–72, 79–80.

[2] Cf. Lavisse, pp. 346–48; Charles Gérin, "La disgrâce de M. de Pomponne (18 Novembre 1679)," *Revue des questions historiques*, XXIII (1878), 68.

[3] Louis XIV, "Relation de la campagne de 1678, et résultat de la paix de Nimègue," *Oeuvres*, IV, 143–76.

[4] Louis XIV, "Réflexions sur le métier du Roi," *Mémoires*, II, 521.

[5] Rousset, II, 571–74.

[6] Tourmont to Feuquières, Feb. 8, 1680, Feuquières, *Lettres*, V, 86.

[7] Mme. de Pomponne to Feuquières, March 21, 1680, *ibid.*, p. 117.

regiments to two of Pomponne's sons and an abbey to a third.

Pomponne's old demon, idleness, did not lose the opportunity afforded him by Pomponne's fall from power. The erstwhile minister soon complained of being "out of affairs and almost out of news," though he would gladly forgo "for all time" the knowledge of secrets of state.[1] To keep his mind busy, he began to write a series of memoirs. These are not the story of his own life, but relations of his Dutch and second Swedish missions giving a strikingly impersonal and objective analysis of the policy and character of all the more important states.[2] Recalling that in 1671 he had received news of his appointment as foreign minister with thoughts of the fickleness of fate, he wrote:

> I cannot praise God too greatly for having then inspired such sentiments in me, and for having maintained them in me for the eight years during which I filled that post, for it is to them that I owe, I do not know whether I can say the firmness, but at least the submission and the tranquility with which God caused me to accept the overturn of my fortune and a disgrace which I may believe with justice I did not in any way deserve.[3]

Pomponne soon disappeared from the arena of public attention. His name was seldom mentioned; his retirement seemed permanent, though now and again he was seen at court and received by the king.[4] The years passed by, filled with the violent, arrogant diplomacy favored by Croissy and Louvois and more in keeping with Louis' image of himself than Pomponne's system had been. Then, in 1691, Louvois at last drew upon himself the wrath of the monarch: the success of William III's Grand Alliance was proof that Louvois' bullying, for all its moments of triumph, ended ultimately in disaster. Louvois' brusqueness, too, won him the enmity of the ever more influential Madame de Maintenon. Worst of all, he had forgotten that a royal servant, always subordinate, must portray his successes as the king's, not his own, that Louis XIV would brook no new Richelieu or Mazarin. In August, 1691, Louvois died on the eve of public disgrace, unregretted by his master.[5]

On the very day of Louvois' death,[6] Louis XIV astounded the world

[1] Pomponne to Feuquières, March 9, 1680, *ibid.*, p. 102.
[2] Cf. Varin, II, 43; Pagès, "L'histoire diplomatique du règne de Louis XIV: Sources et état des travaux," *Revue d'histoire moderne et contemporaine,"* VII (1906), 658.
[3] Pomponne, "Relation de Suède 1671," fo. 154.
[4] Saint-Simon, VI, 348.
[5] Cf. Léon Lecestre, ed., *Mémoires de Saint-Hilaire* (Paris, 1903–06), II, 200; La Fare, pp. 297–305.
[6] Saint-Simon, III, 142.

by calling Pomponne back into active political life. His purely honorific status of minister of state was transformed into actual membership once more in the *Conseil d'en haut*. Croissy was not dropped from the council or from his secretaryship of state, but shared with Pomponne, now past seventy years of age, the function of debate and advice on foreign affairs, so that they were actually co-ministers for foreign affairs. The grueling task of preparing dispatches and running the foreign office as secretary of state remained Croissy's. The king also took the occasion to abolish all ranks of precedence within the council; the actual seating placed Pomponne in the middle position.[1]

Louis XIV used the opportunity of Pomponne's recall to office to devise an end to the hostility between the Colberts and the Pomponnes—though when he had begun his personal rule he had looked upon dissension among this ministers as assurance that none would aspire to Mazarin's post. The king now sponsored the betrothal of Pomponne's daughter, Catherine Félicité, and Croissy's son, the marquis de Torcy. Though Pomponne sought to overcome Croissy's hostility,[2] his grumpy, gouty colleague did not really forget bygones. The marriage of their children was not performed till after Croissy's death in 1696, and then the king insisted that the intervening period of mourning be shortened to a few weeks.[3] Torcy became secretary of state for foreign affairs; Pomponne remained minister of state for foreign affairs and superintended Torcy's performance of the workaday tasks of his office. Torcy drafted dispatches, but Pomponne presented correspondence to and from ministers abroad in the council. Ambassadors were received at Pomponne's residence, with Torcy in attendance, except at Versailles, where they shared the lodgings assigned to the foreign secretary. The young couple were not wealthy, but the king saw to the improvement of their fortunes. In the joint lodgings, as Saint-Simon noted, "they all lived in great and praiseworthy unity."[4]

Pomponne's tasks thus kept him busy without exceeding the limited energies of a septuagenarian. He clung to office. On learning of the retirement of Claude le Peletier, he told the king, "This retirement, Sire, makes M. le Peletier as worthy of praise as I am of shame, at my age, for not having the courage to imitate him."[5] Pomponne and Torcy

[1] *Mémoires de l'abbé de Choisy pour servir à l'histoire de Louis XIV*, ed. de Lescure (Paris, 1888), I, 106.
[2] Saint-Simon, VI, 349.
[3] Bishop Bossuet to abbé Bossuet, July 29, 1696, J. B. Bossuet, *Correspondance*, ed. C. Urbain and E. Levesque (Paris, 1909–25), VIII, 15–16.
[4] Saint-Simon, III, 141–44.
[5] Sainte-Beuve, IX, 138.

between them directed the negotiation of the compromise peace of Rijswijk (Ryswick) in 1697 and of the treaties of partition of the Spanish monarchy which marked the next two years.[1]

In the ninth month of the year 1699, in the eighty-first year of his age, Pomponne died suddenly of a gastric ailment.[2] The marquis de Sourches, in his usual terse style, recorded that he was "universally regretted, and it was certainly a great loss for the king, the state and all good men *(honnêtes gens)*." The king granted his widow a pension of 12,000 *livres*, and Torcy became minister of state at once.[3] Only Torcy, his son-in-law, lived up to the ambitions which Pomponne once held for his family: his own children did little of note.[4]

In retrospect, Pomponne's career appears as a sustained effort to refute the Machiavellian image of politics. His answer to the vexing casuistry of political and moral life was to stress the uncertainty and limitedness of all human things, but to act within those limits, for good if possible but always seeking to avoid evil.

It was this character, these ideas, these values which Pomponne brought with him when, in the bleak winter of early 1669, he traveled across the plain of northern France and Belgium, and then by ship to Holland, to represent in a fateful hour the interests of France in a land of erstwhile friendship.

[1] J. B. Colbert, marquis de Torcy, *Mémoires* . . . (The Hague, 1756), I, 43.
[2] Saint-Simon (VI, 351) tells us he ate too much cold veal and peaches.
[3] *Mémoires du marquis de Sourches sur le règne de Louis XIV*, ed. G. J. de Cosnac and A. Bernard (Paris, 1882–83), VI, 187–88.
[4] Saint-Simon, VI, 353–54.

CHAPTER II

THE TRIPLE ALLIANCE
1667–1669

The specific causes of the war of 1672 can be traced back no further than the Triple Alliance of January 23, 1668, in which the Dutch republic joined with the kingdoms of Great Britain and Sweden to oppose the conquest of the Spanish Netherlands by France. In no sense whatever was the war the culmination of a long enmity between the two states of France and the United Provinces. They were, to the contrary, traditional friends and allies.

Ever since the beginning of the Dutch war of independence a century before, their common hostility to Spain had bound them to each other. In many a moment of peril, each had been saved from the triumph of Spanish arms because the other was also fighting Spain, on the other side of the Low Countries. By the middle of the 1630's, the initiative, and hence the hope of final victory, began at last to pass to the two foes of Spain. In 1635 they agreed to join in the conquest of the Spanish Netherlands, affirming their will to seek only their mutual advantage in the promise not to make any separate peace with the enemy. But, as the hope of victory came closer to realization, a new spirit rose in the United Provinces. The princes of Orange remained constant in their adherence to the French alliance, but the merchant oligarchs increasingly felt that defeated Spaniards would be less dangerous neighbors than victorious Frenchmen. The old proverb, *Gallus amicus non vicinus*,[1] became popular again. The Spaniards were ready to conclude peace with the United Provinces in order to continue more effectively their war with France. Their negotiators at Münster, playing with masterly skill upon Dutch anxieties, at last persuaded the representatives of the States General to sign a separate treaty of peace. Dutch violation of the pledge of 1635 came at the very time when

[1] Einhard, the biographer of Charlemagne, spoke of a "Greek (Byzantine) proverb": *ΤΟΝ ΦΡΑΝΚΟΝ ΦΙΛΟΝ ΕΞΕΙΣ, ΓΕΙΤΟΝΑ ΟΥΚ ΕΞΕΙΣ.* (*Vita Karoli*, 16, 4.)

Spanish collapse seemed imminent. Victory was snatched away from France.[1]

France and Spain fought on for years in single combat. Mazarin made one brief effort to win back the Dutch as allies by supporting the stadholder William II in his bold drive to make the States General do his bidding. But William died in that same year, 1650, before he could consolidate his gains, and the republican (States) party thrust its Orangist adversaries from every place of power. The posts of stadholder in the five leading provinces and captain general of the Union were left vacant. Mazarin then desperately sought to prevent any alliance between the States General and the republic just established in England. Was not Cromwell the foe of the Stuarts in the same way that John de Witt, the new councilor pensionary of Holland, was the enemy of the princes of Orange in the United Provinces? The Orangists, for their part, sought assistance in France. The outbreak of the first Anglo-Dutch war in the mid-1650's eased the French fears, but the Dutch republicans were again roused to a fever of anxiety as the course of war turned definitely and finally to the advantage of France. Not only did the Dutch regents fret at the thrust of the armies of France into the Low Countries, but they also feared that the Bourbon king, as his strength and influence grew, would support the aspirations of the House of Orange. Signs of French commercial rivalry perturbed them too.[2]

In 1659 France was at last victorious. Philip IV signed the Peace of the Pyrenees in which he accepted defeat at the hands of the ancient foe.

In the following year Charles Stuart, who had been a suppliant exile at the peace conference in the Pyrenees, journeyed back to England to resume his throne as Charles II. In the Netherlands the Orangists, who had sought French succor for the past decade, now looked to London for aid in their domestic struggle against the republican party. In order to counteract English influence, the advocates of a stadholderless regime turned to France.[3]

Louis XIV, who took over personal direction of the French government in 1661, on the death of Cardinal Mazarin, was ready for an

[1]. P. J. Blok, *Geschiedenis van het Nederlandsche Volk* (Groningen, 1892–1908), IV, 444.

[2] Report of Chanut, French ambassador at The Hague, on departure from his mission in 1655, *Recueil des instructions données aux ambassadeurs et ministres de France . . ., Hollande*, ed. Louis André and Émile Bourgeois (Paris, 1922–24), I, xv–xix.

[3] Pieter Geyl, *Oranje en Stuart* (Utrecht, 1939), pp. 184–86.

alliance with the United Provinces. He feared a combination of English and Dutch power against France, on the principle later formulated by Colbert that any two of these three powers could normally defeat the third.[1] Because the restoration of the power of the prince of Orange would have certainly resulted in a league of England and the Dutch republic, Louis concluded a treaty of alliance with the States General in 1662. He then assigned Godefroi count d'Estrades, his ambassador at London, to the French embassy at The Hague. Estrades, who knew the northern Netherlands well from previous service there, had the task of strengthening the republican government under the leadership of John de Witt. Louis trusted and relied upon the grand pensionary as the friend of France.[2]

A crack remained in the alliance—there was still no agreement between France and the United Provinces on the Spanish Netherlands. De Witt therefore proposed to Estrades in 1663 that the two allies join in establishing a republic in the Low Countries, after the model of the Swiss cantons. "Cantonment,"[3] he urged, would offer security to both the Dutch and French states on the frontiers where they had hitherto known their greatest perils. Louis XIV seemed interested, and discussion continued throughout the year. When De Witt finally let the proposal drop, Estrades suspected that Amsterdam had refused to approve any change in the political status of Antwerp which might open the river Scheldt to seagoing ships.[4]

In 1665 war broke out between the States General and England. The Dutch expected that the alliance of 1662 would bring them swift French support. To their surprise, Louis XIV did not at once send them aid. He anticipated that if England and the Netherlands fought each other to a stalemate, his own strength at sea, where his fleet was increasing steadily, would be all the greater. Only after naval action began in the Channel and the bishop of Münster, Bernhard Christoph von Galen, invaded the eastern Dutch provinces, did Louis XIV fear that the Dutch might be defeated and his own alliance system endangered. He sent them aid, but left them still to bear the brunt of the fighting. He was convinced that he had fulfilled his obligation to the United Provinces under the 1662 treaty; the States General, on the

[1] Pierre Clément, ed., *Lettres, instructions et mémoires de Colbert* (Paris, 1861–82), III, 208.

[2] *Lettres, mémoires et négociations de Monsieur le Comte d'Estrades*... (new ed., London [actually The Hague], 1743), II–V, *passim*.

[3] The French "cantonnement" also carries overtones of confining or isolating a difficult or sick person.

[4] Estrades, II, *passim*; Japikse, *Johan de Witt* (Amsterdam, 1915), ch. xi.

other hand, believed he scamped his promise in fact if not in form.[1]

In 1667, while the Anglo-Dutch war was still under way, Louis XIV sent his troops across the Belgian frontier with the announced purpose of establishing the right of queen Marie Thérèse to territories in the Spanish Netherlands under the tenuous principle of inheritance of crown lands by devolution. His intention was not only to wrest some immediate gains of territory from Spain, but also to demonstrate to the Dutch that he would not cancel his claim to the Spanish throne if the king of Spain, Carlos II, died without children.[2]

The rapidity and power of the French advance dismayed the Dutch, who quickly made peace with England at Breda on July 31, 1667. But harsh feelings between the States General and England continued. Sir William Temple called the treaty a "snarling peace" which impeded understanding and trust between the two powers.[3] Nonetheless, even before conclusion of the treaty, deputies from Zeeland, the province where the influence of the Orangists was strongest, proposed that the question of joint action to halt the French invasion in the Low Countries be discussed with the English deputies at Breda.[4] At the same time, the Dutch asked Louis XIV what territories he demanded from Spain as the price of peace. He gave them his terms, assuring them he would be grateful for their intercession on his behalf, but insisted that they promise to take up arms against Spain if she rejected these conditions.[5] Coenraad van Beuningen, a leader in the Amsterdam municipality who was just then taking the lead in warning about the dangers from France, opposed such a promise, as did many other powerful leaders in the republic. De Witt warned them that the willingness of Louis XIV to halt the march of his armies depended upon their making this pledge. When the Spanish government spurned the French terms, the Dutch finally agreed to aid France. Their promise was embodied in resolutions of the States of Holland of December 10, 1667, and January 14, 1668. The terms of these resolutions were almost parallel to a program for settlement of the Spanish-French conflict which De Witt had worked out with prince Wilhelm Egon von Fürstenberg, a German diplomat who spoke and acted for the French

[1] N. Japikse, "Louis XIV et la guerre anglo-hollandaise de 1665–1667," G. Pagès, "À propos de la guerre anglo-hollandaise de 1665–1667," *Revue historique*, XCVIII (1908), 22–71.

[2] Mignet, II, 496ff; Japikse, *Johan de Witt*, p. 256. I use the Spanish form "Carlos," to distinguish the king of Spain from the king of England, also "Charles II."

[3] Sir William Temple to his brother, Sir John Temple, Oct. 10, 1667, *The works of Sir William Temple Bar*[t] (new ed., London, 1757), I, 311.

[4] Japikse, *Johan de Witt*, p. 257.

[5] Lionne to Estrades, Sept. 9, 1667, Estrades, VI, 35.

foreign office.[1] The resolution of January 14, however, incorporated one additional point, providing that an effort would be made to bring the English and Swedes to an agreement to exert pressure, together with the Dutch, upon Spain to accept the French demands. Louis XIV would be compelled to observe his terms for peace if Spain accepted them. This final clause was, at least indirectly, in conflict with the provision of the treaty of alliance of 1662 that neither the States General nor the king of France would enter into any league directed against the other.[2]

All this while, Charles II was negotiating with both France and the United Provinces. In December, the earl of Arlington, his principal minister, proposed to Ruvigny, the French ambassador at London, a secret treaty for an offensive and defensive league against the Dutch.[3] Louis XIV rejected it, primarily because he would not break his alliance with the Dutch.[4]

In October and December, 1667, Temple, who was English resident at Brussels, made two visits to The Hague. He proposed to De Witt that the two states combine to oppose France vigorously. De Witt remained noncommittal. Temple then went to London, where early in January he received instructions to go back to The Hague to press the States General into an alliance.[5]

It is impossible to penetrate Charles II's intentions at this moment with complete certainty. To judge by what we know of his prior and subsequent policy and actions, his purposes were devious, subtle, and realistic. If Louis XIV granted him the subsidies he demanded as the price of his alliance, he could resist more successfully the encroachments of parliament upon his prerogative. Otherwise, he could make allies of the Dutch, thus mollifying parliament and demonstrating to Louis that he was able to find support elsewhere. In addition, he would be able to create French resentment and wrath against De Witt, who stood in the way of the advancement of Charles' nephew, prince William.[6] This final point was stressed later by Pomponne, who was

[1] Leonhard Ennen, *Frankreich und der Niederrhein* ... (Cologne and Neuss, 1855–56), I, 191.

[2] Geyl, *Oranje en Stuart*, pp. 370–71.

[3] Mignet, II, 537.

[4] Louis XIV to Ruvigny, Jan. 4, 1668, *ibid.*, p. 542.

[5] Temple to Sir John Temple, Jan. 2, 1668 (O.S.), Temple, I, 313.

[6] Wicquefort, II, 177. Cf. Sir John R. Seeley, *The Growth of British Policy* (Cambridge, 1895), II, 162–64; Osmund Airy, *The Restoration and Louis XIV* (New York, 1895), p. 168, and the same author's *Charles II* (London, Paris and New York, 1901), p. 152; Geyl, *Oranje en Stuart*, p. 368; Richard Lodge, *The History of England from the Restoration of Charles II to the death of William III (1660–1672)* ("The Political History of England," ed. W. Hunt and R. L. Poole, VIII) (London, 1910), pp. 89–90, for similar modern evaluations of Charles' intentions.

following events from his post at Stockholm. There, since he had no secret sources of information, he was compelled to make sense out of Charles' conduct by his own knowledge of affairs, men and motives. This is how Pomponne, in his Dutch relation, explained the English rôle in the Triple Alliance:

> I shall not say what intentions motivated England on this occasion, nor whether, at the time when she appeared to enter more deeply into the sentiments of the States and to second more sincerely their ardor for the Triple Alliance, she had in mind vengeance upon them or upon France. But as her hatred against Holland must needs have been greater than against us, I have always believed that the good understanding which London made show of maintaining with Holland was only an artifice in order to drive her further and further from France, so that, having once been deprived of that great support, she would remain exposed to a vengeance which necessity alone constrained England to dissimulate.[1]

The proposal which Temple brought disrupted De Witt's own plans. During October and November, 1667, De Witt had thought that the French king was showing greater restraint.[2] In January, 1668, he was still confident of Louis' agreement.[3] He hoped, therefore, that French moderation would enable him to escape the pressure from his adversaries in the States General for outright collaboration with England.[4] He joined with Estrades in exerting pressure upon deputies to the States General to support his program of compelling the Spaniards to accept the French terms.[5]

So strong was De Witt's distrust of England that Temple found himself forced to defend the honesty of the proposals which he carried to The Hague. He asked De Witt to believe him as a man of personal honor that, though he, Temple. "could not pretend to know anybody's mind certainly but my own... on this matter I was as confident of his Majesty's, of your lordship's [Sir Orlando Bridgman, Lord Keeper], and My Lord Arlington's, as I was of my own."[6] De Witt voiced belief that the States General "would think it like to prove too sudden a change of all their interests, and that which would absolutely break

[1] Pomponne, *Relation de Hollande*, p. 64.

[2] Japikse, *Johan de Witt*, p. 258.

[3] Temple to Sir Orlando Bridgman, Jan. 27, 1668, Temple, I, 331.

[4] Japikse, *Johan de Witt*, p. 262. Japikse's account is followed here rather than the superficial analysis by W. J. Knoop, "Oordeel van Lodewijk XIV over 1672," *Verslagen en Mededeelingen der Koninklijke Akademie van Wetenschappen, Afd. Letterkunde*, 2nd. ser., IV (1874), 128–29.

[5] Estrades to Lionne, Jan. 12, 1668 (not Jan. 21, as printed), Estrades, VI, 222.

[6] Temple to Bridgman, Jan. 27, 1668, Temple, I, 333–34. Cf. De Witt to Johan Meerman and Johan Boreel, Jan. 8, 1668, De Witt, *Brieven*, IV, 610.

them off from so old and constant a friend as France, to rely wholly upon so new and uncertain a friend, as England had proved."[1]

This was a fear, however, which De Witt felt far more strongly than the majority of members of the States General. The Swedish envoy, Count Christopher von Dohna, who promised the entry of the Swedish crown into a Dutch-English league, was doubtful that De Witt would support it, in view of English support for the Orangists. Dohna told Temple that the councilor pensionary would not overtly oppose his proposal, "because the States and people might run into it; yet... would find some means to elude the conclusion or effect of it, without appearing himself in any such design."[2]

But De Witt did not attempt to prevent the conclusion of the treaty. On January 23, Temple, De Witt and other deputies of the States General signed a treaty embodying the principles of the resolutions of the States of Holland of December 10 and January 14. The point in the latter resolution concerning the possibility of hostilities against France was incorporated into the last of the three secret articles appended to the treaty.[3]

Estrades, the French ambassador, was taken aback. The negotiations for the final conclusion of the treaty, instead of being relayed to the provinces and cities for decision, were completed by the States General, at Temple's insistence, without the required prior approval of their constituents. Estrades had anticipated that he—and apparently De Witt with him—would manage to hold off acceptance of the treaty. His error was understandable. He could not foresee that Temple would demand the evasion of the constitution of the United Provinces,

[1] Temple to Bridgman, Jan. 27, 1668, Temple, I, 331.

[2] Temple to Bridgman, Jan. 27, 1668, *ibid.*, p. 336.

[3] *Ibid.*, pp. 362–84. An excellent summary of the provisions of the treaty is given by Pomponne in his *Mémoires* (I, 512–13): "Its purposes were these: the king [of France] having expressed his willingness to bring the war to an end provided that the Catholic king would cede one of the alternatives to him, the king of England and Holland would promise to obtain this from him; and in the event that the council of Madrid rejected their intercession, they would employ more effective means to compel them to comply; but the King would leave this burden so completely to them that he would not be permitted to send his troops into Flanders, to attack towns or even to receive the surrender of those towns which might voluntarily desire to give themselves to him. Besides these articles which they wished to make public, and which the States sought to color with the single intention of procuring peace when they communicated them to Count d'Estrades who had his first knowledge of these articles from them, they also signed secret articles on the same day.... These articles, the secrecy of which was penetrated only some months later [actually, only a month], included a specific stipulation that they would wage war jointly with England against France if the King did not make peace under the conditions which they should declare they considered to be reasonable. But, in the event that they took up arms, they then accepted the obligation not to lay them down until they should have re-established Spain in all that she had just lost in the Low Countries."

precisely in order to avert that tampering with the decisions of the sovereign provinces upon which Estrades counted.[1]

The French ambassador had relied too much upon bribery. He had spent large sums for the purpose of controlling votes of deputies of various provinces. This was an easy but spurious solution of the problem of overcoming Dutch unwillingness to have France as a neighbor. Once the alliance was approved by the States General, the provincial and municipal bodies cast their votes in favor. In view of the tremendous outpouring of popular enthusiasm, no one dared earn the money of France.[2]

It was not merely the pressure of public opinion which made De Witt accept the violation of the constitution of the land. He had also been compelled to accept the offer of an English alliance because he had already counted upon impressing Louis XIV with the availability of such a league to the States General. He had more and more depended upon the French king's desire to prevent formation of a coalition of the two great maritime powers against France, in order to persuade Louis to display moderation in the southern Netherlands. To reject the English proposal of an alliance when it was actually made would mean giving up an essential weapon in his diplomatic armory. If an alliance with England were the only way to restrain and restrict France in her ambitions to conquer the Low Countries, De Witt would not balk at it.

He would not trust to it, either. Instead, even after the conclusion of the Triple Alliance, De Witt continued with his basic program of maintaining the alliance with France, while limiting French conquests in the Spanish Netherlands. On the very day on which the alliance was signed, he wrote to Fürstenberg, the French agent, to assure him that the league with England was intended to obtain Spanish compliance with the terms they had agreed upon.[3] He envisaged hostility to

[1] Temple, "Observations...," Temple, I, 128–29; Temple to Arlington, Jan. 24, 1668, *ibid.*, pp. 318–19; Estrades to Louis XIV, Jan. 12, 19, Feb. 2, 1668, Estrades, VI, 222, 229–31, 258.

[2] Estrades to Lionne, Jan. 12, 26, 1668, *ibid.*, pp. 223, 250–51. Geyl, in his article, "D'Estrades' beweringen omtrent de omkoopbaarheid der Nederlandse regenten," *Nederlandsche Historiebladen*, II (1939), 163–73, may have missed the point of Estrades' essential failure in his bribery activities. Despite Geyl's efforts to exculpate the Dutch regents from Estrades' imputation of widespread venality among them, it seems difficult to deny that many of them were open to bribery; the practice was neither novel nor confined to the Netherlands. What was significant was that, on issues which were felt to involve fundamental interests, bribery failed to work. Many of the Dutch regents seem to have been willing to take money to do what they would have done anyway.

[3] De Witt to Fürstenberg, Jan. 23, 1668, *Brieven van Johan de Witt*, ed. Robert Fruin, G. W. Kernkamp and N. Japikse ("Werken uitgegeven door het Historisch Genootschap te Utrecht," 3rd ser., nos. 18, 25, 31, 33) (Amsterdam, 1906–13), III, 389.

France only in the improbable event that, if Spain accepted Louis' demands, the French monarch would still not make peace.[1]

De Witt considered that "a little more civility and complaisance in the outward form" would have made the Triple Alliance more agreeable to France.[2] He endeavored to persuade Estrades that the treaty was "advantageous and glorious for the King his master," that his intentions "will be to conserve for all time, and in preference to all other things, the friendship of the King," and that the intentions of the States General were "upright" and did not diverge from the stated desires of Louis XIV himself. He gave repeated assurance that "the good intentions of the States, and his own as well," would be demonstrated by the results of the treaty, that "the effects themselves should speak."[3] The grand pensionary did not try to exculpate himself by telling Estrades that he had not really intended to make an alliance with England. It was hardly possible to explain he had wished to "blackmail" Louis into peace by the threat of such an alliance. Nor could he admit he had lost some of his grip over the States of Holland and the States General.

De Witt explained his policy to Van Beuningen, then on official mission to Paris. It would be a "disservice" to the States General, he warned his colleague, to break off good relations with France, since in the probable event of the resumption of the "usual insolence of the English nation," the Dutch would then be left without friends. On the one hand, the alliance with England and Sweden should be retained, to keep France from "breaking out again"; on the other, the alliance with France should not be abandoned, lest the English thereby "be led once more into evil principles."[4]

De Witt acknowledged to both the English and French ambassadors that the Dutch would take up arms if Louis XIV demanded more than his own stated terms for peace. But he also succeeded, after some delay, in inducing the States General to accept the necessity for military action against Spain if Madrid rejected the peace terms.[5]

[1] A. Lefèvre-Pontalis, *Vingt années de république parlementaire au dix-septième siècle: Jean de Witt, grand pensionnaire de Hollande* (Paris, 1884), I, 450; Japikse, *Johan de Witt*, p. 265.

[2] De Witt to Meerman, Feb. 10, 1668, De Witt, *Brieven*, IV, 650.

[3] De Witt to Meerman, Feb. 4, 10, March 2, 1668, De Witt, *Brieven*, IV, 646, 650, 685; Estrades to Lionne, Jan. 28, Feb. 16, 23, 1668, to Louis XIV, Feb. 2, 1668, Estrades, VI, 258–59, 273, 287; De Witt to Van Beuningen, March 1, 1668, *Brieven van Johan de Witt*, III, 398.

[4] De Witt to Van Beuningen, May 31, 1668, *ibid.*, p. 411.

[5] Temple to Bridgman, Jan. 27, 1668, Temple, I, 331; Estrades to Lionne, Feb. 16, 1668, Estrades, VI, 274; De Witt to Temple, Feb. 25, 1668, *Correspondance française du Grand Pensionnaire Jean de Witt*, ed. François Combes ("Collection de documents inédits sur l'histoire de France, Mélanges historiques," I) (Paris, 1873), pp. 307–08;

To Temple, De Witt indicated that if France forced war upon the Dutch, they would wage it with extreme vigor, particularly at sea. He even proposed invasion of the French coast. But this would be only the final result which De Witt wished not to obtain but to avert; he would not be led by the wiles of Castel Rodrigo, the Spanish governor general in the Low Countries, "to that point where we do not wish to come except in the event of inescapable necessity."[1]

For some weeks, indeed, it seemed that De Witt might yet redeem the harm the Triple Alliance had done to the Dutch cause in France. The court of Saint-Germain, impressed by the territorial gains promised for France in the treaty of January 23, was slow to take deep offense at it. To be sure, at the first official report of the alliance, Turenne and Condé, the French army commanders, and Louvois, chief of the department of war, urged continuation of the war. But the counsels of Colbert and Lionne on behalf of moderation won out, for they were reinforced by the inadequacy of the French forces for a major campaign at that moment.[2] Perhaps most important of all was Louis' interest in the possible acquisition of the selfsame territory by the treaty of partition concluded with emperor Leopold I four days before the signing of the Triple Alliance. But this treaty was surrounded by such elaborate secrecy that it went virtually unmentioned in all the records by which we can trace the ideas of Louis XIV and his close advisers during the years until the outbreak of the war in 1672. It is not even certain that Pomponne knew of the treaty of partition after he became foreign minister in 1672.[3]

Estrades, when informed by De Witt and Temple of the conclusion of the treaty, replied "coldly." His words, as reported by Temple, were prophetic of the three great wars that ensued during the reign of Louis XIV: "... if we thought to prescribe him (Louis XIV) laws, and force him to compliance, by leagues between ourselves, or with Spain, though Sweden and the German Princes should join with us, he knew his Master *ne flecheroit* (sic) *pas*, and that it would come to a war of forty years."[4] He admitted, however, that Van Beuningen's forthcoming mission to Paris might improve matters.[5]

Lionne, the French foreign minister, also thought that Van Beuningen could "easily rectify" the shortcomings of the Dutch proceedings

De Witt to Van Beuningen, March 8, 1668, *Brieven van De Witt*, III, 399.

[1] De Witt to Temple, Feb. 25, 1668, De Witt, *Correspondance française*, pp. 306–07; De Witt to Meerman, Feb. 25, 1668, De Witt, *Brieven*, IV, 681.

[2] Rousset, I, 138–39; Picavet, pp. 226–29.

[3] Pomponne, *Mémoires*, II, 177.

[5] Temple to Arlington, Jan. 24, 1668, Temple, I, 323–24.

[4] Estrades to Lionne, Jan. 26, 1668, Estrades, VI, 252–53.

in the Triple Alliance. His own personal view, he told Estrades, was that "its principal foundation appears to me to be good and advantageous to the king, its manner somewhat distasteful, and the terms of the convention could be more seemly (*honnêtes*); but the sequel will prove whether the intentions with regard to this crown were good or ill: in which respect M. de Witt can contribute greatly by continuing to give His Majesty indications of his friendship, in which he (Louis XIV) will always have confidence until we shall have evidence to the complete contrary." A week later, he repeated these ideas to Estrades.[1]

Estrades, who had a spy among the clerks of the *griffier* (secretary) of the States General, learned not only of the existence of the secret articles, but also what they contained. He berated De Witt for not revealing them to him. The councilor pensionary minimized the importance of the third article, with its menace of war against France. He told Estrades that he "had refused to include this article within the (public) treaty, although Temple had urged it very strongly, but that it was true that it was included among the secret articles, for there it would not be seen by the public, and furthermore it had no force, since the King was satisfied with the alternative (territorial cession), as he had again promised the States by his most recent letter."[2] De Witt later reiterated his assertion to Estrades that "the king of England would not sign the treaty unless the States gave him prior assurance that the King (Louis XIV) would be content with the alternative; that the States did not wish it inserted in the treaty, for it is known to the whole world and these terms might be interpreted by the public in ways which could alter the existing good understanding between the King and the States." He thought a secret article providing for a case "which can never occur" ought not to offend Louis XIV.[3]

Lionne felt differently. On the very last day of February, he had a portentous interview with Van Beuningen, who had just arrived in Paris. The Dutch ambassador consented to read briefly the first two of the secret articles but refused to read the less innocent third. He already knew its provisions, Lionne informed him, giving a stern warning of its probable effect upon the ruler of France.[4]

Meanwhile Estrades was presenting to De Witt a report from Ruvigny in London, saying that he had received a copy of the secret articles from Arlington. This the grand pensionary reported to the Dutch envoys at London and Paris with surprise and indignation.

[1] Lionne to Estrades, Feb. 3, 10, 1668, *ibid.*, pp. 263–64, 266–68.
[2] Estrades to Lionne, Feb. 16, 1668, *ibid.*, pp. 271–72.
[3] Estrades to Lionne, Feb. 23, 1668, *ibid.*, p. 284.
[4] Lionne to Estrades, March 2, 1668, *ibid.*, pp. 303–04.

Arlington denied his responsibility for this breach of faith.[1] It has apparently never been determined who was specifically at fault, but clearly the breach of secrecy was committed in England to Ruvigny some time in the latter half of February.[2] It seems probable that Charles II did not anticipate the moderate attitude taken at first toward the Triple Alliance at the French court and found it necessary to divulge the secret articles in order to disturb this French equanimity.[3]

The conclusion of the treaty of Aix-la-Chapelle between France and Spain on May 2, 1668, brought the War of Devolution to an end. The official French position was that only the moderation of Louis XIV induced him to put down the arms which victory invited him to keep employed, and that the Triple Alliance had "no part in halting his conquests."[4] But this was dust to be thrown in the eyes of the public: the bitterness felt at the French court, and Louis' fear of alliances against him, showed that it played some very real part in the French decision to halt their conquests for the time being.

During May and June of 1668 De Witt continued his efforts to recapture the friendship of France. He indicated that he was ready to support French ambitions to all the Spanish succession *except the Low Countries* in the event of the death of the Spanish king without children.[5] Thus, when Estrades left The Hague on June 8, 1668, preparatory to formal recall from his mission, the change in the relationship between France and the States General was evident, though it was not yet clear which way events would move. A compromise of the interests at conflict was possible, but neither government was ready to take the steps necessary to persuade the other at once of its good intentions. Actually, both Louis XIV and John de Witt were compelled to look across the Channel and the North Sea for an indication of what they would be able to do. The French king needed the alliance of England to be able to punish his ungrateful allies; the councilor pensionary depended upon it to keep the United Provinces safe from France. So the two rivals courted Charles II, each uneasy about what he would decide and what they must do in turn. This was as far as matters had gone when Estrades began his homeward journey and word went up to Pomponne at Stockholm to come back to France.

[1] De Witt to Van Beuningen, March 1, 1668, *Brieven van De Witt*, III, 398; De Witt to Meerman, March 2, 1668, Meerman to De Witt, March 12, 1668, De Witt, *Brieven*, IV, 685–86, 706.

[2] Wicquefort, II, 451; Meerman to De Witt, Feb. 15, 1668, De Witt, *Brieven*, IV, 668; N. Japikse, note in *Brieven van De Witt*, II, 398, note 2.

[4] Airy, *Charles II*, p. 152.

[3] Pomponne, *Mémoires*, I, 562.

[5] Mignet, III, 560–61.

CHAPTER III

PURPOSES AND PLANS

February, 1669

Estrades, the soldier-diplomat, returned to France to resume the simpler duties of mere soldiering, as governor of the fortress of Dunkirk.[1] Already selected to replace him was the administrator-diplomat, Arnauld de Pomponne. Pomponne's letter of recall reached him at Stockholm in mid-July. He boarded ship for Hamburg in August, but it was late September before a tedious journey brought him to Saint-Germain.[2]

Estrades' official recall, which had been delayed till after Pomponne's arrival, could now be completed. Estrades journeyed back to The Hague. On October 17, he took formal leave of the States General, and not long after quit the city where he had served both his own king and the Dutch republic in many capacities.[3]

On October 25, 1668, came the official announcement that Pomponne would go to the States General as ambassador extraordinary from Louis XIV.[4] The Dutch leaders heard this news with mixed feelings. "We shall not gain by the exchange," wrote Pieter de Groot from Stockholm. He reflected a general belief that Estrades, bound to the republic by habit, friendship and pecuniary advantage (he commanded several regiments in the States' service), was their true friend. On the other hand, as De Groot put it, Pomponne had no particular reason to feel "tender affection" for a land and a nation which he did not know personally. Yet De Groot did not doubt that Pomponne would do his best in the new post, "which he had desired more than any other that

[1] Pomponne, *Relation de Hollande*, p. 73.

[2] Ludwig Bittner and Lothar Gross, eds., *Repertorium der diplomatischen Vertreter aller Länder seit dem Westfälischen Frieden* (Oldenburg and Berlin, 1936–), I, 234; Pomponne, *Mémoires*, I, 562, 566, 569; Pomponne, *Relation de Hollande*, p. 29; Arnauld, p. 330.

[3] Pomponne, *Relation de Hollande*, p. 29; Wicquefort to Lionne, Oct. 18, 1668, Arch. étr., Holl., vol. 88, fo. 257.

[4] *Recueil ... Hollande*, I, 259.

might be given him."[1] Abraham de Wicquefort, who had become Lionne's principal source of information about events in the Netherlands since Estrades' departure, also felt sure that Pomponne would do good service at The Hague, but warned of the difficulties he would face.[2]

These difficulties were summed up in the person of Coenraad van Beuningen. He had just returned from Paris, having failed utterly to retrieve the Dutch position at the French court. Though every effort had been made to keep his report on his mission secret, Wicquefort soon discovered what he had said and informed Lionne at once. According to Wicquefort, Van Beuningen declared

> that there was in France, when he departed, a strong inclination to maintain peace, but also a firm resolution to complete the conquest of the Low Countries if the king of Spain should die; that there was in France profound dissatisfaction with this State, without any concealing of the king's intention to take revenge without fail for what has been done here; that enemies will be raised against this State from every side, those already her foes will receive support, factions will be fomented by which this State may be divided, and an effort will be made to ruin its trade, with everything possible already being done in this last respect by placing excessive import duties upon goods from this country, for it was as yet not desired to contravene openly the treaty of 1662. In a word, he has proclaimed that neither friendship nor confidence can exist any longer between France and this State and that friends must be sought elsewhere; that, as for trade, it is impossible to continue it with France if entry duties upon the manufactures of this country are not reduced, and they never will be reduced unless excessive duties are placed upon the manufactures of France as well as upon the wine, salt and other things which that kingdom produces, so that they can no longer be brought here.[3]

Wicquefort warned that Van Beuningen was not alone in spreading the belief that "France no longer has any affection for this State," and that Pomponne would bring only threats. Therefore, "since the inhabitants of this country are very susceptible to such ideas," he wrote, "M. de Pomponne will have to set them right as soon as he arrives."[4]

Pomponne was anything but eager to leave at once for The Hague.

[1] De Groot to Wicquefort, Nov. 10, 1668, De Groot, p. 3; De Groot to De Witt, Nov. 29, 1668, De Witt, *Brieven*, II, 598–99. Wicquefort later contrasted Pomponne's fundamental probity with Estrades' deceitfulness. Wicquefort, *L'ambassadeur et ses fonctions* (Amsterdam, 1730), II, 202.

[2] Wicquefort to Lionne, Oct. 4, 18, 1668, Arch. étr., Holl., vol. 88, fos. 244, 257, 259.

[3] Wicquefort to Lionne, Oct. 18, 1668, *ibid.*, fo. 257.

[4] Wicquefort to Lionne, Nov. 1, 1668, *ibid.*, fo. 272.

For three years he had been far from home and homeland; while he could, he wished to enjoy their delights.[1] As soon as he had been able to break away from court, he withdrew to his estate at Pomponne.[2] But when the ambassador-designate tarried for months, Wicquefort renewed his warnings. The Dutch would judge French intentions by whether Pomponne came without delay or dawdled in France.[3]

When Pomponne did not leave by New Year's, as had been expected,[4] Wicquefort became even more perturbed. He poured out his anxieties in a letter to a friend traveling with Bonzy through Pomerania. To permit Pomponne to delay his going until better weather made traveling easier for his wife was to "display indifference to everything happening here." The Spaniards would be delighted to replace the French in the "interests and affections" of the Dutch people. To be sure, Colbert de Croissy, Louis' ambassador in London, was busy wooing Charles II, but the French should not gamble upon being able to win back the Dutch to their first maxim, alliance with France, if Croissy failed. "This might well turn out to be an error and a miscalculation, for while France has no one here to speak for her, our involvement with Spain is becoming so deep that we shall not be able to pull out of it," he lamented. No one had contradicted Van Beuningen; it would take all of Pomponne's skill to persuade the Dutch that Louis XIV had no plans for an attack upon the Low Countries. Dutch policy was based on the assumption that such plans existed, so that even "those who were once most zealous for the interests of France now hold the view that this State is obliged to give a guarantee to the king of Spain for all his states and realms." The French court knows all this and does not act, Wicquefort moaned. Were his reports suspect? Or was Louis so scornful of the republic that he thought her unable to oppose any effective obstacles to his designs? Why else should he have been without a diplomatic representative at The Hague for seven months?[5]

Writing to Lionne three days later, Wicquefort repeated these ideas, though in a milder tone. Not everyone was ready to accept a Spanish

[1] Pomponne, *Relation de Hollande*, p. 29.

[2] Chapelain to Heinsius, Oct. 11, 1668, Chapelain, II, 599.

[3] Wicquefort to Lionne, Dec. 13, 1668, Arch. étr., Holl., vol. 88, fo. 309.

[4] Chapelain to Heinsius, Dec. 11, 1668, Chapelain, II, 607.

[5] Wicquefort to someone in Bonzy's party, Jan. 7, 1669, Arch. étr., Holl., vol. 89, fos. 13–14. Mignet (III, 563) identifies the addressee as "M. de Bondy," which sounds suspiciously like Bonzy. Mignet, here as elsewhere, omits significant portions of the letter. C. F. Haje identifies this letter as one to Lionne, and asserts, without indicating his evidence, that it was written at De Witt's instructions *(De geheime correspondentie van Abraham de Wicquefort met den Franschen Minister de Lionne* [The Hague, 1901], p. 116).

orientation. Yet De Witt, who two years before had not been interested in the suggestion of the imperial diplomat Lisola that the Dutch and Hapsburg causes be linked together, now had to listen to the proposals of the imperial diplomat. Plaintively Wicquefort told the French minister, "It would be a good thing for M. de Pomponne to be here."[1] A fortnight later, he wrote again in a more optimistic note. There was "utter disgust" with Spain's delay in paying the subsidies promised to Sweden for entering the Triple Alliance, and disapproval of Sweden's conduct. England for the moment was true to the alliance, but her fidelity and her ability to support it were equally dubious. Thus, wrote Wicquefort, the situation was one in which "a skillful minister" could do good service for his own cause.[2]

Whether Wicquefort's querulous pleas were merely an expression of his own narrow interests and views, or, as is more probable, they also gave voice to the hopes and fears of his friend, the grand pensionary, they did not change the pace at which things were done at Saint-Germain. Pomponne continued to take his ease. Lionne worked on the instructions for Pomponne. When he completed the first draft in December, he submitted it to Turenne for his judgment. Though not a member of the *Conseil d'en haut*, the marshal perhaps counted more with the king than any of the ministers. His view of Dutch affairs carried special weight: he had begun his military service in the army of the States General, learning the art of war from Frederick Henry; as the most influential Huguenot in France, he had had especially close relations with the leaders of the republic; yet his conversion to Catholicism that same autumn of 1668 was proof that his judgment would not be warped by sympathy with the Netherlanders. After examining Lionne's draft, Turenne set down his own ideas in a report which he read to Pomponne. The ambassador-designate made his own transcript, which he took to The Hague together with his official instructions.[3]

Because the marshal, though approving the general tenor of Lionne's draft, felt it necessary to sharpen the assumptions on which the in-

[1] Wicquefort to Lionne, Jan. 10, 1669, Arch. étr., Holl., vol. 89, fos. 18–19.

[2] Wicquefort to Lionne, Jan. 24, 1669, *ibid.*, fo. 21.

[3] Turenne's holograph original is in Arch. étr., Holl., vol. 88, fos. 297ff. Pomponne's copy, which varies somewhat, primarily in the direction of logical clarity, is in his own handwriting, in Bib. Ars., MS 4712, fos. 1–3. Another copy, apparently based on Pomponne's version, is in Arch. étr., Holl., vol. 88, fos. 303ff. Two excerpts from Turenne's copy were printed in *Recueil... Hollande* (I, 262, note 1) by André and Bourgeois. Pomponne's version differs materially, though not fundamentally, from Turenne's; it was quite possibly what the great soldier, never gifted with facile or precise command of the written word, actually said. In any event, it is more important to us as the form in which Pomponne received and preserved Turenne's ideas.

structions rested and to clarify the policy which it projected, we must read the two documents together to understand clearly the exact import of the instructions which Pomponne took with him to The Hague.

The mission which Pomponne was taking up was "no less thorny than important." This was the first principle set forth in his instructions.[1] The decisions and deeds of the States General were the "most important" of those of any foreign power. As Pomponne later said in his Relation, "Holland then appeared as the scene of the most important political dealings in Europe and seemed to have greater need of a minister to observe feelings which there was reason to believe were anything but friendly to France.[2]

There was no need to tell Pomponne much of what he should say in his formal speech on presenting his credentials to the States General. The usual assurances of "affection and esteem," a "most sincere" affirmation of the king's intention to maintain the peace established by the treaty of Aix-la-Chapelle—beyond these points, Pomponne could speak as his customary "prudence and discretion" suggested.[3] These were mere formalities; no one would be swayed by them. In serious talks, Pomponne must try to remove the "hostile and for the most part very[4] false impressions" of Louis' policy towards the Dutch which Van Beuningen sought to instill among them. After paraphrasing Wicquefort's summary of Van Beuningen's report to the States General on his return from France, the instructions added the general charge that he wished to persuade the Dutch "that there are no limits to the king's ambition." However much Van Beuningen's "malevolence... toward this crown," his "outbursts of wrath" and his cabals at the French court justified complaint, Pomponne should not attack him personally. He should draw on his own devices for arguments with which to "destroy or at least to weaken" Van Beuningen's influence.[5]

[1] *Recueil... Hollande,* I, 271. References to the instructions are made to this collection, which is generally available. The editors transcribed the copy in the archives of the French foreign ministry (Arch. étr., Holl., vol. 89, fos. 28–42). Noting that there were difficulties in determining the order of materials toward the end of the document, they depended upon pencilled notations for the order of the final six paragraphs. The sequence thus established (*Recueil...*, *Hollande,* I, 286–90) does not correspond, however, to the actual order in the final form of the instructions, preserved, as André and Bourgois note, among Pomponne's papers in the Bibliothèque de l'Arsenal (MS 4712, fos. 8ff). Some forty differences exist between the transcription in the *Recueil...Hollande* and the manuscript in the Arsenal. Most of these are inconsequential; none invalidates the general accuracy of the printed text.

[2] *Relation de Hollande,* p. 29.

[3] *Recueil... Hollande,* I, 271.

[4] The word "très" is omitted in the *Recueil... Hollande* (I, 271), which makes a vigorous phrase a weak one.

[5] *Ibid.*, pp. 271–73.

This concentration upon Van Beuningen as the single great foe of France in the United Provinces troubled Turenne. In his commentary on the instructions, he stressed that De Witt still played the leading rôle in the republic. The grand pensionary was responsible for its present policy of preventing French expansion in the Low Countries, and regaining her losses for Spain if at all possible; he was also behind Dutch efforts to restrict France's commerce, Turenne implied. To be sure, De Witt seemed "more willing to serve the king's interest" than most Dutchmen, but his motives were personal and political. He feared the resentment of Louis XIV ("for his own person," says Turenne's draft), and hoped to lull French animosity by presenting the policy he favored as being really forced upon him despite his opposition to it. Nonetheless, Turenne recognized that De Witt might truly seek the friendship of France. The grand pensionary, he said, acted on the precept that "a quarrel is much more easily patched up with those to whom one has to some extent shown proper respect in word and form, if not in deed."[1]

Lionne, to be sure, also presented De Witt as "the originator *(premier mobile)* of all that is done and decided in their state." He gave a detailed outline of what Pomponne must say in his first conference with De Witt. Significantly, the first point concerned the Triple Alliance. Louis XIV had saved the republic from near-destruction during the war with England and Münster; "to meet their interest alone and their desires," he had halted his campaign at the very moment when it promised him the greatest gains. Was the Triple Alliance the king's "retribution" for this aid? Dutch ingratitude was deepened by their continued quest for "other friends than France, even at the cost of their purse," and by their unremitting efforts to form "leagues and unions which, at least in appearance, are directed against this crown." If "vain errors about things of which His Majesty neither thinks nor wishes to think,"[2] were the source of their conduct, the Dutch were the victims of "pure misunderstanding." The king desired, sincerely and truly, to keep the peace.

To keep the peace, yes, but not to abandon, once and for all, whatever claim France might have to the Spanish succession in the Low Countries, though such a promise would instantly calm the Dutch terrors. Pomponne should merely remind the councilor pensionary that, in the event of the death of Carlos II, the king of France could

[1] Bib. Ars., MS 4712, fo. 1.

[2] Pomponne, in summarizing the instructions in his Relation, took out this note of warning, by saying that these were thoughts the king "does not have and has never had." (*Relation de Hollande*, p. 72.)

not in honor and justice "totally abandon the interests of the queen and her children." Louis was ready, however, to discuss his claims with the Dutch. Van Beuningen, it was true, had proposed such talks while in Paris, but such a delicate affair could not be conducted with one "so ready to anger," so unreasonably and persistently hostile to France. Louis would conduct such a negotiation with De Witt, for he knew his "prudence, capacity and affection," and had recalled Pomponne from Sweden as better fitted to represent him than the soldier Estrades.

This was as far as Pomponne might commit himself formally. But he should ask De Witt, as if on his own initiative, "what present advantages" the king would gain by agreeing to some arrangement with the republic over the Low Countries. For, Pomponne was warned, unless such steps could "wholly re-establish the confidence of the States and oblige them to change their conduct in many things, His Majesty might perhaps not believe he ought to give much attention to such a negotiation." Specifically, the States General would have to abandon the Triple Alliance and their efforts to obtain payment of the promised subsidies to Sweden. Pomponne must not present these ideas to De Witt as a proposal, but seek to elicit them from the pensionary.[1] Turenne emphasized how delicate such discussions with De Witt on the succession to the Spanish monarchy would be. The question could not be neglected. "An ambassador whose great ability is well known" was being sent to The Hague; if he refused to take up the central issue in dispute between the two countries, De Witt's suspicions would be instantly aroused.[2]

Turenne brought to the surface what the instructions here hinted at, that the further course of relations between France and the United Provinces would really be determined by what happened in England. The French had only one reason to seek an alliance with England, to inflict harm upon the Dutch. The way must be left open for a war against them in combination with England and Sweden, except if the States General promised some great profit to the king. Unless they made some such pledge, Pomponne should avoid any commitment to them. He should lead De Witt on without becoming involved in his toils.[3]

Some fifteen years later, when Pomponne recalled this problem in writing his Relation, he vacillated between a statement of French policy in the terms actually used in his instructions, and a belief that

[1] *Recueil... Hollande*, I, 273–78. Cf. Wicquefort, *Histoire*, IV, 23.
[2] Bib. Ars., MS 4712, fo. 1.
[3] *Ibid.*, fo. 2.

Louis' intentions had already become hostile to the States General beyond any possibility of change. The king, he wrote,

> sought, by this embassy, more to give the appearance of continued friendship than to regain the support of the States by a genuine negotiation. The warmth of novelty in the Triple Alliance was still too great to permit the hope that it might be broken up so early. More time was necessary till its bonds should come loose.... This is not to say that in the event that I found the States adhering to sentiments contrary to whose which they had displayed until then, or that the realization of the unwise policy they had followed in separating themselves from France had caused them to seek in all earnest a rapprochement with her, and to renounce sincerely the league which France had only too much reason to suspect, His Majesty, exercising the same prudence, would not have been induced to take new steps with them once again. But there was so little reason to expect this from their disposition at the moment that the wisest policy appeared to be to oppose their hostile purposes by dissimulation and to await favorable circumstances for giving expression to his resentment.[1]

Hindsight seems to have deceived Pomponne's memory. Clearly, Louis XIV, in February of 1669, still considered that a Dutch change of heart was possible and desirable. It was not so probable that he would gamble his policy on it, but he would strive to bring it about and to profit by it if he succeeded. Thus, the friendly policy which Pomponne was directed to take toward De Witt would do dual service. It might cause the Dutch to modify their policy, and then renewal of friendship between the French monarchy and the Dutch republic was feasible. Otherwise, Pomponne's conduct would serve to mask the hostile intentions of France.

Whether the Dutch would change their fundamental attitude toward France would be the central question of Pomponne's whole mission. But many lesser problems would come before him and require his skill and subtlety, though they would not bear the immense burden of the decision for war or peace. On these subordinate questions the instructions also laid down Pomponne's line of conduct.

The most important of these was what should be done if Spain were admitted to the Triple Alliance as an equal partner. Spain had sought to join the league, but De Witt, anxious to soothe France as much as possible, had persuaded the States General to rebuff her. If Van Beuningen's agitation had changed the situation, Pomponne was told not to oppose Spain's admittance. The king would demand that France

[1] Pomponne, *Relation de Hollande*, pp. 70–72.

be accepted as well: this would compel the league to decide whether it was directed against France or merely against any state breaking the peace.[1] As Lionne was bringing the instructions to a close, he received word from Wicquefort that De Witt had succesfully obtained rejection of the Spanish demand. If Pomponne, on arriving at The Hague, found this report to be true, he should praise De Witt in the king's name, for admittance of the Spanish crown would indeed have been offensive to France. After Spain received her guarantee, Pomponne should request an exact copy. Louis XIV would then decide whether to seek a similar guarantee from the Triple Alliance.[2]

This modification of French policy took into account the sharp criticism Turenne made of the earlier provision. It would be dangerous, he warned, to give any indication that France would approve Spain's entry into the league. To do so would remove the only obstacle to acceptance of Spain and destroy the last chance of undermining Arlington's influence in England. Furthermore, why should the king tie his hands when opportunity might soon come his way?[3] Pomponne, if we may judge by his comments in the Relation, was impressed by Turenne's argument. The king, he wrote, "changed his mind upon considering that he would strengthen that side too greatly if by joining it he indicated that he approved it, and judged it wise to retain his freedom to complain upon occasion of an alliance so manifestly being formed against him."[4]

Another problem on which the French attitude changed while Pomponne's instructions were being written, resulted from the treaty of Aix-la-Chapelle. France claimed that Spain had ceded three important places, Condé, Linck and the sluices of Nieupoort, because they were "dependent" (feudally subordinate) upon towns specifically named for transfer to French sovereignty. Spain argued, on the contrary, that only the towns, and not their dependencies, were covered. The issue was not unimportant, for the places were strategically located: Condé lay at the fork of the Haine and Escaut rivers; Linck, a fortified village southwest of Dunkirk, protected the rear of the French-held town of Bergues[5]; the sluices of Nieupoort controlled the low-lying seaboard north of Dunkirk. Since the middle of 1668, French and Spanish delegates had been conferring at Lille, but without reaching any settle-

[1] *Recueil... Hollande*, I, 278–79.
[2] *Ibid.*, pp. 286–87.
[3] Bib. Ars., MS 4712, fos. 1–2.
[4] Pomponne, *Relation de Hollande*, p. 77.
[5] The exact position of the fortifications is no longer known. M. A. Bonvarlet, "Notes sur la commune de Capelle-Brouck," *Annales du comité flamand de France*, XV (1883–86), 178–83.

ment of the dispute. At first Louis was willing to include the States General among arbitrators to whom the dispute might be submitted, because they might thus be persuaded to change their general attitude, "if that is possible."[1] Turenne criticized this position sharply. It would make it difficult to avoid arbitration by which the king would bind himself unnecessarily: Let the Spaniards worry about the safety of these provinces. Then they may feel compelled to "make overtures to the king which he does not expect"—by which Turenne meant proposals for an exchange of the Spanish Netherlands for lands elsewhere.[2]

Another possible exchange of territory between France and Spain, but one which would be to Dutch advantage, was discussed in Pomponne's instructions. The marquis de Castel Rodrigo had deliberately selected between the alternative plans of cession to France put forward at Aix-la-Chapelle that which gave France lands closest to the United Provinces.[3] If the Dutch persuaded the Spaniards to accept exchange of the whole area ceded to France, or of selected places within it, for lands elsewhere, Louis XIV would be ready to state his own intentions, but not before. The pensionary could be told, however, that "if between now and then confidence between him (Louis XIV) and them (the States General) can be renewed, and their friendship and union reestablished, to which he, for his part, is wholly favorable," the king would strive to satisfy the Dutch in this matter.[4] Turenne thought well of such negotiations with De Witt. The least they would do would be to deceive him. In any event this problem, which would certainly lead to interminable discussions, should be taken up before the more ticklish "dependencies" question.[5]

Pomponne would also have to deal with the efforts of duke Charles IV of Lorraine to win Dutch support. The duke, as commander of a large force of troops on the frontier of France, had long been a source of anxiety to Louis XIV. He had been compelled to promise disbanding of his army, but evaded actually doing so. Instead, he merely dispersed his troops among friendly powers nearby, so that they could be brought together under his own command in the event of conflict. Even more disturbing to Louis XIV was a report that duke Charles was seeking admission into the Triple Alliance. The Dutch, knowing him to be a "restless, muddle-headed, fickle and faithless prince," would never accept him, Louis XIV believed. But if they should, Pomponne must

[1] *Recueil...Hollande*, I, 275–76. Cf. Wicquefort, *Histoire*, III, 438–39.
[2] Bib. Ars., MS 4712, fo. 1.
[3] Cf. De Witt to Temple, June 4, 1668, De Witt, *Correspondance française*, p. 328.
[4] *Recueil...Hollande*, I, 276–77.
[5] Bib. Ars., MS 4712, fo. 1.

warn them that such action "might indeed give His Majesty the occasion to thrust the duke out of a state where he keeps busy only in preparing to trouble the repose of Christendom."[1]

The instructions had remarkably little to say about the attitude Pomponne should take toward the prince of Orange. They revealed that France had no positive policy toward the struggle being waged in the Dutch state over appointment of the prince to high office. If an alliance with England were achieved, Louis thought that he could control young William by means of his uncle, Charles II. But there was no assurance that the negotiations in London would succeed. Pomponne was left to give the prince some vague encouragement to seek support from France. The king of France, Pomponne should tell him, expected that the prince's actions would soon win for him that esteem in which his father had been held. Louis would gladly contribute "insofar as he can, to all his advantages." Pomponne should observe closely the actions and inclinations of the prince and seek to discover "what things he may render himself capable of performing." Beyond this, he must rely on his own judgment. He need only keep in mind that in view of the present hostile policy of the United Provinces, "any disunity which may occur within their state would be of some advantage to his (the king's) service."[2] Turenne, too, was aware of the importance which the prince could assume for France, but he had no clear policy to suggest. He assumed, as did the instructions, that if Charles II made an alliance with France, the prince would be subservient to French interests.[3]

This was the assignment with which Pomponne went to The Hague. It would tax his skill as a diplomatist to the utmost. If his task was to "amuse" the Dutch, it would not be easy to deceive "able and distrustful" men, least of all De Witt. If serious negotiations became possible' many questions, involving widely divergent interests, would have to be settled. Pomponne counted on Lionne to support him in the face of inevitable difficulties.[4]

[1] *Recueil...Hollande,* I, 287–88. Cf. Pomponne, *Relation de Hollande,* pp. 75–76.
[2] *Recueil...Hollande,* I, pp. 288–89.
[3] Bib. Ars., MS 4712, fos. 2–3.
[4] Pomponne at Lille to Lionne, Feb. 16, 1669, Arch. étr., Holl., vol. 89, fo. 52.

CHAPTER IV

DUTCHMEN AND THEIR POLITICS
February, 1669 – May, 1670

On February 9, more than four months after his return from Stockholm, Pomponne left for The Hague. His children remained behind in France, in the care of their grandfather, Arnauld d'Andilly. His wife, Catherine, although four months pregnant, accompanied Pomponne; The Hague was less distant than Stockholm, where he had gone alone. A new carriage eased the discomfort of her journey across France in mid-winter, when the roads were either all ruts or all mud. Her sister, Charlotte Ladvocat, came along to assist her, and to indulge her own wish to see strange places.[1]

The journey took the party across Île de France, Picardy and Artois. Sometimes they found lodgings "good enough so that one need not say anything bad," as Pomponne wrote his father. When they crossed into French Flanders on February 15, the change in the character of the land and the roads astounded Pomponne. How rich and beautiful the country is, he wrote. This was a portion of the Low Countries which Spain had ceded to France the year before. Because it was heavily garrisoned, Pomponne began to meet with ceremonious receptions. He found it easier to accept the tedium of reviews, banquets, toasts and speeches, if afterwards he laughed at these delights of officialdom. At Lille, Pomponne was not spared the round of ceremonies. The interminable harangues of the town magistrates were followed by "numerous troops of bottles of Spanish wine." He also received several visits from local Jansenists, who came to meet him in "his quality only of being the nephew of M. Arnauld."[2] The town itself, which he was able to inspect in some detail, was for Pomponne an eloquent demonstration of the value of the Low Countries. France should not lightly abandon

[1] Pomponne's brother, the abbé Arnauld, remarked that she "preferred to satisfy her love for her sister, and her natural curiosity, at the risk of marrying somewhat later." Arnauld, *Mémoires*, p. 333.

[2] Pomponne to Andilly, Feb. 17, 1669, Bib. Ars., MS 6037, fo. 194.

her claims to such wealth, he thought. It was an easy conquest too: had not Lille, so large and populous, been captured only nine days after the French besiegers had opened their trenches?[1]

The remainder of the journey went smootlhy. The five leagues of highway between Lille and Courtrai were paved. Pomponne proclaimed them "the best in the world," utterly unlike the ruts and mire of French roads. At Courtrai the local commander of the French troops would not relax any part of the review he had planned, and Pomponne sourly watched two thousand troops parade before him. But to his surprise and delight the customary present at the customary banquet proved to be not the usual wines, but bolts of the famous local damask cloth.

At Deynze, Pomponne and his party at last left the territory of France. Deynze was less than twenty-five miles from the frontier of the United Provinces, and the great fortified city of Ghent was only three leagues across the frontier. At Ghent, Pomponne once again sought to evade the burden of ceremony, but the Spanish officials were as insistent on the full measure of their duty as the French commander at Courtrai had been. Delayed in his progress, Pomponne spent the day in sightseeing. The contrast between the "ancient" Gothic cathedral and the "modern, Italianate" church of St. Peter in the abbey of St. Benedict struck him vividly.

From Ghent he moved on to Antwerp. Unwilling to be accompanied by a large body of guards, Pomponne accepted a trumpeter to warn off Spanish troops who might be encountered on the highway. The countryside through which he passed now stirred Pomponne to even greater praises. The finest parks in France do not approach the open road here in beauty, he wrote. "The avenues, not just of Pomponne, but anywhere in France, do not compare with the least of these highways," he assured his father. The fair at Saint Nicholas, in the center of the Waas country, reminded him of the landscapes painted by the great Flemish artists. It was an "enchanted land."

At Antwerp a yacht sent by the States General awaited him, but he went sightseeing first in the famed city on the Scheldt. At the Jesuit church, he found its baroque style "reasonable" and its library admirable. He had to undergo one more bout of ceremony, but at last he and his party were able to board the States' yacht. The scrubbed cleanliness of the Dutch ship delighted the ladies: Mademoiselle Ladvocat thought it too bad they would spend only a night aboard so splendid a vessel. But the yacht grounded on a sandbar, and it was two days

[1] Pomponne at Lille to Lionne, Feb. 16, 1669, Arch. étr., Holl., vol. 89, fo. 52.

before they landed at Rotterdam, completing their journey to The Hague by land.[1]

His mere presence in the Dutch capital did not enable Pomponne to begin his mission formally at once. Until his equipage was complete, he could not make a formal entry and be received by the States General. But several of his carriages, and much other gear, had not been ready when he had left Paris. He thought it would be only a few weeks before they arrived, and by then the necessary horses could be bought in Friesland.[2] The delay was an obstacle only to the form, not to the fact of his mission. His "private" talks with De Witt and other leading Dutchmen, his "personal" meetings with fellow-diplomats, began the day after his arrival, although he took two days to settle down. His quarters, which were the embassy of France for the period of his residence, were very comfortable, he wrote his father.[3]

From the beginning of his mission, Pomponne was caught up in a conflict with Abraham de Wicquefort, whose talents he had hoped to use. Minor diplomat, historian and prolific writer of news dispatches to half a dozen European courts, Wicquefort had been a regular correspondent of Lionne's since 1661. Pomponne assumed that he could settle Wicquefort's quarrel with Pierre Bernarts, a secretary and translator who had served Pomponne's predecessors.[4] He did not realize how sharp their enmity was, nor that it reached back to the days when Jacques Auguste de Thou was the French ambassador at The Hague.[5] Bernarts had aroused Wicquefort's hatred by his opposition to De Witt, the latter's friend and supporter. Political anger was intensified by private resentments. He could not tolerate Bernarts' "swaggering" over him,[6] and, to make matters worse, when he went to visit Pomponne, he found Bernarts serving the ambassador as a translator, the very post which Wicquefort had come to request for his own son. As long as his foe remained in the French embassy, he would not enter it. Even after Pomponne went in person to Wicquefort's home to urge the irate newsgatherer to change his stand, he would not budge.[7]

[1] Pomponne, aboard ship, to Ladvocat and Andilly, Feb. 22, at The Hague, to the same, Feb. 25(?), 1669, Bib. Ars., MS 6037, fos. 203–11; Pomponne to Louis XIV Feb. 28, 1668, Arch. étr., Holl., vol. 89, fo. 57.

[2] Pomponne to Louis XIV, Wicquefort to Lionne, Feb. 28, 1669, *ibid.*, fos 58, 70; Pomponne, *Relation de Hollande*, p. 78; Pomponne to Andilly, March 7, 1669, Bib. Ars., MS 6037, fo. 212.

[3] Pomponne to Andilly, March 7, 1669, *ibid.*, fos. 212–13.

[4] Pomponne to Lionne, March 21, 1669, Arch. étr., Holl., vol. 89, fo. 101.

[5] Wicquefort, *Histoire*, IV, 84.

[6] Wicquefort to Lionne, Oct. 18, 1668, Arch. étr., Holl., vol. 88, fos. 259–60; cf. Wicquefort, *Histoire*, IV, 84.

[7] Haje, ch. III; Wicquefort, *Histoire*, IV, 248–49.

At first Louis XIV instructed Pomponne, as better able to judge "on the place," to do as he pleased with such little folk.[1] Small as Wicquefort was, his pinpricks could be painful, for his newsreports were read far and wide through Europe. On the surface, he seems only an adventurer with slippery loyalties, eager to serve any prince who would pay him. Mazarin had jailed him and expelled him from France in 1659 even though he was accredited by the elector of Brandenburg. Yet Wicquefort had gone on to The Hague and re-entered the service of France as a news correspondent. In the interim between the embassies of De Thou and Estrades, he served as unofficial representative of France, while continuing to send news reports to Lionne, who had become foreign minister on Mazarin's death in 1661. Lionne had found Wicquefort's newsletters highly useful. The Dutchman was very well informed: he spent most of the pay he received from the recipients of his accounts to buy news from informants whose consciences were at least as flexible as his own. He managed to serve not only many masters, but also frequently hostile ones; among these were Brandenburg, the ducal house of Brunswick-Lüneburg, France and England.[2] Yet, within this seeming faithlessness, there lurked an elemental fidelity to the republican cause and to the United Provinces. Wicquefort was De Witt's friend and served him gladly as a secondary and unofficial channel of communication with the French court. If De Witt succeeded in regaining the amity of France now that Pomponne was at The Hague, Wicquefort could except that his own pension from France would probably continue to be sent him.

Though Wicquefort's letters to Lionne reveal a narrow emphasis upon petty and personal motivations, he was, as Pomponne recognized, "as well informed a person as there is in the country." But the envoy doubted that he would tell all he knew, and so preferred to keep Bernarts, who was "very careful" and gave "good counsel," in his employ.[3] Lionne approved this decision.[4] A pension of 1200 *livres* annually was granted to Bernarts. Colbert sent the first year's sum early in the summer.[5]

It shocked Pomponne that Wicquefort, who was also minister resident at The Hague for the dukes of Brunswick-Lüneburg, refused to acknowledge the French ambassador's announcement of his arrival.

[1] Lionne to Pomponne, March 15, 1669, Bib. Ars., MS 4712, fo. 41.
[2] Albert Waddington, *Le Grand Électeur Frédéric Guillaume de Brandebourg: Sa politique extérieure, 1640–1688* (Paris, 1905–08), I, 161–65; Haje, *passim.*
[3] Pomponne to Lionne, March, 21, 1669, Arch. étr., Holl., vol. 89, fo. 101.
[4] Lionne to Pomponne, Aug. 26, 1669, Bib. Ars., MS 4712, fo. 54.
[5] Colbert to Pomponne, March 29, July 19, 1669, *ibid.*, MS 4586, fos. 10, 51.

A split between them as individuals little perturbed Pomponne, but, as he wrote to Lionne, he did not believe Wicquefort wished for a division "between crown and crown."[1] Wicquefort further weakened his position by using his newsreports to Lionne to argue in favor of De Witt's policy. His claim to be acting without prompting, with "no orders from anyone whatsoever," did not carry weight. Lionne's answer to him was blunt: Make your proposals, whether yours or anyone else's, to the king's envoy at The Hague.[2] Pomponne thought it obvious that De Witt and Wicquefort had concerted this action beforehand, and that Wicquefort's independence was "feigned."[3]

Before long, Lionne decided that Wicquefort had become "useless" to Pomponne.[4] The Hollander took offense at Lionne's preference for Pomponne over him. He kept aloof from the ambassador, visiting him seldom and telling him little. Pomponne consoled himself with the thought that the loss would have been greater had Wicquefort proved of more use, "but a man who throws together so many interests rarely contributes much to any one of them."[5] Lionne warned his friend that Bernarts could be used but not trusted. If Bernarts thought it to his interest, he would slip the traces as easily as Wicquefort. Pomponne should not tell him anything he did not want repeated at once: De Witt had told Estrades that Bernarts was the Spanish ambassador's leading spy. Lionne compared Bernarts to the foreign diplomat whom Richelieu presented to Louis XIII with the words, "Sire, this is M. David, who serves both sides faithfully."[6] To the money-hungry Wicquefort Lionne sent a warning he could understand: Until he halted his "skirmishing" and voluntarily subordinated himself to Pomponne, he would not get a penny of his pension from France. The foreign minister reminded him that Pomponne was "one of the best friends I have in the world."[7]

Wicquefort's reply did more credit to his sense of personal dignity than to his usual concern for his pocketbook. In a truly regal manner, he proclaimed, "I find myself compelled to take my own justice." He would not beg for his pension. "I will do whatever I am ordered to

[1] Pomponne to Lionne, June 6, 1669, Arch, étr., Holl., vol. 89, fos. 224–25.
[2] Copy in Lionne's hand of letter sent by Wicquefort to him, and of Lionne's reply, Aug. 28, 1669, Bib. Ars., MS 4712, fo. 55.
[3] Pomponne to Louis XIV, May 2, 16, to Lionne, May 9, 1669, Arch. étr., Holl., vol. 89, fos. 161, 176, 190.
[4] Lionne to Pomponne, May 3, 1669, Bib. Ars., MS 4712, fo. 59; cf. Haje, pp. 118ff.
[5] Pomponne to Lionne, May 9, 16, 1669, Arch. étr., Holl., vol. 89, fos. 173, 176–77, 194–95.
[6] Lionne to Pomponne, May 17, 1669, Bib. Ars., MS 4712, fos. 62–63.
[7] Lionne to Pomponne, May 31, June 7, to Wicquefort, June 7, 1669, *ibid.*, fos. 70, 74–75.

do, without reservation, provided that Bernarts is not given the advantage over me of having forced me to bend the knee. That I will never do for any consideration whatever."[1] Meanwhile Louis XIV ordered Lionne to suspend all correspondence with Wicquefort until he had settled his quarrel with Pomponne and gone to visit him. The foreign minister wondered how Wicquefort, "pulled between his vanity, the greatest there is in the world, and his interest," would react.[2] When the angry Dutchman replied only by silence, Lionne sarcastically wrote off the loss of his newsreports. The king would save the thousand crowns a year he had paid for "a little whipped cream" which Wicquefort peddled every week.[3] Pomponne agreed that the loss would not be great. Bernarts, he indicated, had penetrated the secrets of the States General; this had been Wicquefort's true value. He doubted, in any event, that Wicquefort would find anything De Witt would not want him to discover.[4]

Wicquefort did not take his rebuff lightly. Pomponne soon heard that he had denounced Bernarts as the conveyor of the resolutions and correspondence of the States General to the French embassy.[5] The king approved the issuance of a document declaring Bernarts to be in the royal service and thus covered by diplomatic immunity.[6] Pomponne defended Bernarts against the accusation of disloyalty on grounds which, though they may surprise the modern reader, did not shock seventeenth-century sensibilities. "As he holds no office in the State, no guilt is involved if he penetrates its secrets" in performing his duty to the king of France, Pomponne averred. Louis XIV approved Pomponne's plan to protect Bernarts against arrest.[7]

Meanwhile Wicquefort proved that he would seek to hurt France if she would not pay for his help on his terms. Late in 1669, Grémonville, the French ambassador at the imperial court, began to report that the Dutchman was sending to Vienna anti-French newsletters "written with great skill and deliberate purpose to persuade this court" against the "great designs" of France.[8] News that Wicquefort had become an advisor of Lisola and Temple in their ceaseless agitation against France caused Lionne to turn against him with savage wrath. His

[1] Wicquefort to Lionne, June, 6, 1669 (copy to Pomponne), *ibid.*, fos. 85–86.
[2] Lionne to Wicquefort, June 14 (copy to Pomponne), to Pomponne, June 21, 1669, *ibid.*, fos. 78, 84.
[3] Lionne to Pomponne, July 5, 1669, *ibid.*, fo. 90.
[4] Pomponne to Lionne, July 11, 1669, Arch. étr., Holl., vol. 89, fo. 280.
[5] Pomponne to Lionne, July 18, 1669, *ibid.*, fo. 290.
[6] Lionne to Pomponne, July 28, 1669, Bib. Ars., MS 4712, fo. 97.
[7] Pomponne to Louis XIV, Feb. 20, 1670, Arch. étr., Holl., vol. 90, fos. 72–73; Louis XIV to Pomponne, Feb. 28, 1670, Bib. Ars., MS 4712, fo. 202.
[8] Grémonville to Pomponne, Dec. 1, 1669, Feb. 23, 1670, *ibid.*, MS 4713, fos. 78, 98.

impertinence deserved a thrashing, but it would be better to let things be with "this vain and spiteful" fellow, Lionne wrote to Pomponne.[1] Scorn rather than indignation was Pomponne's reaction; he proposed that Wicquefort's news informants within France be hunted down.[2]

Most of Pomponne's attention during this mission was directed not to small folk like Wicquefort, but to the great ones of the land. Most important of these was John de Witt.

Pomponne had to cope with the complexity and subtlety of the grand pensionary's position in Dutch political life. The novelty of his administration lay in the refusal of the dominant political forces in the republic after 1650 to fill the offices of stadholder and captain and admiral general. The republican (States) party had assumed leadership, however, not by defeating the party of the prince of Orange in open battle, for William II's assault upon Amsterdam in 1650 had been terminated by a compromise which excluded his most vigorous foes from office; the republicans had seized the opportunity of William II's death, and the disruption it caused among his supporters, to continue the government of the country without replacing him. The stadholderless régime, which the republicans called "The True Freedom" *(De Ware Vrijheid)*, had quickly come under the guidance of John de Witt, son of that Jacob de Witt who had been imprisoned by William II in Louvestein castle as one of his most implacable foes. The young De Witt, still only twenty-seven years of age, had been elected councilor pensionary of the province of Holland and West Friesland, or grand pensionary as it was usually called abroad, in 1653.

It was significant that De Witt was a citizen not of Amsterdam, the greatest city of the province and the republic, but of Dordrecht. He was not simply the agent of the great commercial metropolis on the Zuyder Zee, as too many foreign historians have assumed. As a Dordrechter, he represented the middle towns of the province. When, as was often true, the interests of Amsterdam were those of the whole province, De Witt acted for her. When Amsterdam's narrow urban loyalism conflicted with wider, provincial and republic-wide interests, De Witt upheld, as much as he could, the interests of the rest of the province against Amsterdam. He usually tried to solve difficulties between towns and provinces by directing the flow of their interests into a single channel.

De Witt's strength derived fundamentally from the skill, knowledge

[1] Lionne to Pomponne, holograph, May 20, 1670, *ibid.*, MS 4712, fo. 262.

[2] Pomponne at Courtrai to Lionne, May 26, 1670, Arch. étr., Holl., vol. 90, fos. 207–08.

and diligence which he placed at the service of the republic. Within the province of Holland, he functioned as an executive secretary; he did not have any portion of sovereign authority. Yet he led the province in a way that no single member of the States of Holland did. Each of them was delegated by a single town (except for the representative of the nobility), and possessed only a temporary and limited mandate. But the deputies came and went, while De Witt stayed permanently at The Hague, enabled by his superior knowledge of events, their past and present scope and future possibilities, to fulfil his duty of proposing policy to his masters. Thus, though his leadership rested not on authority or even primarily on connection, but on persuasion, he could think, speak and act for the whole province of Holland in most situations.

De Witt's tasks as an official of his own province were, however, only the smaller part of his duties. He was regularly named a deputy from the States of Holland to the States General, and therefore had a vote in the body which represented for other states the sovereignty of the United Provinces. Although each individual province had a veto in the formulation and conduct of foreign policy, decisions once adopted became the policy of the Union. When De Witt, unofficially but with the tacit consent of all the provinces, assumed direction of the foreign relations of the republic, he spoke for all the provinces jointly.

Functionally, John de Witt symbolized the triumph of the appointive bureaucrat, although politically he represented the spirit of the patrician regents who traditionally ruled the Dutch towns. For most purposes, he was the moving spirit of policy, though in no sense whatever was he the source of power and authority in the republic.

Unlike Pomponne, therefore, De Witt spoke for many masters. Where the French diplomat's policy rested upon the single, apparently more stable will of the king, and only a few ministers of state contributed much to Louis' judgments and decisions, De Witt always had to operate upon the basis of the various needs and desires of many authorities. He might well have envied the single sovereignty of the French state, as clear and distinct as one of Descartes' self-evident ideas. There was no locus of sovereignty in the United Provinces. In foreign affairs, to be sure, the States General acted *as if* they were sovereign, but their decisions were always subject to recall by the provinces. The provinces, too, seemed each sovereign within itself from the standpoint of the States General; but within each province the rights of a town could not be simply overridden by a majority in the provincial States. We must simply say that town and province somehow shared sovereignty. When De Witt was able to count on good will, he cut the corners of strict legality in order to solve practical problems quickly. The towns and provincial States could undo what he did in their name, and any violation of their sovereignty thus required at least tacit indemnification.

There were even greater difficulties in evaluating the position of the prince of Orange, De Witt's greatest rival within the republic. William was a youth not yet nineteen when Pomponne came to The Hague, so that it was a question of knowing not what he had done but "what he is capable of performing," in the language of Pomponne's instructions. Though he possessed not a tittle of power or authority in the republic, he was still a dynast born. In his own mind he was before all things else the head of the House of Orange. As sovereign ruler over the pocket principality of Orange, wedged into the Rhône valley in southern France, he was formally equal to all other sovereign princes. By itself this was little better than being *roi d'Yvetot*. William's forebears had become members of the class of almost-sovereign princes of Germany by marrying into the House of Nassau. Since the days of William I, the Silent, the princes of Orange had drawn their essential strength from leadership of the Dutch republic. From William the Silent down through his grandson William II, four princes of Orange had succeeded each other in election to the stadholdership of the leading provinces and to the posts of captain and admiral general. Frederick Henry and William II felt such dependence on election to be something of a blow to their pride. But they had accepted the power given to them and used it to lift themselves into the loftiest class in European society. In 1641 William, Frederick Henry's son, married Mary Stuart, daughter of Charles I of England. Their son, William Henry, was granted no office after his father's death in 1650, but his forebears' power became his own dream, from which he drew high pride and vaulting ambition. Despite the rule of the "True Freedom," the name of "Prince of Orange" continued to stir Dutchmen deeply. Even principled republicans could not wholly forget the services which the family had rendered to the cause of a free Netherlands, and the lesser folk preferred the simplicity of government by stadholders to the newfangled rule without a visible single leader of the state.

It was obvious when Pomponne came to The Hague that much depended on the kind of person the prince would show himself to be. When Pomponne described William III in his Relation more than a decade later, he still could maintain an admirable objectivity, as if the man he was limning had not for six years thwarted not only Louvois' armies but his own diplomacy. Pomponne might have been penning the portrait of someone wholly foreign to France's interests; its subtlety, insight and honesty merit for it a place alongside the reminiscences of other contemporaries like Bishop Burnet. William, wrote Pomponne,

> had been born with intelligence, and no less judgment. He was able to conceal his opinions behind the dissembling character natural to him. Except for hunting, he had none of the passions customary in youth. In his personal conduct, he followed the strictest discipline; his character was settled, humane and affable. He knew well what his interests were, and how to further them with skill. His bent of character—or, it may be, the disorder in which he found his business affairs—seemed to encourage him to be somewhat too thrifty and economical. It was amazing to see the intelligence and competence with which he worked to pay off the debts of his House, to control his expenditures, and to re-establish his revenues. These activities, combined with his naturally reticent and withdrawn personality, kept him a bit too removed from society and did him no service among the people. The love they bore him (they never called him by any name except "Our Prince") should have been cultivated by friendliness, familiarity and caresses, and it seemed that he did not make enough use of such means, always so helpful to those who have risen in popular republics. Those attached to him were grieved to see that this taciturnity was harming his interests, and those opposed to him were not annoyed to be able to attribute to the pride he felt on his alliance with England, the small value he seemed to place on his own countrymen. It is certain that greater ease in making himself seen, in speaking to all sorts of persons, even in having more social commerce with women, who in Holland more than anywhere else in the world have power over their husbands, would have been of great advantage to him, and it might have been wished that he had had, in addition to the many qualities unusual for one his age, the ordinary zest of young men for companionship, public festivities, and pleasures.[1]

The political controversy raging about the person of William III when Pomponne began his mission concerned the position the youth would hold in the Dutch political system. What offices should he be given? Some said all his fathers had held: the stadholdership of the leading provinces, and the posts of captain and admiral general. As little as possible, said others, who recalled that the princes, by virtue of these offices, had retained important rights of appointment from the

[1] Pomponne, *Relation de Hollande*, pp. 55–56.

time when the stadholders and captains general were officers of the crown, not of the States; by these rights, they selected new aldermen and magistrates from lists submitted to them by the town magistrates, and named captains and colonels in the military forces. As a result, the very agencies from which they drew their authority after the abjuration of Spanish sovereignty tended to fall under their influence. When, after 1650, the stadholderate was discarded and no new captain general was named, the various sovereign bodies retained these valuable rights of appointment wholly to themselves. As Pomponne observed, they were not minded to forgo "favors which before they had been obliged to solicit."

Pomponne believed that De Witt, having assured the leadership of the republican party in this manner, thought it wise to give "some mark of consideration" to the prince as a sop to the populace. By compelling him to take a lesser post at the permanent sacrifice of the greater ones traditionally held by his fathers, the republicans could prevent that joint tenure of the highest civil and military offices in the land which they so feared.[1]

The prince could take no office over which the States of Holland had any say except by accepting the Eternal Edict of 1667. This edict confirmed as a permanent institution the right of the town magistracies to choose their own successors. It also barred any person from holding at the same time the posts of stadholder of any province and captain general. When William reached the age of twenty, he would be given a seat in the Council of State, the branch of government under the States General concerned with military administration and the government of the Generality lands.[2] The province of Holland would henceforth appoint no stadholder, and all officials subject to its approval must take an oath to support this edict. Lastly, it provided that William, by forgoing the stadholdership, would be assured the captain generalship of the Union when he reached the age of twenty two.

The choice before the prince and his advisers was not an easy one. To accept the edict meant abandoning the provincial stadholderships to which several provinces would gladly name him. To reject the terms

[1] It may be noted that Pomponne's account, based upon what he learned about this situation between 1669 and 1671, confirms in general spirit, though not in detail, the subtle analysis of the problem of the origin of the "Eternal Edict" of 1667 given by Pieter Geyl in his article, "De wording van het Eeuwig Edict van 1667," *Nederlandsche Historiebladen*, II (1939), 378–92.

[2] These were the conquered lands in the south and southeast owned by the States General rather than any individual province.

of the edict meant, however, that William could be elected to the lesser stadholderships only at the price of abandoning the captain generalship. The prince and his counselors therefore decided to submit to the edict. In Pomponne's words, they "judged quite rightly that however he made his first steps toward returning to official posts, it was important that he do so, for once he was established in command of the armed forces, it would provide him with a stairway on which to climb to all the other posts."

The prince of Orange had been for some years under the legal tutelage of the States of Holland, with the title of *Kind van Staat.* William's own suite of counselors and friends was dismissed, and in their place as his tutors came De Witt and other servants of the States of Holland. Pomponne recognized that the arrangement might be explained in part as resulting from De Witt's realization that the prince could not be permanently excluded from Dutch political life. It would be wise, then, "to instruct and to train" him in the methods and problems of government, to the eventual benefit of himself and of the state he would serve. But Pomponne thought this was not De Witt's true purpose. He really wished to permit only those to be close to the prince "in whom he felt confidence, and to keep away those who maintained their accustomed love for his House and desired to see it return to the heights from which it had fallen."[1]

At the time Pomponne came to Holland the prince was still the reluctant pupil trying to throw off the control of "would-be" tutors. Without De Witt's permission, he secretly made his way to Middleburg, the capital of Zeeland, in order to take over in person the post of "First Noble," which belonged to him. As marquis of Flushing and Veere, William already controlled two votes in the States of Zeeland; an additional vote as first noble meant that he needed only one additional voice in order to have a majority in the provincial government and hence a powerful position in the States General as well.[2]

It is not surprising that Pomponne should have stressed signs of conflict such as these, rather than the potentialities for the prince to achieve a place for himself in the republic, by which he could serve its interests as well as his own. Not only would cold calculation have shown little likelihood that such objectives could be achieved in a way satisfactory to De Witt, but the development of dissension within the republic was a prime purpose of French policy at this time. It was the guiding rule for appraising the Orangist problem laid down in

[1] Pomponne, *Relation de Hollande,* p. 56.
[2] *Ibid.,* pp. 54–56.

Pompone's instructions and reaffirmed by Turenne. On the other hand, if De Witt and Pomponne succeeded in re-establishing friendship between their countries, France would inevitably insist that the prince, as the instrument of English policy, be barred from office.

The Orangists were traditional foes of De Witt, but perhaps even more troublesome for him were new opponents from his own republican camp. Forming what Dutch historians now call the "middle party," they were ready to join with the Orangists against De Witt. Their leaders were Van Beuningen, Hieronymus van Beverningk, former treasurer general of the Union and one of the most skilled of Dutch diplomats, and Gillis Valckenier, whose principal sphere of activity was the municipality of Amsterdam. The movement was no more than two years old.[1] In 1669, in the period when Pomponne first began his duties at The Hague, Valckenier broke with the faction in Amsterdam that supported the leadership of Andries de Graeff, with whom De Witt was connected by family relationships. Valckenier and Van Beuningen together were able to gain control of the municipal government.[2]

In this conflict, Pomponne's sympathy lay with De Witt rather than with the Valckenier-Van Beuningen group. For the grand pensionary he had praise: his authority rested on his "capacity and merit." Those opposing him were motivated by "great jealousy in a state where petty interests of many persons are almost considered to be higher than those which concern the general welfare." The only reason the new party joined hands with the Orangists was to obtain tactical advantage over De Witt.[3]

Early in March, 1669, less than two weeks after his arrival, Pomponne would still not venture "a firm and certain judgment on this state in general or De Witt in particular," but he began to record the interplay between the domestic dissensions of the Dutch and the foreign policy the republic pursued. Their squabbles made them fear for their power. Pomponne observed a general doubt that prince William, whose "great intelligence and diligence" everyone praised, would permanently accept the status of a "private person without a post in the government." Some leaders of the States party were over-confident because of the prowess the republic had displayed in her recent war

[1] Pieter Geyl, in his article, "De wording...," refutes the view that this middle party arose in the period of the second Anglo-Dutch war (1665–66) (e.g., A. Bredius *et al.*, *Amsterdam in de zeventiende Eeuw* [The Hague, 1894–1904], I, 218.)

[2] Johan E. Elias, *Geschiedenis van het Amsterdamsche Regentenpatriciaat* (2nd ed., The Hague, 1929), 160–61.

[3] Pomponne, *Relation de Hollande*, p. 57.

with England. But De Witt was not one of them. Nor did the grand pensionary make the mistake of those leaders who carelessly trampled on French sensibilities; in this he was more prudent and skillful than the present leaders of the cities of Holland, especially Amsterdam, where Valckenier and Van Beuningen fanned the resentment over Colbert's high tariff of 1667 and his other measures to hamper Dutch trade.[1]

In early 1669, the problem of the Orangists emerged for the moment in the form of a quarrel between the provinces of Holland and Zeeland over their joint high court of appeals, the *Hooge Raad* or high council. Zeeland sought to break loose from this arrangement by establishing its own final appellate jurisdiction, but Holland resisted the change. The leaders in Holland believed that the initiative for Zeeland's action actually came from the prince of Orange, and they brushed off a proposal that he be named a mediator in the dispute. The only rôle the Hollanders would permit him in the affair would be that of a delegate to a mediation conference fully accredited by the States of Zeeland.[2]

Pomponne emphasized how intimately this dispute was connected with the general struggle over the prince's position in the state. The Zeelanders' demand for separation of the high council served them as a weapon in their parallel conflict with Holland over the Eternal Edict of 1667. If Holland would show more favor to the prince, the Zeelanders indicated they might modify their stand on the *Hooge Raad.* Before they accepted the Eternal Edict, Holland would have to promise not only a seat in the Council of State for the prince, but that the captain generalship be assured him at once. Holland might accept this proposal, Pomponne thought, provided Zeeland accepted three conditions: 1) the prince would not assume the functions of captain general until he reached the age of twenty-two, in the year 1672; 2) even then, his competence to hold the office must be re-examined; 3) the prince must enter into no alliance not approved by the States General. The latter two provisos were specifically designed to hamper the prince of Orange in his activity as a quasi-dynast. William would be subject to the limitations of a private citizen for whom high office was not a birthright. These conditions made it unlikely, in Pomponne's opinion, that the prince would actually receive the captain generalship in 1672. Though conciliatory in appearance, Holland was deftly preparing, he thought, to prevent the prince from ever receiving authority.

[1] Pomponne to Louis XIV, March 7, 1669, Arch. étr., Holl., vol. 89, fos. 78–79.
[2] Wicquefort to Lionne, March 7, 1669, *ibid.*, fo. 82.

The obstacles which would turn up in 1672 would prove as great as those of 1669.[1]

Pomponne was impressed by the firmness shown by the province of Holland in the affair. Though Zeeland might have to concede now in the questions of the high court and the elevation of the prince of Orange, William's aspirations "may well become one day a source of great divisions within these provinces."[2] By June, the conflict became so sharp that Pomponne anticipated rioting in the republic. Yet the fears that such disorders would do the state harm in its foreign relations helped to bring a compromise in the affair of the high court, Pomponne observed. De Witt worked out a plan with Huibert, the pensionary of the States of Zeeland, by which the high court would continue its function of hearing final appeal in civil cases, while criminal appeals would henceforth terminate within the provincial courts. Pomponne thought Holland was thereby seeking to assure its ability to punish violators of the Eternal Edict within its boundaries. The ambassador also noted that De Witt was abandoning his reported hopes of becoming president of the high council. De Witt was too wise to risk civil disorder for such personal gains, Pomponne commented, "when their needless involvement in so many foreign concerns makes internal tranquility all the more necessary to them."[3]

Pomponne, always alert to signs of Dutch dissension, watched with interest the struggle between the "middle party" and De Witt. When the grand pensionary proposed that Van Beuningen go to England as ambassador extraordinary in order to counter efforts to make an Anglo-French alliance, Pomponne heard that the Amsterdammer suspected his rival's motives. Did De Witt want him out of the country because his influence was growing? Was De Witt afraid of his support for the election of William to the Council of State?[4] Pomponne instructed Bernarts to hunt out the hidden facts of the case, and drew from his report thoughtful conclusions about the relationship between the "middle party," on the one hand, and the prince of Orange and England, on the other. The conflict between De Witt and Van Beuningen was still "veiled," Pomponne wrote. Its first signs had come in the debate between Holland and Zeeland over the court of justice. In

[1] Pomponne to Louis XIV, March 21, 1669, *ibid.*, fo. 98.
[2] Pomponne to Louis XIV, March 28, April 4, 1669, *ibid.*, fos. 108–110, 116.
[3] Pomponne to Lionne, June 6, 1669, *ibid.*, fos. 222–23. Pomponne erroneously believed that the *Hooge Raad* was two bodies, a Court of Justice and a Grand Council, with criminal and civil jurisdictions respectively. Actually it was one body with dual functions. See R. Fruin and H. T. Colenbrander, *Geschiedenis der Staatsinstellingen der Nederlanden* (2nd ed., The Hague, 1922), pp. 261–63.
[4] Pomponne to Louis XIV, April 11, 1669, Arch. étr., Holl., vol. 89, fos. 129–30.

persuading Amsterdam to support Zeeland in this issue, Van Beuningen really was working to assist the cause of the prince of Orange, "which he has been eagerly serving for some time." According to Bernarts' information, a very secret plan was afoot in the States of Zeeland to demand an investigation of De Witt's administration on the grounds especially of misuse of the 80,000 guilders furnished him annually for "secret affairs," but really in order to take revenge for his opposition to the election of the prince to the captain generalship. Once this affair was settled, Van Beuningen would then go to England, "so that he might take credit with the king for service to his nephew." Pomponne accepted the report as credible: Van Beuningen was not only seeking to increase his influence within the government of Holland and the republic, he thought, but also, in "his single intention to strengthen the liaisons he has formed against us, will neglect nothing by which England will be indebted to him."[1]

From the point of view of Louis XIV, as Pomponne knew, there was no longer any great choice between De Witt and Van Beuningen: the grand pensionary was more moderate but wilier, the Amsterdammer more open and violent. French advantage lay in increasing animosity between them, rather than in any settlement of their quarrel.[2] Pomponne, recognizing this advantage to France from the domestic broils of the Dutch, saw that De Witt might be able to dissipate the storm clouds. The envoy reported a widespread belief that De Witt would not look amiss at the outbreak of "some great affair" which, by making him necessary, would stifle the cabals against him.[3]

By late April of 1670, De Witt's influence was again increasing. The councilor pensionary, "whose capabilities in this government are all the greater because they are accompanied by more moderation and skill," persuaded several of the lesser towns of Holland, fearful of Amsterdam's ascendancy, to abandon support of the prince. With the votes divided at the moment ten to nine against the prince, it was likely that William would have to accept a deliberative (non-casting) vote if he were to be named to the council. Yet Pomponne recognized that the significance of the struggle lay not so much in the inherent value of the office as in its rôle as a political symbol. It was the occasion for the first open combat of the prince of Orange with the republican party. Any victory would encourage his supporters; the resistance he faced made clear the obstacles he would face in seeking higher office.[4]

[1] Pomponne to Lionne, May 9, 1669, *ibid.*, fos. 175–76.
[2] Louis XIV to Pomponne, Dec. 6, 1669, Bib. Ars., MS 4712, fo. 152.
[3] Pomponne to Louis XIV, Dec. 19, 1669, Arch. étr., Holl., vol. 89, fo. 448.
[4] Pomponne to Louis XIV, April 24, 1670, *ibid.*, vol. 90, fo. 153.

It was also clear that France could not count upon any direct advantage whichever way the decision went. Neither William, who acted throughout the affair with intelligence and skill, nor the grand pensionary discussed his interests any longer with the French ambassador. "Perhaps they both fear they will be suspect if they turn to France," he mused.[1]

Sharp conflict was renewed when the States of Holland, where De Witt remained paramount in influence, proposed that William be granted only a deliberative vote in the Council of State. Such a right to speak, but not to have his vote counted, was a hollow right, of course. Some of the Orangists therefore urged that the prince reject a seat in the council on these terms as beneath his dignity. Others among his supporters urged that he accept and attack the problem of his precise powers later.

The implications of the prince's promised promotion were clear to Pomponne. Where would the nephew of Charles II take his stand if the negotiations between France and England ended successfully, as seemed likely in the spring of 1670? This would be the obvious reason for a visit which Charles invited William to pay him in England. The prince was reluctant to leave until the issue of his seat in the Council of State was settled.[2]

These domestic broils formed the background upon which Pomponne and De Witt spun out their negotiations for the first fifteen months of the Frenchman's embassy. These talks were the main body of his tasks, and it is they which must now hold our attention.

[1] Pomponne to Louis XIV, May 1, 1670, *ibid.*, fos. 164–65.

[2] Pomponne to Louis XIV, April 10, 1670, *ibid.*, fo. 129.

Geyl (*Oranje en Stuart*, p. 409) accepts a contemporary report by a British news writer from Holland that the prince received from Pomponne assurances that his aunt, the duchess of Orleans, would support his interests at Dover. Japikse (*Prins Willem III: De Stadhouder-Koning* [Amsterdam, 1930–33], I, 161) credit's Wicquefort's assertion (*Histoire*, IV, 121) that Pomponne also urged the prince to accept his uncle's invitation, and predicted that the decisions which the duchess would help to make would bring about a revolution in the republic which would change his fortunes.

The absence of any mention of such a meeting between Pomponne and the prince, or of any hint of such encouragement in this dispatch of April 10, or indeed of any other in the Quai d'Orsay archives, makes the whole story almost certainly untrue. Wicquefort was obviously fabricating his tale, as Geyl suspects; the English news reporter, writing the day after Pomponne's dispatch, perhaps had picked up a rumor.

CHAPTER V

POSITIONS EXPLORED AND DEFINED
February-May, 1669

As French policy stood in February of 1669, the first of Pomponne's tasks as ambassador of Louis XIV at The Hague was to keep open the door for renewed amity with the United Provinces. While he was en route to The Hague, Lionne had rushed off to him a reminder that he must try to persuade the Dutch that "the king does not *devour lands and states without rhyme or reason,*" and he underlined the words which summed up the Dutch fears.[1]

Van Beuningen, who led the party of opposition to France, came to see Pomponne the day after the envoy's arrival. He explained that he was leaving at once for Amsterdam, where he had just been elected burgomaster, and wished to meet the new ambassador without delay. He was in fact testing the character of Pomponne's true purpose. Late in 1668 a mutual friend in the Netherlands had received a letter from Pomponne affirming that he was bringing proposals so reasonable that the States General, if their intentions were moderate, could not but be satisfied. Upon being shown the letter, Van Beuningen said that if Pomponne spoke truly, his success at The Hague was assured. But the new ambassador should not expect to "make fools" of the Dutch.[2]

Pomponne easily carried off his task of rebutting Van Beuningen's political ideas without attacking him personally. The French diplomat made his most telling points with a pleasant laugh that kept the interview from becoming a brawl of hot words. It was true, Van Beuningen admitted, that France's neighbors felt fears over her immense power; but it was up to Louis XIV, as the "unquestioned arbiter of Europe," to overcome such difficulties. Had not the king proved his love of peace by

[1] Lionne to Pomponne, Feb. 15, 1669, Bib. Ars., MS 4712, fo. 20.

[2] Haje, pp. 78–79. Haje's comment here that "these are the words of one who knows that war is inevitable and prefers to have it today rather than tomorrow," is a simple *non sequitur*. Pomponne believed that Van Beuningen had been influenced by a favorable account of his mission given by a personal friend, Daunoy, before his arrival. Pomponne to Lionne, Feb. 28, 1669, Arch. étr., Holl., vol. 89, fo. 68. Daunoy may have been the mutual friend, whom Haje does not identify.

accepting terms to end the late war which deprived him of aspirations both great and certain? Pomponne asked. If such proof could not cure distrust, nothing could. Van Beuningen was not deflected from his principal contention. There must be some way to assure the United Provinces against the threat of France's "power and propinquity." Pomponne took this as a hint that agreement between France and the States General concerning the Spanish succession would turn the trick. Since his orders permitted him to discuss this matter only with De Witt, and not at all with Van Beuningen, Pomponne pretended not to understand.[1]

The next day Pomponne saw De Witt for the first time. He was pleased to find the councilor pensionary, who showed "much gaiety" at his arrival, "free, easy and open in spirit." He would present Louis XIV's views on present affairs "baldly" and "without further preparation or that sly, tricky deviousness which forms almost all the mystery of negotiations," he told De Witt. The pensionary replied with assurances of similar frankness: he too would speak as openly. Pomponne was delighted by the prospect that the "useless compliments which ordinarily consume so much time" could be avoided in his conferences with the grand pensionary.

Pomponne and De Witt met squarely the first test of straight talking —willingness to discuss the impact of the Triple Alliance on relations between France and the Netherlands. It was an act of ingratitude on the part of the States General, Pomponne declared. The Dutch had been misled by "false rumors" that Louis XIV "placed no bounds upon his ambition, that he is intent upon renewing the war at any cost, and that it is Holland which has most to fear from the power of his arms." The ambassador then offered to De Witt the gambit which he himself had declined from Van Beuningen the day before. If the king of Spain died, said Pomponne, though Louis XIV would insist upon the rights due to his queen and the dauphin, he "would be happy indeed to give proof once more of that moderation he had just displayed before all Europe, and to defer greatly to the counsel and interests of his friends."

De Witt assured Pomponne that the States General knew full well what they owed to France. But the wars were over now, and the Dutch republic required tranquility "for the security of its trade." The safety of the United Provinces depended upon preserving a barrier between themselves and France, lest the "hundred little quarrels" which spring up between those whose frontiers touch create the danger

[1] Pomponne to Louis XIV, Feb. 28, 1669, *ibid.*, fos. 58–60.

of some mightier conflict. To keep French power at a distance was and had always been the "first maxim" of the republic, De Witt said. He repeated to Pomponne his arguments of 1663 in favor of "cantonment" of the Low Countries. Louis XIV's "interest lay not so much in Flanders" as in keeping the Hapsburgs from joining their forces there in order to invade France during her civil wars, he said. Louis XIV ought to prefer as a neighbor "a small republic necessarily submissive to him." By accepting cantonment he would end all fears that he wished to extend his frontiers to the limit of his strength and "fix in alliance and friendship with him all the powers which fear of his greatness and his nearness had been able to drive from him."

"We would go into the affair in vain," the French ambassador replied, "much as it would please these provinces, if we did not see some prospect for leading them back to the former confidence from which they had departed." Louis XIV was not interested in an agreement upon "one article" if complete understanding upon all of them was not achieved. The king was willing to discuss these matters with De Witt but not with Van Beuningen. De Witt, accepting Pomponne's statement as a basis for discussion, came to his fellow-Hollander's defense: beneath his violence and temper, there were "great qualities" and "good intentions" toward the alliance with France. Though the grand pensionary presented a single front with his great rival, Pomponne detected some estrangement between them, "born perhaps of the jealousy which division of authority usually causes."

De Witt freely admitted that the Dutch ran grave peril in the shift of their alliances, and that their friendships with "old, natural and offended foes" would probably not last long. "He seems to see the difficulties," Pomponne wrote to the king, "and that is why he affirmed his desire that we should be able to establish this state in Your Majesty's good favor." Ruminating on what his first conference had shown, Pomponne concluded that De Witt's skill was obvious, but not as yet his sincerity.[1]

As for the grand pensionary, he seemed satisfied with the way in which the conference with Pomponne had gone—or at least gave Lionne to believe so.[2] Yet, before two days passed, De Witt came to Pomponne again to go over his arguments, as if reiteration brought persuasion.[3]

Further discussions could not remain on this plane of general

[1] Pomponne to Louis XIV, Feb. 28, 1669, *ibid.*, fos. 60–67; Pomponne, *Relation de Hollande*, p. 80. Cf. Wicquefort, *Histoire*, IV, 25.

[2] Wicquefort to Lionne, Feb. 28, 1669, *ibid.*, fo. 70.

[3] Pomponne to Lionne, Feb. 28, 1669, *ibid.*, fo. 69.

principle. The Dutch were afraid that Louis XIV would use the pretext of the dispute with Spain over the Flanders dependencies to renew the war. The pensionary, though reassured by the king's promise to the Pope not to attack Spain during 1669, urged arbitration of the dispute. Pomponne demurred: until every honest effort had been made for agreement between the parties, there was no ground for arbitration. Spain's obvious intention in the affair was to cause new hostilities with France in which England and the United Provinces would be drawn in as her allies, he warned. Had not Castel Rodrigo chosen the "alternative" cession to France most unfavorable to Dutch interests? he asked. The Hollander did not use this opportunity to propose an exchange of territories. The Spaniards would not change their minds, he said. Pomponne let the issue pass lest he make French interest in it too apparent.

The discussion thereupon turned to a frank confrontation of principles. Pomponne and De Witt both realized that decisions on such issues as the guarantee to Spain or the possible exchange of territories ultimately flowed from judgments on two fundamental questions: Was the Dutch principle of *Gallus amicus non vicinus* justified? Did Dutch efforts to enforce this principle by means of the Triple Alliance necessarily destroy good relations between the United Provinces and France?

The Dutch "departed from their true interest" whenever they based their safety on any principle except friendship with France, Pomponne told the grand pensionary. When De Witt presented as the only obstacle to that friendship the danger to the barrier on which their liberty and safety depended, Pomponne replied:

> If I were a Dutchman, I might indeed be disturbed to see the situation of this state, but I would not at all change the ancient maxims by which it had been established. I might well view with anxiety the power of France so nearby, but I should look with much greater fear on the means by which I might be made safe from it. Being unable to keep France at a distance and having only Spain, England and Sweden to set against her, I should consider it a much lesser peril to place my trust in an ally whose affection and assistance I had always known, rather than trust myself wholly to powers, some irreconcilable, others frequently enemies, and several newly offended. It was difficult to believe that a good understanding could be long maintained with so many causes, however deeply concealed, for breaking it,[1] and, adapting myself to a decision of Heaven which I could not change, I should

[1] This phrase, "Que difficilement pourroit-on croire que la bonne intelligence pût s'accorder longtemps avec tant de sujets, bien que cachés, de la rompre," is lacking in Mignet's excerpt from this dispatch (III, 578).

> prefer a lesser to the greater danger, and a powerful and tested friend to reconciled foes who remain always suspect.[1]

A fortnight later, Pomponne presented these views as his own in a letter to Robert de Gravel, French resident at Regensburg:

> The source of distrust remains as always in their fears of having us as neighbors. Genuine illness may be cured, but not fear. Therefore, whatever remedies the king may place in my hands, such as his good faith, his sincere intention to maintain his alliances and his firm purpose to preserve peace, I do not know whether I dare to be sure of curing these sick people. For if it is the reduction of the king's greatness, by which they are stunned, which can return them to health, you may well judge, Sir, that the cure would be somewhat too costly to the doctor. What I do know is that any man of good sense, seeing this state join with those who are really its enemies and turn away from a tried and faithful friend who is alone capable of protecting it, will conclude that fear of a danger is often more hurtful than the danger itself, and that [and here Pomponne picked up a striking phrase from Lisola's *Buckler of State and Justice* in order to turn it against its author's intent] it is like jumping over the side of a cliff to avoid seeing a shadow or a phantom.[2]

Pomponne reaffirmed this judgment in a conference with Van Beuningen and Ghent, who had also been an ambassador from the States General to France. There was grave "peril," he warned them, in the principle which they were coming to take for granted, that "the character of a neighbor of France is incompatible with that of her friend." Should Louis XIV become convinced that they were fundamentally committed to this maxim, then he would have to take his own measures in response. The Dutch in that event would face a difficult choice: either they would become the "slaves of their new allies," or they would have to seek the assistance of France whenever their allies turned against them, without being certain of receiving that aid.[3]

These warnings to De Witt, Van Beuningen and Ghent, therefore, were based not on a denial of the facts of political life—"Opposition is natural between two neighboring powers," he wrote in his Relation[4]—

[1] Pomponne to Louis XIV, March 7, 1669, Arch. étr., Holl., vol. 89, fos. 73–76.

[2] Pomponne to Gravel, March 12, 1669, *ibid.*, fo. 86; François Paul de Lisola, *The Buckler of State and Justice against the Design manifestly Discovered of the Universal Monarchy, Under the vain Pretext of the Queen of France, Her Pretentions* (2nd ed., London, 1673), p. 277.

[3] Pomponne to Lionne, March 28, 1669, Arch. étr., Holl., vol. 89, fos. 108–09.

[4] Pomponne, *Relation de Hollande*, p. 63.

but on the principle that the wise man accepts and makes do with what he cannot change except at greater cost to himself. The problem confronting the Dutch resolved itself into one easy to state and difficult to solve: Were the dangers they were courting by their policy of the Triple Alliance greater than those which they would have faced from France at their very next door, protected from her overweening might only by the fragile, but nonetheless sometimes very real, screen of her friendship?

Just what conclusions could be drawn from these first conferences? Pomponne speculated. De Witt was clearly more aware of the perils which the enmity of France might conjure up for the Dutch republic than were many of his colleagues, "who are puffed up still with the opinion of their strength they gained during the war with England." Pomponne observed how proud De Witt was of his sincerity, but he was reluctant to trust him. The grand pensionary might be the true friend of France he claimed to be, but even if he were not, he would strive to appear so. If any change could be wrought in the attitude of the United Provinces, Pomponne concluded, it would be the result only of time and repose.[1]

Louis XIV approved Pomponne's conduct in these first conferences, especially the speech to De Witt on the theme, "If I were a Dutchman." To Lionne this discourse was both "forceful and tactful," and "as judicious, urgent and well thought out as was possible." He did not expect, however, that these "most convincing arguments" would actually persuade the Dutch to change their conduct. "The harm has already been done," he wrote to Pomponne, "and there seems little reason to expect the States to be willing to withdraw now from this Triple Alliance which they boast was a work of their own making only, and on which they establish their own safety and that of the Low Countries." Of course, if Pomponne's eloquence swayed them to abandon their new policy and "seek their support only from the king," France in turn would have to reconsider her attitude.[2]

Pomponne was not optimistic that such a change would come easily. Rather he came to think that the malady was "beyond hope," because the Dutch fears could be cured not by fact or argument but only by some "great event" which would prove their error in turning away from France. What should French policy be in the meanwhile? To watch for opportunities to demonstrate their "false conduct" to the Dutch, to act "equably and courteously" toward them, and thus to

[1] Pomponne to Louis XIV, March 7, 1669, Arch. étr., Holl., vol. 89, fos. 76–79.
[2] Lionne to Pomponne, March 8, 15, 1669, Bib. Ars., MS 4712, fos. 36, 40–41.

permit the chilling of "that first ardor which impels them to support and to strengthen with great care and vigilance the mechanism of alliances which they deem it an honor to have erected," Pomponne suggested. Some break in the alliance system was bound to come, he thought. Thus Pomponne still assumed that it was to French interest to extract the Dutch from their new arrangements and policies and to make friends of them again on Louis' terms. Much depended, as the envoy saw, on De Witt's intentions, on his "sincerity," to use Pomponne's term. Since he had provided the grand pensionary with an opportunity to discuss the Spanish succession, De Witt would have to show his hand; if he wished to quell Dutch fears of France by an arrangement with Louis XIV, he would have to take the initiative in further discussion of the problem of the succession and the Low Countries.[1]

The immediacy of this question was brought home by the illness of Carlos II early in 1669. When Pomponne tried to reassure Van Beuningen that the reports he had received from Lionne indicated that the king of Spain had recovered, Van Beuningen replied sadly, "The whole state of Europe is to be pitied when its peace depends upon the pleurisy or other illness of a child."[2]

Pomponne was surprised that De Witt did not at once seize upon the opportunity to discuss the question of the Spanish succession. He found an explanation in a conference with Temple. When he remarked that "great liaisons" were being formed for the occasion of the expected early death of Carlos II, the Englishman told him that the Dutch had taken the initiative for such talks with their partners in the Triple Alliance. Pomponne drew the conclusion that De Witt desired to explore this avenue of negotiations before turning toward France.

To wait for De Witt to act was not only the best course, it was the only course to follow, Pomponne wrote Lionne. "Patience must still chill the heated feelings displayed by this state for more than a year, it must loosen the liaisons which they have sought to make, and time must teach them how little safety there is in a league which embraces so many opposing interests."[3]

Patience and time could be aided in their work, Pomponne judged, by his own policy toward the Dutch. On the one hand, he should

[1] Pomponne to Lionne, March 21, 1669, Arch. étr., Holl., vol. 89, fo. 100. This dispatch is one of many where Mignet (III, 580) indulges his practice of modifying material supposedly cited verbatim. Cf. Pomponne, *Relation de Hollande*, pp. 82–83.

[2] Lionne to Pomponne, March 8, 1669, Bib. Ars., MS 4712, fo. 36; Pomponne to Lionne, March 28, 1669, Arch. étr., Holl., vol. 89, fo. 108.

[3] Pomponne to Lionne, March 28, 1669, *ibid.*, fos. 108–09.

continue to assure them of Louis XIV's constant peaceful purpose, and thus to calm them; on the other, by reminding them how useful French amity had been, compared to the manifest unreliability of their new friends, he would enhance their own uncertainty. "We must wait," Pomponne wrote to the king, "until they cure themselves, or until Your Majesty is able by his prudent acts to bring more powerful remedies to bear." Cleavage of interest between the Dutch and their allies might bring the States General to seek Louis' protection again; the question then would be whether to give them succor which they no longer deserved.[1] This pattern of conduct—calming the Dutch with "general assurances of friendship and good intentions," while leaving the initiative for further action up to De Witt—accorded with Louis XIV's estimate of the proper policy.[2]

Lionne was not surprised that De Witt evaded discussion of the succession problem, nor was he troubled by Dutch efforts to strengthen the Triple Alliance: "I hope that the English and the Swedes will not let themselves be led by the nose like bears, and that they will prefer, if the chance presents itself, to profit by the fall of the tree, with certainty and without difficulty, rather than enter a war to please their good friends, the Dutch." He reassured Pomponne:

> Take courage, Sir, from my bold prediction that the more the Dutch bestir themselves, the greater will they make the glory of the king without harming him, and the greater will be, some day, their reason to repent. On the contrary, it is good that they should pile up their faults, since we cannot put them on the right path. For His Majesty will be supported by the world in the justice of his action if, some day, when the opportunity shall present itself, he brings down his fist upon a state which, it may be said, he twice created, lifted up, supported and saved from final ruin only two years past, and which pays all these debts by the fine, silly project of bringing all Christendom down upon His Majesty. Heaven is too just to suffer that such extraordinary ingratitude turn out well for those who have been capable of blackening themselves by it.[3]

In a "quite long" conference with De Witt on April 9, Pomponne explored more deeply with him the implications of the Dutch position toward France and the Low Countries. Two days before, Don Estebán

[1] Pomponne to Louis XIV, April 4, 1669, *ibid.*, fos. 114–16.

[2] Lionne to Pomponne, April 5, 1669, Bib. Ars., MS 4712, fo. 46.

[3] Lionne at Paris to Pomponne, April 12, 1669 (not, as given by Mignet, III, 582, from Saint-Germain April 19), Bib. Ars. MS 4712, fo. 48; Arch. étr., Holl., vol. 89, fo. 136 (minute in Lionne's hand).

de Gamarra, the Spanish ambassador, had presented a memorandum to the States General in which he charged that Louis XIV had sent troops to occupy the disputed "dependencies," and called upon the Dutch to send aid to the Spanish Netherlands as provided by the guarantee. Pomponne replied with a laugh. I am annoyed, he told De Witt, that Gamarra should have received a report before my own arrived by the ordinary mail, and that the French ambassador should be somewhat tardy in informing you that Louis XIV was carrying the war into Flanders. The pensionary replied in the same bantering tone: He did not have to wait for the courier to doubt the truth of Gamarra's memorandum.

Pomponne then steered the conversation to reports that Van Beuningen was going to London. The trip had not yet been decided, De Witt said. The Frenchman, granting the importance of the controversy with England over trade to the Indies, asserted that the affairs of Europe were more involved in Van Beuningen's journey than those of the East. With an air of knowing more than he was saying, Pomponne suggested that the true purpose of the Amsterdammer's mission was at least in part to discuss what should be done in the event of the death of Carlos II. Though De Witt denied that any such negotiation was in progress with England, he was drawn into a discussion of the problem, as Pomponne wished.

How could De Witt square any such conversations with England with article 15 of the French-Dutch treaty of 1662, providing that neither country would engage in a discussion or conclude a treaty inimical to the interests of the other? Pomponne queried. This was a deft thrust at De Witt's argument that the States General were doing nothing harmful to France. De Witt's reply was lame: the treaty of 1662 obligated the signatories to defend each other against aggression, not to refrain from supporting the victim of aggression. Pomponne snapped at the implication: By aggression, did De Witt mean Louis XIV's action in defending the rights of queen Marie Thérèse if her brother, Carlos II, died? The emperor, Pomponne warned, might contest these rights, but neither Leopold I nor Louis XIV "had judges upon the earth" who could adjudicate their claims. De Witt parried: the treaty of Aix-la-Chapelle gave a guarantee to Spain and France; the guarantors had a right to know who the heirs of Louis XIV and Carlos II would be, since only they would have the protection of the guarantee. Thus, as Pomponne wrote to Louis XIV, "by this indirect means he attributed to the Triple Alliance the right to examine the claims of Your Majesty and the emperor." Indeed, De Witt proposed that the two great monarchs accept negotiations with the States General on means to prevent the Spanish succession from upsetting the peace of Europe. Pomponne rebuffed him by a reminder that the Dutch were only concerned in the fate of the Spanish Netherlands. De Witt said he was willing to continue a discussion limited to the Low Countries, but, to Pomponne's surprise, seemed more eager for "general mediation embracing the whole affair."

What was behind De Witt's shift of emphasis? Pomponne thought that his primary concern now was to avoid being separated from England: the Dutch wished to negotiate with France for an arrangement with France regarding territorial exchanges or the succession to the Spanish monarchy, but only in partnership with England. Pomponne drew the conclusion that De Witt feared to enter a separate negotiation with him lest Charles II hear of it and turn against the States or even forestall them by himself joining with Louis XIV. It was not, Pomponne reaffirmed, that the grand pensionary had lost any of his apprehensions: De Witt still feared the propinquity of France and the unreliability of the Dutch means for preventing it. He admitted to Pomponne that, in the event of the fall of the Spanish monarchy, the Dutch would prefer to have the German branch of the House of Austria rather than the Bourbon king as their neighbor, but that, if they had to choose between France and England, they would prefer France. "For nothing in the world would they wish to see her (England) established in Flanders," he said. But the best solution, he continued, would be to form the Low Countries into a republic, as Louis XIV had seemed ready to do some years before.[1]

This was a "most curious" discussion, Lionne thought. It delighted him that Pomponne had drawn from the grand pensionary an admission that he looked upon France as a less dangerous neighbor than England. This avowal might be used against him some day, but for the moment Pomponne must pretend that he had not noticed it. Lionne railed, however, against De Witt's desire to have the States General "informed" of the negotiations which might occur between the emperor and the king of France over the Spanish succession. "By what right do the United Provinces wish to set themselves up as judges" if their imperial and royal majesties dispute the Spanish succession? he asked. It was pushing the seventh article of the treaty of Aix-la-Chapelle far beyond the claim of justice and what the disputants themselves might agree upon for an event "which would change in a moment the face of world affairs." In any case, Lionne added, "it would not behoove

[1] Pomponne to Louis XIV, April 11, 1669, *ibid.*, fos. 124–29.

tradesmen, themselves usurpers, to decide in sovereign fashion over the interests of the two greatest monarchies in Christendom." Therefore, he wrote, De Witt might be told that the king would not explain his own intentions until the emperor had changed his mind.

This last phrase may explain the actual intention of Lionne in the whole passage, which is often cited to prove that Louis XIV's hatred for the Dutch was in large degree that of the aristocrat for the burgher. The high dudgeon of Lionne's words may be better understood, however, as a feigned anger designed to distract attention. For the emperor, by the treaty of partition of 1668, had already promised the Spanish Netherlands to France as its share of the succession of Carlos II. Belgium in the possession of France was precisely what the leaders of the Dutch republic did not wish to see occur. If, as is almost certain, Pomponne was not informed of the highly secret treaty, Lionne's outburst in his letter to his friend may have been intended to deceive him, at least in part. Where the true reason could not be hinted at, this was a makeshift of an argument for not permitting the Dutch to inquire further into the possibility of an agreement by Leopold I and Louis XIV on the succession to the Spanish throne.[1]

Pomponne's ignorance of the partition treaty led to difficulties. When he suggested that he drop the question which De Witt had brought up, Lionne and the king saw a peril which they could not avoid by the simple method of telling Pomponne the truth. They feared that the grand pensionary and his masters might interpret Pomponne's rebuff to mean that such a treaty already existed. The ambassador had to distract the Dutch from such dangerous thoughts. He was instructed to inform De Witt that the king "was very much disposed toward strengthening the repose of Christendom" by means of a treaty on the Spanish succession, but Vienna, and Madrid even less, had "never" had any disposition to accept it.[2]

When Pomponne conferred again with the grand pensionary concerning this question of the emperor's rôle in the Spanish succession, he discovered once more how Dutch foreign policy now revolved around the necessity to keep England a loyal ally. To draw De Witt out, Pomponne asked for his suggestions as to what should be done if the emperor refused to talk about the future of the Spanish monarchy. In that case, De Witt replied, it would be proper and rightful for the United Provinces and France to join in a "partition of some kind which would assure their frontiers." What about England then? Pomponne

[1] Lionne to Pomponne, April 19, 1669, Bib. Ars., MS 4712, fos. 50–51.
[2] Lionne to Pomponne, May 17, 1669, *ibid.*, fo. 62.

queried craftily. Wouldn't she become a neighbor of the United Provinces? Wasn't the need to consult her, as a member of the Triple Alliance, spoiling the whole business? "Not England!" De Witt expostulated. "We do not want her in Flanders!" What more certain proof was needed than this that the Dutch did not expect the English to remain friends for long? Pomponne mused. When the ambassador grimly contrasted, as he had done before, the known advantages of French amity for the Dutch with the uncertainty of their new allies, and predicted that war, by reducing Dutch commerce, would sap their defensive strength, De Witt sadly admitted that this was all true.

Pomponne mulled over the relationship between De Witt's avowal and the development of French policy toward the Netherlands. It was probably true, Pomponne thought, that only De Witt's fear of the consequences in England kept him from responding to his, Pomponne's, own initiative in the matter of the Spanish succession. If the Dutch "could be completely certain that Your Majesty were willing to agree fully on some arrangement for Flanders such as that begun in 1662, they would be overjoyed to enter it," Pomponne wrote to the king. But he did not see that Louis had any intention of doing anything further to bring the Dutch back into the French fold, and therefore he would continue to act as before, reassuring the Dutch with words, but not with the deeds which alone could make friends of them again.[1]

At his next conference with De Witt, on April 30, Pomponne probed even more deeply into this problem of the Spanish succession. His technique was to bring up, "with apparent frankness, as if it came up during the discussion rather than as the result of some obvious premeditation," the surprising failure of the Dutch to act on Louis' first overture. De Witt's reply again depended upon the peculiar relationship he bore to his masters: he himself had often thought of the matter, he said, and he had sounded out in secrecy "the most capable and influential persons in the state." But there was more to the matter than that, he added. For one thing, it was not easy to get a government of many persons—"a plurality of Caesars," Estrades had called it—to deliberate on a specific question except on urgent occasions; for another, there was left over from the War of Devolution, which Louis XIV had begun despite a promise not to act without the participation of the States General, a "mistrust difficult to overcome." Even so, De Witt was confident that if the French assented to the cantonment project, with Aire, St. Omer and Cambrai as French acquisitions, he could win the States General for the plan. The treaty of Aix-la-Chapelle

[1] Pomponne to Louis XIV, April 25, 1669, Arch. étr., Holl., vol. 89, fos. 147–49.

gave to Louis XIV most of what was supposed to form the new republic, Pomponne pointed out. The rest could still be made into a republic, De Witt rejoined. While Pomponne listened, neither approving nor refuting, the councilor pensionary argued that it would be to Louis' advantage to "exchange for all time the vicinity of the House of Austria for that of a little state which would always be dependent on him, to assure the repose of all Europe and to cure his allies of the apprehensions they have of seeing him master of all the Low Countries."

This proposal brought to a head the necessity for the French court to decide which way its Dutch policy would go. Pomponne was certain that the Dutch were "troubled by their present state and their inability to face its perils, and that, in this extremity, they would be happy indeed to discover some compromise by which there could be placed between France and these provinces a small state which England and themselves would be obliged to support by the same interest which now unites them, and which could not give France the umbrage in which till now she has held the House of Austria."[1]

In a dispatch to Lionne, Pomponne spelled out his judgment. By accepting cantonment and the limitation of his claims upon the succession to the Spanish monarchy, Louis XIV could easily win back the Dutch. But, even if the king were ready to make the United Provinces his allies again by these means, as did not seem likely, it would be advisable to compel the Dutch to take the initiative. The "most enlightened" among the leaders of the republic observed with grave qualms the way the republic was falling into dependence upon England. It was obvious to Pomponne that Charles II "could garner every advantage he pleased if he knows how to use his strong position." De Witt knew this, and it was another reason, according to Pomponne, for his seeking the friendship of France.

Van Beuningen, too, whose hostility to France was so much more sharply expressed than De Witt's, was motivated by the same maxim that France was not a safe neigbor. The famous "Joshua medal" incident brought the character of the Amsterdammer's attitude home to Pomponne. On May 1, 1669, a troubled Van Beuningen came to see the French ambassador. In his hand was a private letter from Paris telling of indignation there over a report that a medal had been struck in Holland depicting Joshua stopping the sun—an obvious emblematic play on Van Beuningen's rôle in halting Louis XIV's conquest of Flanders. He assured Pomponne that he had been guilty of no such "extravagant invention"; no one had ever heard him speak of France's

[1] Pomponne to Louis XIV, May 2, 1669, *ibid.*, fos. 161–64.

conduct at Aix-la-Chapelle except with fullest respect. He requested Pomponne to inform Louis XIV of his true feelings, and the ambassador assured him of his own belief that Van Beuningen had had no part in "this ridiculous emblem." But, with the laugh that usually accompanied his most serious and probing remarks, Pomponne suggested that Van Beuningen's public declamations against France all during 1668 confirmed the medalmaker's choice of image.

The Amsterdammer hotly denied this. In reporting to the States General on his return from France in the autumn of 1668, he had acted solely in accordance with his conscience and as the welfare of his country demanded. He had asserted that in view of the immense growth of French power, the United Provinces must either come to a basic agreement with Louis XIV or supinely become his subjects after he conquered the Low Countries. His efforts to begin talks on the Spanish succession had been spurned, and so he came to believe that France intended to conquer the whole of the Spanish Netherlands. The safety of the republic depended, therefore, on bringing together the princes of Europe, especially those close by, since they would all be threatened by the yoke which such formidable power as France's could place upon them. Then Van Beuningen came to the heart of the matter: It was to the interest of the States General to retain the friendship of France, but if Louis XIV would accept no compromise regarding Flanders, they had to choose between two alternatives—either to oppose the expansion of France and therefore to run the risk of perishing at her hands, or to capitulate to Louis XIV at once. Brave men could not choose the latter road, he said. He hoped, however, that it would not be necessary to take the former. Louis XIV's true advantage lay in moderating his claims. France would still remain the "first state in Europe," but her neighbors and friends could then "forever revere her." Pomponne listened, speaking only in order to make his visitor develop his thought, and offered no comment on his own. But to Lionne he sent a full account of the interview for his judgment.[1]

Even before these dispatches reached him, Louis XIV had decided to leave the initiative for talks concerning the Spanish succession wholly to De Witt. As for the pensionary's suggestion that the emperor be brought into such negotiations, Lionne still told Pomponne nothing about the secret treaty of partition. Instead he discussed the problem with him as if the Spanish refusal to approve negotiations on the matter had brought it to a halt. He sloughed off Dutch worries:

[1] Pomponne to Lionne, May 2, 1669, *ibid.*, fos. 165–67.

"If the Dutch were worth the trouble, or merited by their conduct that they should be cured of their anxieties, I would tell you that you could reassure M. de Witt, in the king's name, that there is no negotiation under way for that eventual treaty, neither by their ministers nor by the intermediary of any mediator."[1] This was a plain quibble, of course, since the treaty was already in existence.

Pomponne accepted without complaint Lionne's instructions as the guide for his further conduct. What he had done so far was sufficient to put the States General in the wrong if they did not act. It would be best to permit the Dutch to think that the Low Countries might fall into French hands—then they would be more eager to curry French favor in one way or another. But the initiative now belonged to the Dutch, and Pomponne was amazed that they had not yet used it. He saw through the good face they put on their new alliances and knew how they feared a war with France.

Their fears were justified, Pomponne assured Lionne. Their resources were not inexhaustible and they would find it difficult to sustain for long the expenses of an entire alliance; their territory was too small to permit them to resist a major assault, and "in wartime it would be easy to destroy at sea the sources of a power which resides only in the freedom of trade." Yet Pomponne, who by now had seen enough of the Dutch to size up their potentialities, gave a warning too. If the leaders of the republic should ever steel themselves to the necessity for waging war, "they will bring to it the diligence, steadiness and even stubbornness almost always characteristic of republics fighting in self-defense." Not that they were likely to take the initiative for war themselves. Their own best efforts would be inadequate against French power, and their allies were too unreliable for the safety of the republic to be entrusted to them. Therefore, no matter how bravely they talked, he doubted that they would dare to take up arms against France in the event of the death of Carlos II.[2]

Lionne admired Pomponne's adroit handling of De Witt and Van Beuningen. The king agreed with Pomponne that the Amsterdammer was too skillful to have committed "so great and bold an extravagance" as the Joshua medal. Pomponne should avoid bringing up the cantonment proposal, Lionne warned, though the issue of exchanges of territories in Flanders might well be discussed.[3]

Nonetheless De Witt's cantonment conception became the center of

[1] Lionne to Pomponne, May 3, 1669, Bib. Ars., MS 4712, fo. 58.
[2] Pomponne to Lionne, May 9, 1669, Arch. étr., Holl., vol. 89, fos. 173–74.
[3] Lionne to Pomponne, May 10, 1669, Bib. Ars., MS 4712, fo. 60.

his further discussions with Pomponne. Had Louis XIV said anything about this way of solving the problem of the Spanish succession? De Witt asked the French envoy. His present powers were enough to permit continued talks, Pomponne replied, but specific proposals must come from the United Provinces. If Louis XIV acted first, the world might say he did so because he feared the Triple Alliance. The king might accept some arrangement for the Low Countries, but only with the States General, not with the whole Triple Alliance.

Pomponne thus compelled De Witt to expose his hand more fully. "If Flanders is covered," De Witt declared, the States General would not be concerned with Louis' interest in the Spanish empire elsewhere. Pomponne's fundamental judgment was confirmed, he reported to the king: De Witt distrusted the allies of the United Provinces and feared the consequences of a break with France. Yet "he is, as always, concerned over the ruin of their state and their trade, which they (the Dutch) hold to be inevitable if the remainder of the Low Countries, and Antwerp in particular, fall under his (Louis') domination. They believe their freedom to be linked to the presence of some kind of a state between themselves and France." Doubtful of their ability to protect the Spanish Netherlands, they hoped to persuade Louis XIV to establish such a barrier by his own assent. Therefore, Pomponne concluded, "it lies in the hands of Your Majesty to enter or not into a negotiation which this minister has made only too clear to me he should like to begin, but toward which I have not yet taken the least step." The king should instruct him whether to "seem to understand or continue to elude."[1]

Louis XIV was delighted with Pomponne's skill in drawing from De Witt his innermost feelings on the question of the Spanish succession. He remained firm against the proposal for cantonment of the Low Countries, lest the world think he had capitulated to the Triple Alliance. He preferred to rely "on the weakness which is always inseparable from leagues," and on the probable brevity of this one. Pomponne should not seriously discuss with De Witt the rôle that England and Sweden could play in an eventual treaty of partition, but merely listen; his sole objective must be to hoodwink De Witt and his masters. Furthermore, if the other members of the Triple Alliance heard of this secret negotiation, they would be only the more willing to throw over the league at France's suggestion; it would be a "legitimate reason, or at least a plausible pretext."[2]

[1] Pomponne to Louis XIV, May 16, 1669, Arch. étr., Holl., vol. 89, fos. 189–92.
[2] Lionne to Pomponne, May 24, 1669, Bib. Ars., MS 4712, fos. 66–67.

For Pomponne these orders represented, as he saw, "a new instruction." "I shall listen to all proposals, but make none," he wrote to Lionne. The ambassador cut through to the heart of De Witt's intentions: the cantonment proposal, like the Triple Alliance before it, had been designed to obtain Louis XIV's self-denial of all rights and opportunities by which ownership of the Low Countries might come to him. All that was offered him in return was "mediocre" by comparison. Pomponne doubted that he could trick De Witt into a discussion far enough to do him harm at London and Stockholm: he is "too skillful to give me such an opening," and he knew the importance of keeping the Triple Alliance united. One could not count on Dutch missteps to split the league, Pomponne warned. It was necessary to wait for the outbreak of some quarrel, or on the work of time. Thus, he sadly mused, "I can hereafter expect little to keep me busy." Would not the king give him now some more effective task to perform than this "unpleasant uselessness"? The Dutch were beginning to treat everything he did as constituting "arrogance and threats," and he was finding it difficult to maintain his own "moderation and complete courtesy."

But, if his tasks were becoming those of an observer, Pomponne was able to take pleasure in the lesser joys of such a rôle, such as reporting the silly superstitions of his opponents. He mixed laughter and sound sense in telling Lionne how the people of The Hague continued to believe that the nesting habits of birds were a political augury. But let us listen to Pomponne's own words:

> You believe, perhaps, that since the days of ancient Rome, the flight of birds has ceased to control the fate of empires. Yet some trace of that belief has been conserved here at The Hague. You know the strong reputation storks have as good republicans and loyal imperialists, and you have perhaps heard tell at Metz that, as soon as the Three Bishoprics ceased to be part of the empire, these birds flew away. Last year it was observed in this town, which has the stork as its heraldic emblem, that though these birds returned as usual, they did not produce any young. This year the same thing happened. The storks appeared, though fewer in number, and did not add to the number of their families. You can see, Sir, how much a people fond of reasonings could indulge its taste on this event, what presaging can be based on the way in which this bird, which fears nothing more than monarchy, has changed its residence, and I leave it to you to guess the direction from which they expect it to change further.[1]

[1] Pomponne to Lionne, May 30, 1669, Arch. étr., Holl., vol. 89, fos. 212–14.

Lionne replied in the same bantering tone to Pomponne's gay tale of the storks and to his complaint about his coming idleness. Not only would Pomponne suffer from lack of occupation, but there would be henceforth a lack of essential matter in their correspondence, Lionne moaned. But the king was delighted by Pomponne's account of the storks, and Lionne himself hoped that the augury would prove true, even if it cost Pomponne his post.[1]

[1] Lionne to Pomponne, June 7, 1669, Bib. Ars., MS 4712, fo. 74.

CHAPTER VI

"CANTONMENT"—DE WITT'S SOLUTION
June, 1669—May, 1670

In the first week of June, 1669, Pomponne at last made his formal entry into The Hague. It was for him a week of ceremony no less distasteful because it was necessary and inescapable.

Pomponne and his party left The Hague in the three carriages which had finally arrived from Paris. At a village half a league away, on the road by which travellers usually came from France, he was met by the master of ceremonies of the States General. Then he re-entered the city he had just left, his official rôle formally assumed; with the reception party from the States, he made a grand tour of the town, while the populace thronged to see the spectacle. Pomponne noted that they were especially impressed by the fine horses prancing in their colorful harness, and by his household servants in their bright livery. Days of banqueting followed, with the usual interminable toasts and bouts of drinking, and he was glad each evening when he could return home. On June 6, Pomponne went to his formal audience with the States General, accompanied by the same train of attendants.

He did not fail to inform Lionne how expensive it had all been. He had been compelled to excel the brilliant entries of the English and Portuguese ambassadors. Unlike them, however, he refused a gift of some five hundred crowns from the States, even though he was himself compelled to make many gifts to various Dutch officials who had served him. With a scrupulousness remarkable in that age when a bribe was called a gratification, he felt bound to seek the re-establishment of his purse from his own master only, although he trusted to Lionne to bring at the proper moment to the king's attention the inadequacy of his pay for the expenses he had to meet.[1]

The high point of the solemn entry was Pomponne's delivery of a formal speech on the presentation of his credentials to D'Aspre, pre-

[1] Pomponne, Relation of his entry into The Hague, and letter to Lionne, June 6, 1669, Arch. étr., Holl., vol. 89, fos. 219–22.

siding officer of the States General for the week. Even on this occasion, when there was no compulsion to make his words carry any but the emptiest of formal respects, Pomponne went beyond the letter of his instructions. Not only did he rebut the suspicions which Spain sought to create regarding the king's will for peace, but he also insinuated that Louis XIV's inviolable good faith was an incomparably stronger basis for peace than all the Triple Alliance. The replies given to Pomponne by D'Aspre, as well as by other deputies, remained within the usual generalities which no one took seriously.[1]

Louis was pleased with Pomponne's "harangue" (the term having, of course, none of the invidious meaning of today) to the States General; he found it done in his minister's "usual manner, that is, in terms as judicious in their content as they were eloquent in the form he gave them." But, though Lionne read to the monarch Pomponne's plea of genteel poverty in his private letter to the foreign minister, Louis listened attentively but did not reply. Lionne thought wise not to risk a negative decision then, "which could be of harm to you throughout the course of your embassy," but to wait a more favorable opportunity to call upon the king's "generosity and justice."[2]

The fundamental issues in the controversy between France and the United Netherlands had now been explored and clarified. What remained to be said was either repetition, or discussion of minor conflicts, without effect on the basic relationship between the two states. This was the import of a dispatch early in July, 1669, from Pomponne to Lionne: "As the principal engines seem to come into motion here, and it can be said that they move principally against us, and that as long as there is a Flanders where they will fear to see us neighbors, we shall have no reason to promise ourselves that these folk shall become our friends."[3]

In his next dispatch, Pomponne spelled out the situation created by Louis XIV's rejection of the cantonment proposal. De Witt, according to reports reaching the French ambassador, was convinced now that the king would settle for nothing less than the whole of the Spanish Low Countries; even partition would be inadequate. Therefore, De Witt maintained, the Dutch must prepare to defend the southern Netherlands or themselves accept the yoke of France. Dutch anxieties were multiplied by reports from the South: the population of the great Belgian towns, restive at Spanish exactions, were said to be consider-

[1] Pomponne to Lionne, June 6, 1669, speech to States General, June 6, 1669, *ibid.*, fos. 221, 226–27.

[2] Lionne to Pomponne, June 14, 1669, Bib. Ars., MS 4712, fo. 77.

[3] Pomponne to Lionne, July 8, 1669, Arch. étr., Holl., vol. 89, fo. 276.

ing placing themselves voluntarily under the sovereignty of France, or at least creating an independent state with his support. This proved, Pomponne remarked, how valuable it was to treat the population of newly conquered territories in an easy, gentle manner: those not yet blessed with French rule would be "flattered" into desiring to be conquered in their turn.[1]

Pomponne's main subject of conversation with De Witt now became Dutch efforts to intervene in the relations between France and the Spanish Netherlands. The negotiations at Lille regarding the disputed "dependencies" provided the first matter for such debate between the envoy and the pensionary. Underlying the whole problem, as Pomponne realized, was the effort of the Spanish authorities to anger and embitter France, in the hope that Louis XIV would start a new war and thereby bring the Triple Alliance into action. De Witt sought to play the rôle of mediator, Pomponne considered, in order to have a pretext for extending Dutch arbitration to the question of an exchange of territories.[2] If France could not be kept at a distance by "cantonment," at least the buffer between her and the republic could be widened by exchange of territory.[3]

It was another conflict between French and Spanish authorities in Flanders, however, which brought into the open the hostility between Paris and The Hague which Pomponne's talks with De Witt during the first months of his embassy had not overcome. The controversy concerned mainly French efforts to continue to use Belgian resources in the work of fortification undertaken by Louis XIV in the newly conquered regions. The French fortifications required huge quantities of brick because local supplies of stone were frequently insufficient. The French brickmakers burned coal, brought from the Belgian province of Hainaut, in their kilns. The Constable of Castille, who had replaced Castel Rodrigo as governor general of the Spanish Netherlands, decided that this dependence upon fuel from Hainaut was a weak point in the French military preparations; he thereupon barred the export of coal, hoping to delay the fortifications as much as six years. In June, 1669, bargeloads of coal were stopped by the constable's orders at Condé under the claim that they were contraband. The French protested that contraband may be designated only in wartime, but backed this argument by reprisals upon Spanish territory by some five to six thousand troops under the command of marshal

[1] Pomponne to Lionne, July 11, 1669, *ibid.*, fo. 277.
[2] Pomponne, *Relation de Hollande*, pp. 105, 109–10.
[3] Pomponne to Lionne, July 11, 1669, Arch. étr., Holl., vol. 89, fo. 281.

Humières, commander of the Lille garrison. The government at Madrid ordered the lifting of the ban, though it complained that the shippers had refused to pay the usual duties on exported coal. The constable meanwhile increased the duty from one to twenty shillings, and finally banned export of coal altogether, on the grounds that it was required for use within Belgium; the French, he said, were not satisfied to receive only the amount shipped before the start of their program of fortifications. The French accepted the legality of this means, but foiled the constable's hopes by importing large quantities of coal from Scotland and Liége. Estrades, military governor of Dunkirk, and Humières were ordered to convoy these supplies from stockpiles at Dunkirk and Le Quesnoy to Lille and the region around Ath and Tournai. Several such convoys were delivered by way of roads crossing through Spanish territory without resistance from the Spanish forces, but the constable complained at once that the French were breaking their treaty obligations and demanded assistance from the Triple Alliance.[1]

De Witt admitted that much of the French argument was valid. Contraband was a meaningless concept in peacetime, and in any event coal could not be classified as having military importance, he said. The Constable of Castille might ban export of coal on the basis of domestic needs, but only if the embargo were general. Thus far the envoy and the councilor pensionary could agree, but the convoys led by Estrades and Humières were another matter. De Witt urged that Louis XIV ought not to have used arms but should have appealed to the Dutch, in their capacity as guarantors of the treaty of Aix-la-Chapelle. Pomponne defended the use of military reprisals: they did not necessarily lead to war but might bring justice. Then he warned De Witt that Dutch mediation was not wanted, for Louis XIV "would always gladly spare his friends the task of settling his quarrels."[2]

The affair soon degenerated into a bout of chicanery and devious devices. By placing a tax of a thousand pistoles on each trunk of letters going between Flanders and Spain, the French quickly compelled the constable to withdraw a tax he placed on French coal from other states passing through Spanish territory. But the constable, a stubborn man, was not ready to concede defeat.

[1] Pomponne, *Relation de Hollande*, pp. 106–10; Constable of Castille to Queen-Regent, July 3, 17, 22, 1669, consultation of Spanish council of state, Aug, 9. 1669, J. Cuvelier *et al.*, eds., *Correspondance de la Cour d'Espagne sur les affaires des Pays-Bas au XVIIe siècle* (Brussels, 1923–37), V, 79–84; Wicquefort, *Histoire*, IV, 40–44.

[2] Pomponne to Louis XIV, to Lionne, July 18, 1669, Arch. étr., Holl., vol. 89, fos. 285–87, 290.

On his orders, the passage of a large French coal shipment was held up at Condé. Louis XIV replied by ordering Humières to enter Spanish territory again and to take renewed reprisals until the constable ceased to halt goods which were not contraband.[1]

At first Lionne and Pomponne both tended to minimize the whole affair as a minor wrangle,[2] but its importance became clear when the States General made formal diplomatic representations to France in the name of the Triple Alliance. After agreement with Temple and the Swedish envoys at The Hague, De Witt obtained from the States General a decision to send a deputation to Pomponne. This delegation, of which De Witt was a member, informed Pomponne on August 29 that the English and Swedish envoys and the States General had received from Gamarra memoranda charging France with various infractions of the peace, especially in regard to the coal question. The delegation repeated the Spaniards' allegations and requested clarification of the position taken by Louis XIV. The king would surely accept their mediation, they said, in view of the position of the States General as guarantors of the peace of Aix-la-Chapelle. The deputation also claimed authority to act on behalf of the English and Swedish envoys, and De Witt drew forth a paper as if to show it to Pomponne. When the Frenchman rejected the complaints as either unfounded or unjust, De Witt warned that the Constable of Castille might find this an opportunity for legal resistance to French forces and thereby compel the Triple Alliance to come to his aid. Pomponne's reply was brusque: In such an event, the French would not be aggressors, for the king of France had the right to protect the safety and livelihood of his subjects.

Louis XIV treated the Dutch démarche with haughty disdain, and ordered Pomponne to inform the States General "that the king of France had no answer to make to them, because he saw that for some time past whatever concerned him was taken amiss at The Hague; but that he would gladly listen to the English ambassador residing by his person, if he had to speak to him on behalf of his master."[3] Lionne added that it would be wise to break the Dutch of the habit of troubling Pomponne with all the "plaints" of the Spaniards. The foreign minister strongly doubted that England and Sweden would assent to the principle, which De Witt "establishes so boldly," that a war begun on the issue of the armed reprisals would obligate the Triple Alliance to

[1] Lionne to Pomponne, Aug. 21, 1669, Bib. Ars., MS 4712, fos. 106–09.
[2] Lionne to Pomponne, July 24, Aug. 21, 1669, *ibid.*, fos. 94, 109.
[3] Louis XIV to Pomponne, Sept. 11, 1669, *ibid.*, fo. 115.

act under its guarantee to Spain. "The States may do us harm," Lionne told Pomponne, "but they will never frighten us. If they apprehend war as much as they say, it is up to them to control the Spaniards and to prevent them from doing anything which may cause it to flare up again."[1]

A week later Lionne made his view still clearer. The king would not be induced to seek the mediation of the Dutch. As for Sir William Temple, he would be rendered harmless by the efforts of Colbert de Croissy in London. Charles II had promised Croissy to reprimand Temple so severely that he would never act in that way again. Thus, said Lionne, unless Arlington, on whom it depended to carry out Charles' promise, "finds a way of eluding or applying feebly the intentions of the king, his master," De Witt would have come a cropper with his "false policy." Pomponne should draw out Temple, who would have to admit that he had been disavowed by London; if he failed to do so, Croissy should be informed at once so that he could renew his complaints to Charles II. A similar use of De Witt's tactical error could be made at Stockholm.[2] Lionne awaited impatiently the news of Temple's reply to Pomponne's searching questions.[3]

The affair turned out badly for the Dutch. The other Triple Alliance envoys denied that they had authorized the Dutch to act on their behalf; Temple, admitting to Pomponne that he had been reprimanded, claimed he had only wished the Dutch to present the Spanish complaints, not to defend them. Pomponne, considering that "De Witt... had much power" over Temple, was not impressed by his explanation: "perhaps" the councilor pensionary had exceeded Temple's intentions.

In London Croissy warned Charles II that if Temple continued to act in this way, his own withdrawal would result. Charles formally disavowed Temple, and in the presence of the duke of York called his envoy's action indefensible and ridiculous. He promised that Temple would not repeat this most surprising impertinence. The duke of York added that Temple thereafter would act in Triple Alliance matters only on specific orders from Charles. Louis XIV considered this a satisfactory reply, but Charles' attitude was kept strictly secret: the Venetian ambassador thought Croissy had been rebuffed.[4]

[1] Lionne to Pomponne, Sept. 11, 1669, *ibid.*, fos. 114–16.
[2] Lionne to Pomponne, Sept. 18, 1669, *ibid.*, fos. 117–18.
[3] Lionne to Pomponne, Sept. 28, 1669, *ibid.*, fo. 121.
[4] Croissy to Louis XIV, Sept. 9, 1669, Lionne to Croissy, Sept. 11, 1669, Mignet, III, 95–96; Mocenigo to Doge and Senate, Oct. 11, 1669, Allen B. Hinds, ed., *Calendar of State Papers and Manuscripts Relating to English Affairs Existing in the Archives and Collections of Venice and in other Libraries of Northern Italy*, vol. XXXVI (London, 1937), p. 114.

De Witt tried to reassure Pomponne that he had only intended to prevent accidents capable of troubling public tranquility, but the Frenchman told him that his favoritism to Spain had been only too clear. By early November, these "small matters of dispute," as Pomponne called them, were solved by English and papal intervention.[1]

Proposals now began to be heard in the Netherlands that the States General wage a preventive war against France before she grew too strong. Pomponne reported a wide belief that such a war had become inevitable, and that it would be better to wage it while there was some strength left in the Triple Alliance. Once it had been De Witt who most strongly opposed such "perilous" measures; now, according to reports Pomponne received from persons he considered well informed, there was none bolder than the grand pensionary. Those who knew De Witt well said he had acted similarly during the second Anglo-Dutch war. As long as possible he had sought to solve the conflict with England by compromise, but once he lost hope of such a remedy, he took upon himself, "alone and not without peril," the leadership of war against a great power.

There were many elements of interest and policy involved in De Witt's position. Some believed that he was being pushed by an irresistible torrent, but "others, who penetrate further into his interests and his ambitions, think he may desire war in order to crush various intrigues which idleness and peace enable to form against his authority." Pomponne noted the possibility that in a "popular government" the outbreak of war, by causing individuals to subordinate their private to the general and public interest, would render De Witt's experience and ability more necessary. Furthermore, according to this view, war would in similar fashion weaken the "cabals" of the prince of Orange and eliminate the French regiments in the States' service, a stronghold of his interest. Pomponne presented this report to Louis XIV specifically for his judgment as to what was appearance and what reality, and to utilize his knowledge for his own "interests and glory."[2]

Lionne did not grow fearful at the news that the Dutch might take the first step in outright war. He was pleased to see De Witt squirming at the realization that he "was not as much the master of the will of their new allies as he perhaps thought he was." He assured Pomponne that the French could both parry and riposte, even with so good a

[1] Pomponne, *Relation de Hollande*, pp. 110–13; Mignet, III, 592–95; H. A. van Dijk, *Bijdrage tot de geschiedenis der Nederlandsche Diplomatie*: *Handelingen met Frankrijk en Spanje in de Jaren 1668–1672* (Utrecht, 1851), p. 52.

[2] Pomponne to Louis XIV, Oct. 3, 1669, Arch. étr. Holl., vol. 89, fos. 381–83.

second as Lisola behind De Witt. But, Lionne warned his friend, keep this opinion to yourself and let no hint of threat ever enter your words. "Let us be satisfied to seem the anvil, but omit no effort to become the hammer," he wrote. As for the possibility that the Dutch might take the initiative for war, De Witt was probably only seeking to maintain the appearance of strength and to persuade his masters to prepare for coming events. Nothing would please Lionne better than that the Dutch should begin war against France, for the king did not not want to be the aggressor. Lionne felt certain that if the Dutch took this initiative, they could not carry either England or Sweden with them, and perhaps Spain even less.[1]

Lionne's expectation that De Witt would not take so grave a step as to urge preventive war was soon confirmed. Late in October the grand pensionary came to Pomponne to raise once more the possibility of some negotiation between France and the United Provinces over the future of the Spanish Netherlands. This time De Witt did not confine himself to hints, but on his own initiative and in clear terms brought the matter to a head. The States General had just rebuffed a Spanish effort to assure Dutch support for immediate rupture of the Lille conference, and had insisted that Spain continue to seek a settlement, he informed Pomponne. Though the Spaniards might seek to incite a break, the Dutch would not be dragged into war. Citing this action as proof of his sincere intentions toward France, De Witt returned again to the central problem. Dutch friendship for France needed only one measure to be achieved: the Dutch must be assured of their safety by means of a free republic in the southern Netherlands. Partition could not be considered because England might demand a share. There was nothing more disadvantageous for both France and the United Provinces than to give England any foothold on the mainland—it would be "the greatest of all evils."[2]

Pomponne's reply was general: he saw with joy that De Witt felt he could persuade the Dutch not to let the Spaniards push them over the precipice. To control events, De Witt continued, he needed some assurance from the king that the negotiation would be made swiftly.

Pomponne thought that the appointment of Pieter de Groot as ambassador to France, which now seemed probable, was another sign of De Witt's desire to recapture French amity. They were "intimately united in friendship" and De Groot would probably only accept the difficult and perhaps profitless post because he hoped to change

[1] Lionne to Pomponne, Oct. 9, 1669, Bib. Ars., MS 4712, fos. 123–24.
[2] Pomponne, *Relation de Hollande*, p. 119.

France's policy by important proposals. These would only be a renewal of the cantonment idea, Pomponne predicted, and he saw little likelihood that Louis would accept it. What do you want me to do now? Pomponne asked Lionne.[1]

De Witt specifically requested Pomponne to communicate his proposal to Louis XIV. He wished to be informed in secret of the monarch's intentions, so that he could take the necessary measures. Pomponne considered that he might simply have treated this as an interview rather than as a negotiation, but, "in order to maintain a deception which it was worthwhile to continue," he wrote as requested.[2] Louis XIV's reply could hardly have been less encouraging. The Dutch rebuffed Spain not out of consideration for France but for their own safety and interest only—this was the view at the French court. The matter was an idle problem in any case, for Spain could hardly be brought to undertake the initiative for war during the minority of Carlos II. As for De Witt's request to be informed of Louis' intentions regarding the cantonment proposal, the king instructed Pomponne to inquire whether the pensionary had in mind action at once or only when Carlos II died—and the king of France was not interested in "distant and uncertain cases," Lionne indicated.[3] Louis XIV's attitude toward De Witt was now made clear by his gibe that it "perhaps will no longer depend upon him to direct the activities of other potentates as he pleases."[4]

The question which the king instructed Pomponne to ask the grand pensionary served its purpose exactly. De Witt was compelled to admit that he proposed future, not present, benefits for Louis XIV, but also that his stated "good intentions" for France were not shared by many of his masters and that he was not sure he could sway them to his policy. After repeated examination of the situations in which it would be "legitimate" to strip Spain of her Belgian provinces and give them "a better form of government," De Witt said, he had discovered only two possible cases in which this might be done. The first would occur if Spain broke with France or acted with insulting hostility equivalent to a rupture; the other, if the death of Carlos II, by opening the succession debate between Louis XIV and Leopold I, involved the Dutch by the question of their frontiers. It was in view of this latter possibility that De Witt had persuaded the States General not to take any stand on the validity of the renunciation of queen Marie

[1] Pomponne to Lionne, Oct. 31, 1669, Arch. étr., Holl., vol. 89, fos. 401–04.

[2] Pomponne, *Relation de Hollande*, pp. 119–20.

[3] Lionne to Pomponne, Nov. 1, Louis XIV to Pomponne, Nov. 15, 1669, Bib. Ars., MS 4712, fos. 130, 138.

[4] Louis XIV to Pomponne, Nov. 22, 1669, *ibid.*, fo. 144.

Thérèse; it might be to their interest to decide that it was null and void. But the grand pensionary admitted that his sentiments "were not shared by everyone here." Many took the position that the safety of the Dutch depended on keeping Spain in Belgium, come what may. Otherwise, neither Germany nor England would give much support to the republic, and France would be able to expand as she desired on the Rhine and in the empire, after having "overcome the strongest barrier she has had to combat until this time." So vigorously did De Witt phrase these arguments that to Pomponne he seemed to think them more effective than his own. The pensionary continued to urge as before, however, that there was greater advantage in agreement with Louis XIV than in opposing him, because a cantonned republic would provide them with their necessary security. Apart from the two stated cases, De Witt said he believed that Louis would not break the peace of Europe or attempt to despoil Spain; yet, in order to forestall the Spanish propensity for creating wrangles, a negotiation for the future possibility ought to be undertaken now. Pomponne listened, speaking only to elicit De Witt's views in more exact detail, and waited for Louis' orders.

He did not venture to decide whether De Witt was genuinely seeking a rapprochement with France or, anticipating the king's rejection of his expedients, merely sought a cheap claim to have striven for French friendship without seriously risking anything. Pomponne saw the two factors influencing De Witt: on the one hand, the general opinion, "which may be fed in part by his foes," that "all his intentions are for France"; on the other, "to judge by the Triple Alliance which he created, and by the diligence with which he seeks to maintain it, I find him as afraid as anyone else of seeing Your Majesty the master of Flanders and Antwerp." His good words would then be explained by his "naturally wise and moderate" conduct.[1]

In reply, Louis XIV instructed Pomponne to tell De Witt that his new overture actually hazarded little. Louis wished religiously to observe the peace with Spain, and it was unlikely and unreasonable to expect that Spain would dare to break with France. As for the death of Carlos II, his improved health, the king stated—actually the French court was banking heavily on Carlos' early death and his unexpected recovery at this time dashed its hopes[2]—made that seem too improb-

[1] Pomponne to Louis XIV, Nov. 28, 1669, Arch. étr., Holl., vol. 89, fos. 425–28.

[2] Cf. for attitude of French court on Gourville's negotiations to place the duke of Anjou on the Spanish throne, Jean Hérauld de Gourville, *Mémoires*, ed. Léon Lecestre (Paris, 1894–95), I, xxx, and Lecestre, "La mission de Gourville en Espagne (1670)," *Revue des questions historiques*, LII (1892), 110–11.

able an event for a treaty to be made in anticipation of it. This was made all the more necessary because the secrecy requisite would be impossible; in a "popular state," too many persons would necessarily be involved in such a negotiation.[1]

De Witt, anxious lest the negotiation be completely halted, sought and obtained from Louis XIV power for Pomponne to engage in such discussions "when the occasion should arise." The French monarch indicated that De Witt could suggest the forms and terms of this power. The councilor pensionary tried, however, to continue discussion of specific measures. He proposed that the new state either make territorial cessions to the Dutch and French, its guarantors, as set forth in the 1663 project, or that it retain its existing frontiers. He also suggested exchange of those places conquered by France which projected into Belgian territory for Cambrai, St. Omer and Aire, the traditional points of entry into France by invaders. At this point in the negotiations—if such we may still call these talks—with De Witt, Pomponne displayed the fundamental independence of judgment which he retained within the required subservience of manner toward the king. He explained his delay in communicating Louis' reply to De Witt not merely on the sufficient grounds that a slow convalescence from illness prevented him from going out, but also because "it seems to me" prudent as affairs stood to show no hurry in replying.[2]

The news of Pomponne's illness drew from Lionne an expression of anxiety, indicative of his dependence on his friend's reports and views. The king's service would lose even if Pomponne were only unable to perform his duties for a while—he would not speak of losing Pomponne, "that would be too much." No blow could strike him in a more sensitive spot. The king, too, was concerned, but less personally troubled than Lionne.[3]

It was only on December 19 that Pomponne communicated to the grand pensionary the king's reply on the question of cantonment. De Witt agreed that unprovoked action against Carlos II during his lifetime would be improper. But would Pomponne have power to act if either of the two legitimate cases developed? he queried. Pomponne assured him there would always be time to obtain such authority.[4] Louis XIV, however, decided not to follow Pomponne's tactic of delaying a reply to this question until the eventuality arose. He

[1] Louis XIV to Pomponne, Dec. 6, 1669, Bib. Ars., MS 4712, fo. 152.
[2] Pomponne to Louis XIV, Dec. 12, 1669, Arch. étr., Holl., vol. 89, fo. 438.
[3] Lionne and Louis XIV to Pomponne, Dec. 13, 1669, Bib. Ars., MS 4712, fos. 157, 159.
[4] Pomponne to Louis XIV, Dec. 19, 1669, Arch. étr., Holl., vol. 89, fos. 448–49.

told Pomponne that he would receive such powers at once, and indeed instructed him to inform De Witt that they could discuss together the terms and clauses of such authorization.[1]

Meanwhile both the king and his ambassador began to consider more seriously the growing alarm among the Dutch that the next spring would bring war. Do not quell Dutch perturbations, Louis told Pomponne, for their preparations, being premature, will be a waste of money.[2] As for Pomponne, what struck him now was how the most fantastical of reports shattered the equanimity of Dutch minds and made them fear the worst. A guilty conscience of their misconduct toward France was partly responsible, he thought, but also the deliberate policy of those, like the Constable of Castille, who sought to keep the Dutch in the path they had chosen. The ebb and flow of these fears, he decided, proved the weakness of their régime and the malady of their spirits.[3]

When, shortly before the end of the year, the reports of French troop movements into Flanders proved empty, the Dutch began to be troubled by talk of hostile movements against them along their German frontiers. "The destiny of this state is to pass from one anxiety to another," wrote Pomponne. Not that they did not have every reason to fear the action of the bishop of Münster, especially if he were supported by France, for their frontier on that side remained "weak and open."[4]

The plan which Louis XIV now began to develop—to visit the conquered territories in Flanders for some seven weeks—was bound, he knew, to heighten the alarms in the Netherlands, but he was not perturbed. To be sure, as he told Pomponne, it would be only a "journey of court and not of war," but "I shall do what I deem proper for my service, without troubling overly much to quell their chimerical fears, particularly since all my efforts to cure them would be attributed without fail to a premeditated purpose of lulling them more effectively."[5]

Nor was the king wrong in this judgment. Pomponne's assurances that no more was involved in the royal visit than a desire to see these "fine provinces" and the fortifications under construction in them, did not destroy De Witt's qualms. He spoke of fears that the presence of queen Marie Thérèse might mean that she would proclaim her rights over her Belgian "subjects" in their own capital, and though he said

[1] Louis XIV to Pomponne, Jan. 3, 1670, Bib. Ars., MS 4712, fo. 164.
[2] Louis XIV to Pomponne, Nov. 29, 1669, *ibid.*, fo. 147.
[3] Pomponne to Louis XIV, Dec. 12, 1669, Arch. étr., Holl., vol. 89, fos. 438–39.
[4] Pomponne to Louis XIV, Dec. 28, 1669, *ibid.*, fos. 450–51.
[5] Louis XIV to Pomponne, Jan. 17, 1670, Bib. Ars., MS 4712, fo. 171.

these anxieties were not his own, he admitted they were felt by a majority of members of the Dutch governing class. This was, to Pomponne, a significant admission that most important Dutchmen were now moved by automatic hostility to France. As for the question of cantonment, De Witt sought to bring him to talk of the terms by which a settlement might be reached of the conflicting interests of France and the Dutch republic.[1]

Louis XIV was annoyed when he heard that the grand pensionary had tried to wangle Pomponne into discussing the terms of a draft treaty, rather than merely the clauses of Pomponne's power to negotiate when the proper time came. Do not let De Witt think that we can be drawn "imperceptibly" into a negotiation we do not desire, Louis XIV warned his envoy. He decided that it would be best, after all, to calm Dutch anxieties over his forthcoming journey, and instructed Pomponne to inform the States General that all French infantry companies were being reduced by ten men each, "which is hardly what one does in February if one has some plan to fight when the season is fair." Only the household cavalry, without the French and Swiss guards, would accompany the royal party.[2] The Dutch were chastened in mood when they heard of the reduction of French troop strength. They were also encouraged when Louis XIV accepted Anglo-Swedish arbitration of the "dependencies" dispute, for they thought it was this dispute which might provide the occasion for renewed war.[3]

As tempers relaxed, Pomponne observed "general tranquility" in the Netherlands. We can hear a sigh of boredom in his remark to Lionne that "foreign affairs seem lifeless."[4] His own negotiations with De Witt had entered an impasse. The significant problems, difficult but interesting, now lay in London, in Croissy's hands. However penetrating and precise he might be as an observer, Pomponne could not draw from such a limited rôle the pleasure he found in the very uncertainties of genuine negotiation. He could hardly take joy in the phrase which keeps recurring in Louis' dispatches to him during the next months: "no precise response" is needed to the generalities in Pomponne's letters.[5]

The tendency of the Dutch to suspect every act of France now led them to begin to worry again because the king was taking only the household cavalry with him to Flanders. Are the rest of the guards

[1] Pomponne to Louis XIV, Jan. 30, 1670, Arch. étr., Holl., vol. 90, fos. 38–41.
[2] Louis XIV to Pomponne, Feb. 8, 1670, Bib. Ars., MS 4712, fo. 187.
[3] Pomponne to Louis XIV, Feb. 13, 27, 1670, Arch. étr., Holl., vol. 90, fos. 66, 78.
[4] Pomponne to Lionne, Feb. 27, 1670, *ibid.*, fo. 82.
[5] E.g., Louis XIV to Pomponne, March, 28, 1670, Bib. Ars., MS 4712, fo. 223.

being left behind so that they can be swiftly assembled into an army corps for attack? they wondered. The armament measures which had been allowed to slide were again resumed. Maastricht was reinforced and some fifteen to twenty men were added to the infantry and cavalry companies stationed on the frontiers —about five thousand men in all.[1]

Louis' impending journey into Flanders aroused ideas of a different kind in Pomponne's mind. He requested that he be permitted to go to greet the king at Lille, only three days distant from The Hague. One of the gravest difficulties in embassies abroad, he reminded Lionne, was being out of the king's sight for years on end.[2] The king at once approved Pomponne's journey to Lille, "with the best grace in the world," Lionne wrote. Indeed the monarch suggested that though Pomponne need not go beyond Courtrai, he should accompany him to Lille, because Pomponne "would no doubt be delighted to be with (him) for a longer time."[3] In his own letter to the envoy, the king was more explicit: he would be "most happy to express to you with my own lips the satisfaction I feel with the good services you continue every day to render me with great competence and zeal."[4] Pomponne's pleasure at going to Flanders was not total, however, for Lionne would not make the journey. To see him was, he told his friend, "one of the joys I had expected."[5]

A new element crept into Dutch anxieties. For the most part the Netherlanders had been concerned at how their safety was involved in the preservation of the Spanish Low Countries; now the imperviousness of Louis XIV to their proposals and the rumors of French diplomatic machinations in England, Germany and Sweden, combined to make the Dutch fear for themselves directly. Pomponne found their sensitivity almost ridiculous. Any report of French troop movements, however ill-founded, threw them into "a general emotion."[6]

It was during this period that Van Beuningen returned to Pomponne to protest that any conflict between France and himself lay in principle only, and that he was guilty of no personal delinquency so far as proper conduct and respect for the king of France was concerned. This time it was a report in France that he had been furnishing anti-French material to the gazettes of Amsterdam which caused his visit. He had nothing to do with "such nonsense," he asked Pomponne to

[1] Pomponne to Louis XIV, April 3, 1670, to Gravel, April 14, 1670, Arch. étr., Holl., vol. 90, fos. 116–17, 136.
[2] Pomponne to Lionne, April 3, 1670, *ibid.*, fo. 119.
[3] Lionne to Pomponne, April 11, 1670, Bib. Ars., MS 4712, fo. 236.
[4] Louis XIV to Pomponne, April 11, 1670, *ibid.*, fo. 237.
[5] Pomponne to Lionne, April 17, May 1, 1670, Arch. étr., Holl., vol. 90, fos. 146, 166.
[6] Pomponne to Louis XIV, April 17, 1670, *ibid.*, fo. 144.

inform his master. The king, he hoped, would excuse his acting according to his conscience of his duty to his country. "Except for the fears he feels at having us close, and for the trade of France," Pomponne wrote, "he assured me strongly that there was no better Frenchman than he. In this respect he spoke truly, and I will pay him this justice. For whatever does not concern these two articles, more or less, he is favorable to France and holds the nation in high esteem. Above all, I must speak the truth, which is that he has never spoken of the king except with praise." He could hardly be the author of reports "unworthy of him."[1]

Lionne was not so kind. As burgomaster of Amsterdam, Van Beuningen could either silence ("which would be quite the best thing") or chasten the gazeteer. To Lionne, a good beating would be the proper lesson for the perpetrator of such "insolence and impertinence."[2]

The news that Pomponne might go to Flanders to see the king, and the final appointment of Pieter de Groot as ambassador to France, prompted De Witt to visit the French envoy in order to probe again the chances for reconciliation. Perhaps Pomponne might join with him, he said, in drawing up De Groot's instructions; Pomponne would know the best remedies for Dutch fears and therefore the ways in which Dutch friendship with France, "the most considerable interest of this republic," could be re-established. The Frenchman would not be led where he did not wish to go. De Witt's request still required some reply, for silence would only confirm his suspicions that Louis XIV sought measures against the States General but not with them. Pomponne therefore reassured the pensionary: the king knew that the Francophobe movement in Dutch affairs was not De Witt's doing, and that only the councilor pensionary could bring its transformation.

Though Pomponne did not doubt De Witt's moderation nor his interest in having the protection of France against the rise of the party of the prince of Orange, he asked him a number of hard questions. Had he acted to accept Louis' initiative, at the start of Pomponne's mission, for an accord on the death of Carlos II? Was he any longer the master of his masters? Had he been able to prevent them from taking such steps as the Triple Alliance and the campaign to bring all Germany into "a league all too obviously formed against us"? Yet Pomponne hinted that if De Witt could change the course of Dutch policy, he might "return to the honor of (the king's) graces." By that change he meant "the abandonment of every league and

[1] Pomponne to Lionne, April 24, 1670, *ibid.*, fos. 158–59.
[2] Lionne to Pomponne, May 2, 1670, Bib. Ars., MS 4712, fos. 256–57.

association which might give umbrage to France." De Witt knew this, Pomponne saw, but his reply was one of despair: What had been done could not be undone without too many perilous consequences. The Dutch had gone too far with England and Sweden simply to abandon their alliance. Nor could he see why the guarantee to Spain should trouble Louis XIV when the French monarch made clear by word and deed his own desire to maintain the peace. This was evading the central issue, for De Witt knew that France wanted peace *with territorial gains.* Pomponne merely replied, therefore, that the pensionary would be hard put to persuade him that Dutch conduct had been fair.

Then let us not talk of the past, De Witt replied. Let us see how we can choose the right road in the future. The Frenchman, unwilling to suggest new expedients, urged De Witt to explain what he had in mind. It was, Pomponne wrote to the king with an almost audible sigh, "the same as Your Majesty has seen till now in various dispatches from me: always the interest Your Majesty has in curing their fears of having him as a neighbor and thereby destroying the connections which those fears had caused them to take; always his intention to keep at a distance from their frontiers the greatest power in Europe; always the means of doing both these things by forming what Spain still holds in the Low Countries into a republic; and always the assurances of a junction with Your Majesty in achieving this, either on the occasion of the death of the Catholic King or that of an unjust war which Spain might declare against him."

Pomponne replied more curtly. The grand pensionary knew well that Pomponne was authorized to discuss his powers for negotiations on such an occasion. Again De Witt returned to his demand that England and Sweden be brought in too, and this, of course, was the very stumbling block to any agreement. Pomponne spoke only in order to draw De Witt out, but not to enter himself into the negotiation. He was not surprised, therefore, that De Witt returned to his bone: England should be kept off the continent, the total present territory of the Spanish Netherlands should go to a new "cantonned" republic, and thus the usual quarrels between neighbors would be spared France and the United Provinces. Then nothing would keep the States General from Louis' graces; protected by his alliance, they would need no other leagues for their defense; once his friendship were regained, they hoped trade between the two lands would be resumed as before, to their mutual benefit. The pensionary came back to the point that cantonment would be to France's advantage—at the expense of what the king might gain or inherit in the Low Countries, Pomponne silently noted. Those who put themselves forward as the friends of France and those who knew the pensionary's mind best all secretly urged upon Pomponne the advantages of cantonment, or at least of partition, "as if," he commented to the king, "it would be a great advantage, when a thousand occasions may open up for him the total control of the Low Countries, to place all his hopes upon the repose and good will of friends as grateful and faithful as these folk here."

Pomponne thereupon analyzed De Witt's position more closely. The connection with England was quite uncertain, not so much because of the past wars, in which De Witt had done so much to England's hurt, as because of his ever-present fear that England would favor the prince of Orange. "This is the first affair in importance for him." The wisest and most skilled of all the Dutch, De Witt foresaw better than any other how little aid he could expect from the Triple Alliance, yet till now, Pomponne said, he had seen no sign that any rights to the Low Countries which Louis XIV might assert would reconcile the pensionary to accepting France as master of those provinces. Therefore the news of the fragile health of Carlos II and the debility and misery of Spanish Flanders would always drive him to renew his proposals for cantonment.[1]

Writing to Lionne, Pomponne grew sarcastic. When De Groot reached Paris, he would no doubt soon persuade Lionne by his eloquence "that the sovereign advantage of His Majesty is to renounce the just claims which may attach provinces of such beauty and importance to his crown, and that it is to his service to assure the repose of this republic by forming a new one at Cambrai and Brussels. This is what they call here the best intentions in the world, and you will be disarmed, Sir, by these arguments." But Lionne would no doubt reply that one could as soon persuade him that quartan fevers improve our health.[2]

The ambassador and the grand pensionary met again on May 14, for the last time before Pomponne's departure for Lille. A note of outright boredom marked his dispatch. The same topic—cantonment—came up. The same arguments were used in its favor by De Witt. Pomponne replied in the same generalities designed to keep the pensionary from despair. "Much as I saw how strongly he hoped to be able to take steps now to determine the future of Flanders," wrote Pomponne, "equally did I avoid putting before him any but vague and distant prospects."[3]

[1] Pomponne to Louis XIV, May 8, 1670, Arch. étr., Holl., vol. 90, fos. 188–92.
[2] Pomponne to Lionne, May 8, 1670, *ibid.*, fo. 194.
[3] Pomponne to Louis XIV, May 15, 1670, *ibid.*, fos. 202–03.

On this dull note of disillusion the first portion of Pomponne's mission as a negotiator came to an end. He had come to The Hague to engage in negotiations if possible, but both sides had proved intransigeant. Louis XIV and his counselors, entranced by the prospect that the imminent death of Carlos II would open up for France the acquisition of all the Spanish Low Countries, were unwilling to settle for what the Dutch offered. The grand pensionary, eager to regain the friendship of France at any price but one—abandonment of the Triple Alliance—sought, always in vain, to persuade the French king that his truest interest lay in an independent Belgic republic between the two erstwhile allies.

Pomponne left for Lille eagerly. Perhaps what he could guess from his dispatches would be confirmed by word of mouth—that England had been won for war against the United Provinces and all seemed sure for France.

CHAPTER VII

SPAIN, SWEDEN AND SUBSIDIES
February, 1669—May, 1670

Pomponne, at The Hague, was not directly involved in the French efforts to win England and Sweden away from the Triple Alliance. Yet, as the representative of France at the hub point of the league, he had to note the responses there to the maneuvers conceived and directed by Lionne. As for the foreign minister, he looked to Pomponne perhaps more than to any other French diplomat for help in evaluating the changing events and in judging what should be done. Pomponne was a model of ambassadorial competence and sagacity; he was also a personal and intimate friend without hidden motives, who gladly followed his advice to the letter.[1]

The first object of Pomponne's attention as observer and commentator at The Hague was the relationship between Spain and the Triple Alliance. The interest of Spain and the States General in their mutual support, as Pomponne saw, "derived in neither case from a former feeling of friendship."[2] At the moment, however, Spain was fearful of French progress in the Low Countries and wished to persuade the Dutch that they had "an interest of their own" in the defense of these provinces. The Dutch needed no convincing; they viewed the Spanish Netherlands not only as a barrier between themselves and France, but also "as a chain which still retained that crown (Spain) in the North, whereas if once it were taken from her, her assistance would be implored in vain, for, her interest having been detached from it, and with so many countries separating them, all her thoughts would remain in the South and extend no further than Italy and the Indies."[3]

For all her high hopes in the Triple Alliance, Spain had not received its official guarantee of the Spanish Netherlands by the time that Pomponne reached The Hague, more than a year after the con-

[1] Pomponne to Lionne, Jan. 30, 1670, Arch. étr., Holl., vol. 90, fo. 45.
[2] Pomponne, *Relation de Hollande*, p. 66.
[3] *Ibid.*, pp. 85–89.

clusion of the original treaty. The difficulties holding up its final approval centered about the subsidies which had been promised to Sweden in return for her commitment to join England and the Netherlands in defense of the Low Countries. The money was supposed to be paid by Spain as the beneficiary. The sum involved was very large, 300,000 crowns for Swedish expenditures until the time of ratification of the treaty, and 18,000 crowns for each quarter-year thereafter. After the conclusion of peace with France at Aix-la-Chapelle, the Spanish council indicated its willingness to make good the promise to Sweden, provided that the Triple Alliance undertook a new obligation to protect not only the Spanish Netherlands, but any Spanish territory attacked, and that the size of the forces promised be set forth in specific terms. Spain's refusal to pay Sweden before the act of guarantee was signed was "the single difficulty" which halted the affair. Spain would pay only for future assistance, the Triple Alliance desired her payment to cover the past obligations. In Pomponne's opinion, if Spain had conceded this point, the Triple Alliance would readily have granted her other demands.[1]

From the start, De Witt felt that both the Swedes and the Spaniards were in the wrong. The Swedes, in his view, were pressing too hard,[2] but it was the Spaniards who placed a major dilemma before him. Spain, in refusing to pay the Swedes the subsidies promised by England and the States General, gave proof, he felt, that she wished to have the defense of her Belgian provinces taken in hand by the Triple Alliance. However, if France were to attack the Low Countries and Spain did not do her part in their defense, England and the United Provinces should attempt to prevent their conquest by France, if possible by means of a treaty "by which France and Their High Mightinesses would promote their own interests."[3]

This matter of the Spanish subsidies was discussed at the first conferences between Pomponne and De Witt. When Pomponne predicted in jest that Sweden would go awhile before receiving her money, De Witt criticized the lack of dignity with which the northern kingdom hunted after subsidies.[4] Pomponne soon received news from Stockholm that power to conclude was being sent to Harald Appelboom, the Swedish resident at The Hague. He sent Lionne a suggestion on how to minimize the effects of the treaty in Sweden. Magnus de

[1] *Ibid.*, pp. 65–66. Cf. Cuvelier, V, 47–68.
[2] De Witt to Temple, at Brussels, April 4, 1668, De Witt, *Correspondance française*, p. 319.
[3] De Witt to Meerman, at London, May 18, 1668, De Witt, *Brieven*, IV, 793.
[4] Pomponne to Louis XIV, Feb. 28, 1669, Arch. étr., Holl., vol. 89, fos. 65–66.

la Gardie, the Swedish chancellor and leader of the Francophile party, should be allowed to accept the subsidies from Spain, especially since France had promised peace for the present year. But, "in a wholly separate affair," De la Gardie should be persuaded to "take measures with us instead of with England and these provinces." Pomponne hoped that the proffer of French subsidies would strengthen the chancellor's hand against English influence in the Swedish senate.[1] Though Rousseau de Chamoy, Pomponne's former secretary who had remained behind in Stockholm as the French agent, reported that De la Gardie had promised to send a power of negotiation to Count Wilhelm Otto von Königsmarck, then at the French court,[2] Lionne expected that Sweden would first ratify the Triple Alliance in order to get Spain's money. They would "skip over the difficulties in order not to miss so fine a morsel, which comes to them by the grace of Heaven, without being earned," he predicted.[3]

The Spanish government was in fact growing more willing to pay something, provided the guarantee and the "concert of forces," as the agreement on specific military obligations was called, were settled to her satisfaction; the Council of Finances at Madrid was ordered to prepare to make payment.[4]

Late in April the Swedish diplomat Jürgen Marschalk arrived at The Hague to conclude the affair on terms acceptable to Sweden. Pomponne noted with pleasure that Marschalk explicitly limited the obligation to Spain to that which ensued from the treaty of Aix-la-Chapelle. His demand that England and the United Provinces, rather than Spain, guarantee the subsequent payments, caused uneasiness, Pomponne noted. It might be a means to escape the full obligations of the Triple Alliance or at least to obtain more coin for Sweden from her allies.[5] Pomponne agreed with Lionne's judgment that the French had best count on Sweden's listening to France's siren call only after she had pocketed Spain's money. He reported without perturbation, therefore, that the guarantee arrangement had been signed on May 7. Even Dutch refusal to stand behind Spain's future payments played into French hands, since any delay could always serve to justify a Swedish breakaway.[6]

Sweden continued to maintain that her business had been not with

[1] Pomponne to Louis XIV and Lionne, March 14, 1669, *ibid.*, fos. 88–90.
[2] Lionne to Pomponne, April 5, 1669, Bib. Ars., MS 4712, fo. 46.
[3] Lionne to Pomponne, May 3, 1669, *ibid.*, fos. 58–59.
[4] Queen-Regent of Spain to Constable of Castille, March 7, 1669, Cuvelier, V, 71.
[5] Pomponne to Louis XIV, April 25, 1669, Arch. étr., Holl., vol. 89, fos. 149–50.
[6] Pomponne to Lionne, May 9, 1669, *ibid.*, fo. 174.

Spain but with England and the States General. She demanded their surety not only for the 280,000 crowns which would remain due after the first payment of 200,000 crowns was paid, but especially for the 60,000 crowns monthly to be paid in the event of military action.[1] The Dutch were willing to furnish such surety, and the municipal administration of Amsterdam offered to underwrite it; De Witt sought, however, to make use of this demand to push again his plan to induce the Spaniards to borrow the money by mortgaging Upper Gelderland to the States General. His overtures were received with indignation by Gamarra. If the Dutch were thus capable of profiting by Spanish hardship instead of alleviating it, Gamarra warned, the Spaniards would be capable of seeking an accommodation with France. The king of Spain would remain a great monarch without his possessions in the Low Countries, but the Dutch would face the French, alone and without friends. De Witt's "insinuation and skill" were of no avail, though he continued to hope that future necessities would make the Spaniards readier to enter this arrangement.[2]

Subsequent negotiations between Madrid and the Triple Alliance concerned not so much the terms of the subsidy agreement itself as the conditions under which the act of guarantee—the document, ratified and in good form—would be turned over to Spain.[3] Rumors of Spanish readiness to discuss some total exchange of the Spanish Netherlands for some other territory spread in the United Provinces and elsewhere in October and November, but Lionne discounted them; he expected that the Spanish ministers would use these rumors as a means of pressure upon the Dutch.[4] Pomponne was surprised when these rumors recurred in December,[5] and by January 1670, Louis XIV found the notion of such an exchange "fabulous."[6] But the reports, true or not, were an effective Spanish weapon against the Dutch, as Lionne expected. Pomponne observed that whenever the Dutch found themselves clamping hard upon the Spaniards, they began to fear that they were driving them to accept, or perhaps even to suggest, such a general exchange. "There is no doubt here," he commented, "that the consequence would be the downfall of these provinces."[7]

[1] Pomponne to Lionne, July 11, 1669, *ibid.*, fo. 278.
[2] Pomponne, *Relation de Hollande*, pp. 89–90.
[3] Pomponne to Lionne, May 30, 1669, Arch. étr., Holl., vol. 89, fo. 214.
[4] Lionne to Pomponne, Nov. 28, 1669, Bib. Ars., MS 4712, fo. 135. Cf. a report of such rumors at Vienna in a dispatch of Grémonville to Pomponne, Nov. 10, 1669, *ibid.*, MS 4713, fo. 72.
[5] Pomponne to Louis XIV, Dec. 19, 1669, Arch. étr., Holl., vol. 89, fo. 447.
[6] Louis XIV to Pomponne, Jan. 3, 1670, Bib. Ars., MS 4712, fo. 164.
[7] Pomponne to Louis XIV, April 3, 1670, Arch. étr., Holl., vol. 90, fo. 116.

The grand pensionary, irked at the Spanish dilly-dallying, finally suggested that England and the Dutch republic each pay a fourth of the subsidy, thereby avoiding "breaking of the business."[1] But Charles II had no intention of paying money in that cause. Arlington warned Temple that, come what may, the king would "never be at charge by reason of the League."[2] As for the Spaniards, they remained firm. The Constable of Castille received instructions to pay the 200,000 crowns only after the act of guarantee had been given and the "concert of forces" had been arranged.[3] The constable, who was not dismayed at the possibility of the alliance breaking up over this question, relayed these orders to Gamarra, who was urging concessions. The Spanish government was in the right, the constable affirmed, and the Triple Alliance had no reason to reject its demands. Only formal orders from Madrid would change his stand, he informed Gamarra. The orders which were soon on their way to him only confirmed his position.[4]

By the end of November, however, Louis XIV began to expect the imminent conclusion of the accord. He was not perturbed, at least for the moment, by the provisions in the "concert" for action only on behalf of Spain. He instructed Pomponne to be on the watch, however, for any action to convert this "simple guarantee" into a treaty of alliance; this would be an overt infraction of the French-Dutch treaty of 1662.[5]

The king's equanimity with regard to the guarantee could only be heightened by Pomponne's report on the way in which De Witt looked upon Spanish delaying tactics. The pensionary admitted his irritation and "chagrin" to Pomponne. The Dutch were anxious over the prospect of having to bear the total burden of the Triple Alliance, Pomponne reported. "There are some who perhaps might wish now that the things which estranged Your Majesty from them had not been done, or that things be done now to win back his friendship, but as yet we can hardly expect anything certain from a situation which is so uncertain. Only this is sure, as Your Majesty sees more clearly than anyone else, that the Triple Alliance, near as it still is to its origins, is growing neither in the mutual comprehension of its members nor, consequently, in its strength."[6]

[1] Temple to Arlington, Sept. 2, 1669, Temple, II, 65.
[2] Arlington to Temple, Aug. 24/Sept. 3, 1669, *The Right Honourable the Earl of Arlington's Letters to Sir William Temple...*, ed. T. Bebington (London, 1701), pp. 412–13.
[3] Queen-Regent to Constable of Castille, Oct. 12, 1669, Cuvelier, V, 85.
[4] Constable of Castille to Gamarra, Nov. 21, 1669, Queen-Regent to Constable of Castille, Nov. 23, 1669, Cuvelier, V, 86–87. Cf. Pomponne to Lionne, Oct. 31, Nov. 28, 1669, Arch. étr., Holl., vol. 89, fos. 404, 428.
[5] Louis XIV to Pomponne, Nov. 28, 1669, Bib. Ars., MS 4712, fo. 147.
[6] Pomponne to Louis XIV, Dec. 5, 1669, Arch. étr., Holl., vol. 89, fos. 433–34.

This was also Louis XIV's view. He believed that the Spaniards were gambling safely in incurring Dutch wrath, for the United Provinces were inextricably committed to the defense of the Low Countries, even at their own cost. Indeed, a hint to the Constable of Castille, if Pomponne had some means to give it, might well result in further depleting the purse of the States General.[1]

To get Spain to pay Sweden continued to be, in Pomponne's words, the "principal affair" of the United Provinces. Though Lisola was not officially involved, it was his too. As Pomponne said, his "great occupation" was "the quest for expedients and the art of persuading the parties" in an endeavor to break the deadlock.[2] Aghast at the danger to his pet plan, Lisola hastened to Brussels in order to soften the implacable resolution of the Constable of Castille. But, as Mocenigo, the Venetian envoy in London, put it, Lisola was running one course and the constable another.[3] The Dutch tried to persuade England to join them in pressure upon the constable, but instead met English displeasure at the prospect of having to pay 15,000 crowns to Sweden. Thus, saw Pomponne, the Dutch "still see that the expenses of the league will fall principally upon these provinces."[4]

Early in the new year, 1670, reports from Spain began to show a growing readiness there to relax from the stiffness which the constable had been ordered to assume, and Louis XIV expected an early conclusion to the affair.[5] Finally, on January 30, Pomponne reported the conclusion of the business the day before. The constable authorized payment of the 200,000 crowns to Sweden, but the money would remain at the Bank of Amsterdam under the surety of the States General until the Swedish instrument of ratification arrived. Meanwhile the States General handed over to Gamarra the act of "concert of forces," with its provisions that England and the United Provinces should each provide 40 warships, 4,000 infantry and 600 cavalry, and Sweden 11,000 infantry and 5,000 cavalry. As always, De Witt explained the guarantee as deriving only from the treaty of Aix-la-Chapelle. Pomponne requested that its text be transmitted to him; De Witt promised to do so as soon as the Swedish assent was received.[6]

The conclusion of the agreement brought public outbursts of joy at The Hague from "all who support the House of Austria and oppose

[1] Louis XIV to Pomponne, Dec. 6, 1669, Bib. Ars., MS 4712, fos. 152, 155.
[2] Pomponne to Louis XIV, Nov. 28, 1669, Arch. étr., Holl., vol. 89, fo. 428.
[3] Mocenigo to Doge and Senate, Jan. 3, 1670, *Calendar of State Papers, Venice*, XXXVI, 146–47.
[4] Pomponne to Louis XIV, Dec. 19. 1669, Arch. étr., Holl., vol. 89, fos. 447–48.
[5] Louis XIV to Pomponne, Jan. 17, 1670, Bib. Ars., MS 4712, fo. 170.
[6] Pomponne to Louis XIV, Jan. 30, 1670, Arch. étr., Holl., vol. 90, fos. 41–42.

France." Pomponne, however, twitted De Witt with the triumph of the Spaniards, who had obtained their demands for the "concert of forces." The grand pensionary frankly admitted that their conduct, in which "stubbornness had prevailed over reason," had not been to his liking; yet he claimed that all that they had actually achieved was to have the aid promised in the event of an attack upon the Low Countries fixed at a public figure, whereas the Triple Alliance before had promised to support them with all its strength. In his report to the king, Pomponne commented, "perhaps he (De Witt) spoke quite truly in saying that the troops now stipulated by the Triple Alliance would not suffice for a war of some scope, and it was, no doubt, in the belief that this engagement would carry with it a more considerable one that the Spaniards insisted on it so vigorously." But Pomponne did not share the confidence of the ministers of the House of Austria that the new treaty was unbreakable. "I cannot, in any event, imagine that there is much solidity in a liaison which so many opposing interests may weaken so easily," he wrote, "nor can I envisage much vigor in a body, every part of which has natural weaknesses."[1]

Others felt differently. The Queen-Regent of Spain was delighted when she heard of the settlement.[2] De Witt, too, believed that the affair had come to a "good end."[3] Temple likewise felt satisfaction, and commented that the danger of retreat was obviated by this "consummation in matrimony." With the Dutch historian Japikse, we may say that Temple "forgot that untrue husbands and wives are beyond counting."[4]

Early in March the final exchange of papers was apparently completed at The Hague between Spain and the Dutch. Even then Pomponne made two observations of significance. The first was that, even at this last moment, the Constable of Castille attempted to diddle the Swedes of a portion of the subsidies by paying it at the current rate of exchange, about four per cent less than the official bank rate. More important was the insistence of the Swedish minister on staying away from the ceremony of the exchange of documents. His ground was that his government was involved only with England and the States General, not with Spain.[5] After repeated efforts, the Dutch deputies at Brussels were able to persuade the constable to pay Sweden the full sum. But the 200,000 crowns, however eagerly the Swedes desired it, was allowed to

[1] Pomponne to Louis XIV, Feb. 6, 1670, *ibid.*, fos. 52–53.
[2] Queen-Regent to Gamarra, Feb. 18, 1670, Cuvelier, V, 89.
[3] De Witt to Boreel, March 14, 1670, *Brieven van De Witt*, IV, 69.
[4] Japikse, *Johan de Witt*, p. 299.
[5] Pomponne to Louis XIV, March 6, 1670, Arch, étr., Holl., vol. 90, fo. 88.

remain in Dutch hands. Appelboom refused to accept delivery until word came from Stockholm that all the conditions had been accepted.[1]

Louis XIV decided at this point not to ask the Triple Alliance for a similar guarantee. Not only was it morally as well as physically impossible for the Spaniards to attack him, but he feared that by accepting a guarantee, "various princes of the empire who are today restrained from joining this alliance by fear of disobliging me, might abandon these compunctions." Nonetheless, Pomponne should refrain from letting this decision become known. If questioned, he should merely say it was being put off to a later date.[2]

Now that the occasion had arisen for renewed negotiations with Sweden to steal her from the Triple Alliance, Pomponne knew he would be more closely involved than before, even though he was in another land. He was in direct correspondence with Rousseau, whom Lionne ordered to act upon his instructions in the whole business.[3] But, though Lionne had earlier been restive and eager to begin his efforts to win back the Swedes, now that negotiations with England were going so well there seemed to be little need to recruit Sweden on the basis of paying her whatever Spain was obligated to give. Even the monthly sum of 60,000 crowns for the action of an army of 16,000 seemed excessive to Louis XIV, "whatever may be my need for it."[4]

Pomponne meanwhile anticipated further conflict over the subsidies question between Sweden and her friends. For one thing, it was improbable that Spain could ever pay the 60,000 crowns a month it had promised. Learning that Lisola was proclaiming his distrust of Sweden, Pomponne wrote to Louis XIV that he "hoped that these apprehensions are well founded." If Magnus de la Gardie re-established his influence and held the same good intentions for France he had had when Pomponne left Stockholm, he would perhaps be able to regain Sweden's adherence "to her true interests and to the solid advantage she can receive from the friendship" of Louis XIV.[5]

Pomponne's hopes were not without basis. Rousseau's dispatches from Stockholm indicated some possibility that the Swedes might not ratify the subsidy agreement if her loss would be made up by France.[6] This last-minute chance to prevent the guarantee for Spain from becoming reality enticed Louis XIV into a sudden decision. He

[1] Pomponne to Louis XIV, March 13, 1670, *ibid.*, fo. 95.
[2] Louis XIV to Pomponne, March 7, 1670, Bib. Ars., MS 4712, fo. 207.
[3] Lionne to Pomponne, Oct. 23, 1669, *ibid.*, fo. 125.
[4] Louis XIV to Pomponne, March 14, 1670, *ibid.*, fo. 213.
[5] Pomponne to Louis XIV, March 20, 27, 1670, Arch. étr., Holl., vol. 90, fos. 102–03, 107, 109.
[6] Lionne to Pomponne, March 28, 1670, Bib. Ars., MS 4712, fo. 222.

abandoned his refusal to match Spain's promised payment, and assured count Königsmarck, who had been idling away his time at the court of Saint-Germain awaiting developments, that France would be willing to pay both the 480,000 crowns due Sweden under the new guarantee, and even the 280,000 crowns due for Swedish arming before the conclusion of the peace of Aix-la-Chapelle. Königsmarck rushed off to The Hague to persuade Appelboom to delay delivering the ratification documents, at least until word came from Stockholm as to whether the regency had acted on this offer. Louis gave Königsmarck full powers to work with Pomponne in these belated efforts to spoil the Triple Alliance agreement with Spain. Lionne wrote out an enciphered certificate attesting to these powers, and a covering letter to Pomponne, in his own hand, rather than entrust them to a clerk.[1]

When Königsmarck arrived at The Hague on the morning of April 3, 1670, ostensibly on private business, the ratification had not yet arrived from Stockholm. Pomponne at ounce rushed off to Rousseau the packet of dispatches from France. For the moment, Königsmarck did not reveal his secret to Appelboom, and Pomponne hoped the material for Rousseau would reach the Swedish capital in time to delay the transmittal of the ratifications. Pomponne admitted to Louis XIV that he remained uncertain how the Swedes would act. He was somewhat optimistic because latest reports indicated that Biörnclou, till then De la Gardie's chief antagonist, was moving to his support, and their conjoined strength should be enough to push the French plan through. If this occured, Pomponne exulted, the time would be near for "punishing the ingratitude of these people and silencing the insolence which their Triple Alliance has already inspired in them."[2]

Louis XIV committed himself fully to this new Swedish policy. The first danger was that the ratification had already left Stockholm before Rousseau received the French offer. Therefore, in order to permit the Swedes to reconsider while the tempting delight of a more certain French subsidy dangled before them, Louis ordered Pomponne to join with Königsmarck in attempting to persuade Appelboom to hold off delivering the instrument of ratification until the regency had considered the French offer. But, as the king realized, Appelboom would not be easy to win; De Witt's authority over him might be too strong. Appelboom had lived in Holland for thirty years with his family, and all his property was located there. Yet he "was not in-

[1] Lionne to Pomponne, and certificate noted, March 28, 1670 (holograph), *ibid.*, fos. 226–27.

[2] Pomponne to Louis XIV, April 3, 10, 1670, Arch. étr., Holl., vol. 90, fos. 117–18, 123.

sensitive to his own interests," and might be tempted by a "gratification." Three to five thousand crowns, perhaps even as much as seven thousand, might be offered to him.[1]

Königsmarck found Appelboom difficult to drive to a decision. Appelboom used as an argument against acting on his own initiative the importance for Sweden not to break with England, since the Swedish state needed the friendship of at least one of the sea powers. Pomponne had anticipated this line of reasoning, and Königsmarck fell back upon the pecuniary argument. He reminded Appelboom that his back pay was assigned to the second installment of the Spanish subsidy, which might never come, while French cash was always certain. Pomponne expected, however, that the more forthright offer of a bribe would have to be employed.[2] Appelboom persisted in his refusal to take upon himself the responsibility for delaying the delivery of the ratification documents once they arrived, although he admitted it might be to Sweden's interest to turn toward France. Pomponne agreed with Königsmarck that it was advisable to seek a delay even of a few days, since the materials from France must have reached Rousseau by mid-April and, even if the ratification had been sent, a countermanding order could reach Appelboom without much delay.[3]

So eager was Louis XIV for the Swedish alliance that he imagined Appelboom was closer to doing Königsmarck's bidding than Pomponne's dispatches actually gave reason to believe. Indeed, the king thought that the Swedish resident would leap at the chance to get his back pay from France, and decided that no bribe should be offered him for the time being. Louis was not as yet ready to assent to the proposition that Sweden receive in peacetime from France what the Triple Alliance had promised for the occasion of war—but he was willing to discuss even such a proposal.[4]

Meanwhile, at The Hague, the affair grew stickier. Pomponne heard from Rousseau that the ratification had already been sent off, but thought that if Appelboom could delay actual delivery for about twelve days, there would be time to hear from Stockholm after the documents for Rousseau had been placed in the hands of the Swedish government. Pomponne lauded Königsmarck's skill and zeal, but doubted whether he could move Appelboom. On April 24, just as Pomponne was about to close his dispatch, Königsmarck hurried in with news that Appelboom had received the ratification documents,

[1] Louis XIV to Pomponne, April 4, 1670, Bib. Ars., MS 4712, fo. 231.
[2] Pomponne to Louis XIV, April 10, 1670, Arch. étr., Holl., vol. 90, fos. 123–27.
[3] Pomponne to Louis XIV, April 17, 1670, *ibid.*, fos. 139–42.
[4] Louis XIV to Pomponne, April 18, 1670, Bib. Ars., MS 4712, fo. 246.

together with precise orders to deliver them. The count had spared "neither arguments nor threats" to persuade Appelboom to delay anyway, but to no avail.[1]

Lionne continued to hope that some way could be found to achieve the delay. Perhaps the courier from Stockholm might join with Königsmarck in persuading him, for then he could be told, "*ne Hercules quidem contra duos*."[2]

Aid came to Königsmarck from a most unexpected quarter, Appelboom himself. The resident suggested that a delay until the arrival and delivery of the Spanish ratification could be justified, and held out firmly with this argument against De Witt and Temple. But Pomponne, remembering that the Swedes would probably be absent from Stockholm over the Easter vacation, feared that the dispatches from Sweden would not bring the desired orders. An additional week, during which Spanish ratification would almost certainly arrive at The Hague, would be needed. But now he felt that Appelboom's intentions were good, though "fear makes him unwilling to accept responsibility."[3]

Louis XIV recognized that much depended on Pomponne's judgment and initiative in this affair. While journeying into Flanders, accompanied by the marquis de Berni, Lionne's son, the king sent Pomponne a letter of change for 10,000 crowns, to be used as the ultimate argument with Appelboom. The confidence which the monarch felt in Pomponne was reflected in Berni's comment, "You are a great master, and if it is possible to do anything, it will be you who without doubt will accomplish it."[4] Actually, the decision to send the letter of change was taken at Lionne's initiative, after he received Pomponne's letter of April 24, with the news of the arrival of the Swedish ratification at The Hague. He convoked a council meeting with Le Tellier and Colbert in the king's absence, and with his colleagues' approval sent to Louis a draft of the letter which the king sent to Pomponne in his own name on May 1. The letter of change, Lionne thought, would do better work than the arguments Königsmarck was using; it could be used at Pomponne's discretion.[5]

The affair reached its height on May 3, when Gamarra turned up with the Spanish ratification—although Pomponne suspected he might

[1] Pomponne to Louis XIV, April 24, 1670, Arch. étr., Holl., vol. 90, fos. 150–52, 155–57.
[2] Lionne to Pomponne, April 25, 1670, Bib. Ars., MS 4712, fo. 250.
[3] Pomponne to Louis XIV, May 1, 1670, Arch. étr., Holl., vol. 90, fos. 161–63.
[4] Louis XIV and Berni, at Noyon, to Pomponne, May 1, 1670, Bib. Ars., MS 4712, fos. 252, 253.
[5] Minute by Lionne of dispatch of Louis XIV to Pomponne, May 1, 1670, Arch. étr., Holl., vol. 90, fo. 167; Lionne to Pomponne, May 2, 1670, Bib. Ars., MS 4712, fo. 256.

have fabricated it at The Hague. Appelboom was torn between the incessant demands of Temple, De Witt and Gamarra, who realized what Königsmarck was seeking, and the resident's own promise to delay if at all possible until the arrival of the ordinary courier from Stockholm in two days. De Witt threatened to report his delaying tactics to Stockholm, but Appelboom pleaded illness to gain every possible hour. Thus, though the Swede remained timid and fundamentally irresolute, Pomponne was satisfied that he would hold firm at least for one day. Pomponne refrained from using the letter of change, doubting it would prove of any effect.[1]

That same afternoon and evening the affair came to a head. Temple and Gamarra descended upon Appelboom to make their arguments, then De Witt came to loose his thunder upon him. The grand pensionary warned him officially that he knew that the ratification had come with plain orders that it be delivered, and that Königsmarck was trying to prevent it. Do not think that I have 80,000 florins for secret affairs without being well informed, he told the Swede. If Appelboom delayed any longer, the States General would declare him persona non grata and so inform Stockholm at once.

Though little more than twenty-four hours remained until the scheduled arrival of the courier from Stockholm, De Witt's arguments and threats shattered Appelboom's never very firm resolution. He quaked under Königsmarck's indignant denunciation and threat to hold him responsible for the failure of the affair, but decided, in Pomponne's words, that "if he had to be lost, he preferred it be for following orders rather than for disobeying them." He knew he would probably lose his post, but in his far advanced age, he needed a place to live, and that could only be in the United Provinces.

This remark gave Pomponne cause to suspect that De Witt had promised him assistance if a revengeful Königsmarck did him harm. But the French envoy made a judgment of wider consequence: Appelboom had become almost a "natural subject" of the States General during thirty years of residence in the United Provinces, and this showed the danger in permitting ministers to reside too long in one country, lest they come to "feel that the land in which they served had become their own."

At nine o'clock that night, an hour after Königsmarck stalked from Appelboom's home, the documents were exchanged at Temple's residence. Sweden's guarantee to Spain was in effect. The next day brought an anticlimax.

[1] Pomponne to Louis XIV, May 3, 1670, Arch. étr., Holl., vol. 90, fos. 176–81.

A dispatch from Rousseau arrived with the paradoxically encouraging news that De la Gardie had decided that the time was not propitious to take up the offer from France. Thus old Appelboom had been subjected to his torment to no point. But Pomponne saw some advantage from the affair for France. The Dutch could not rely on the Swedes, who, if they did not accept the French offer of subsidy, would certainly raise their demands on Spain and the States General in the event of war. Pomponne thought De Witt was as aware as himself of the fundamental weakness of Sweden, which could not maintain 16,000 men by her own efforts, especially in a war which would leave her exposed to attacks from Denmark or Muscovy.[1]

Pomponne did not abandon hope that De la Gardie would sooner or later change his mind, either because of Spanish delays or for other reasons.[2] On reconsideration, and after receiving further information about the situation at Stockholm from Rousseau, Pomponne decided that the Swedish senate would not act without England, so that a change in Swedish policy would depend on what could be done to win over England.[3] This only added importance, therefore, to the negotiations under way with England, already so close to success. Disappointment in the French king's council was great, nonetheless. Colbert expressed his disappointment that the letter of change for 10,000 crowns had not been used.[4]

Pomponne's involvement in the elaboration of the Swedish policy of France was left here, while the ambassador journeyed to Flanders to see Louis XIV. What Pomponne learned in Flanders was central to what he had observed thus far regarding developments in England, and by derivation, in Sweden. Before we can turn our attention to this topic, however, we must watch as Pomponne and De Witt debate the issue of Germany, the land where both France and the States General sought allies.

[1] Pomponne to Louis XIV, May 6, 1670, *ibid.*, fos. 185–88.
[2] Pomponne to Lionne, May 8, 1670, *ibid.*, fo. 193.
[3] Pomponne to Louis XIV, May 15, 1670, *ibid.*, fo. 198.
[4] Colbert to Pomponne, May 16, 1670, Bib. Ars., MS 4586, fo. 113.

CHAPTER VIII

ALLIES TO THE EAST?
February, 1669 – May, 1670

From the first, Louis XIV planned to bypass the Spanish Netherlands in any invasion of the United Provinces. He wished, of course, to spare the feelings of the English, whose maxim, like that of the Dutch, was to keep France out of the Low Countries. But equally, because he did not wholly trust his Britannic cousin, he desired to avoid giving him any pretext for bringing the Triple Alliance into action.

The obvious pathway for French invasion of the Netherlands, under this territorial limitation, was western Germany. There the river Rhine, historically the bulwark of the Dutch republic against Spanish *reconquista*, provided an easy avenue of access from Germany. In the autumn of 1668, Wilhelm von Fürstenberg, to whom Louis XIV and Lionne gave their confidence in German matters, led his Gallic masters to believe that a boulevard could be cleared through the Rhineland for the passage of French troops. The German princes formerly linked to France in the Rhine league were ready, he asserted, to join with her again, provided her target lay outside the empire.[1]

However, most of the German princes, including emperor Leopold I, found it difficult to choose between France and the Triple Alliance. Louis XIV offered them friendship sweetened with subsidies for helping him. They were greatly tempted, but could not easily dull the fear that they would later face alone the demands of a greedy king of a powerful France.

In January 1668, Leopold I and Louis XIV had agreed to parcel the Spanish inheritance between themselves if Carlos II died without a direct heir. Yet, as Grémonville's dispatches from Vienna showed, it it was uncertain how faithful the emperor remained to that settlement.

[1] Hans Böhmer, "Forschungen zur französischen Bündnispolitik im 17. Jahrhundert: Wilhelm Egon von Fürstenberg und die französischen Diplomatie in Deutschland, 1668–1672," *Rheinische Viertelsjahrblätter*, IV (1934), 225–29.

To most onlookers, who knew nothing of the highly secret treaty, the emperor's policy was outlined, if not defined, by the activity of Leopold's representative at Brussels, François Paul baron de Lisola. Lisola, in his famous pamphlet, *The Buckler of State and Justice*, had invoked the principle of balance of power against the threat of French hegemony. But to Louis XIV and Lionne he was the screech-owl of Francophobia. Though the foreign minister assured Pomponne that "Lisola's scribbblings trouble us little,"[1] he felt bitter hatred for the active and tireless Franc-Comtois.

Lisola had long urged his imperial master to join the Triple Alliance. This plan was the very special bugbear of Louis XIV, for if realized it would infuse new life into the Triple Alliance and block his pathway through Germany to Amsterdam and The Hague. Consequently, a major portion of Pomponne's task consisted in reporting on Lisola's negotiations and in thwarting them if possible.[2]

Neither the Viennese court nor the Dutch had been receptive at first to Lisola's proposal. All through the winter of 1668, he had plagued the emperor and his ministers for authorization to enter negotiations with the Triple Alliance, but without success.[3] As for De Witt, he had suggested instead that Leopold and the princes of the empire join in their own league, parallel to the Triple Alliance, to protect the Spanish Netherlands. The imperial court gave thought to this proposal, but wanted to know what guarantee the emperor and his allies would receive from the sea powers. Concerned lest Lisola be falling under De Witt's influence, Vienne ordered him to return from The Hague to his regular post at Brussels.[4]

In conference with Pomponne, De Witt sought to minimize Lisola's project. It concerned only the "concert of forces" for the guarantee to Spain, he said, denying that the emperor had either asked or been asked to join the Triple Alliance. However, he did admit that the States General had invited Denmark, the Swiss cantons, the elector of Brandenburg and the dukes of Brunswick to enter the league—on the grounds of article seven of the treaty of Aix-la-Chapelle, of course.[5] Pomponne did not discount the dangers to France in a league of German princes under the aegis of the emperor. When he heard of negotiations at the imperial diet for such an alliance, he wrote at once to Gravel, the French resi-

[1] Lionne to Pomponne, March 15, 1669, Bib. Ars., MS 4712, fo. 41.

[2] Pomponne, *Relation de Hollande*, p. 116.

[3] Alfred Francis Pribram, *Franz Paul Freiherr von Lisola, 1613–1674, und die Politik seiner Zeit* (Leipzig, 1894), p. 460.

[4] *Ibid.*, p. 469; Grémonville to Pomponne, May 5, 1669, Bib. Ars., MS 4713, fo. 17.

[5] Pomponne to Lionne, Feb. 28, 1669, Arch. étr., Holl., vol. 89, fo. 69.

dent at Regensburg, to ask if the report were true.[1] Lionne, relying on his knowledge of the secret treaty of partition with the emperor, gaily reassured Pomponne. Have no fear, he told his friend, nothing will happen—but don't let any hint of this drop, and no boasting![2]

Pomponne was soon able to test Lionne's judgments as to the course of events at Vienna when he began to exchange dispatches with Grémonville, the French ambassador to Leopold I. Grémonville was not as blithely confident as his superior about the emperor's firmness. "I cannot yet say what will be decided," he wrote Pomponne at the end of March.[3] In May he warned Pomponne: "Things are not in as good a state here as Lionne gives you to believe." The imperial court, importuned by the Spanish ambassador, the marquis de Malagón, was seriously considering joining the Triple Alliance.[4] But Grémonville wrote with delight six weeks later that the Spaniard's insistence had turned to insolence and spoiled his success.[5] Grémonville continued, on occasion desperately, his efforts to prevent the emperor from taking a step which, as he told Pomponne, "could lead to strange and unpleasant consequences for us." Nor did he scoff at Lisola's influence. Hearing that the Franc-Comtois, exasperated by his squabbles with the Constable of Castille, had requested leave to return to his native province, Grémonville commented, "I would rather have him there than in Brussels."[6] Lionne, too, admitted that Lisola, "chimerical troublemaker" that he was, could do France more harm than anyone else in the service of the House of Austria.[7]

Grémonville, reporting that the Viennese court had just decided to pacify the Spaniards by sending Lisola back to The Hague, sent Pomponne another warning "between ourselves." His troubles were not accidental, he declared. As long as French policy, by its actions and its appearances, aroused "continual alarm and jealousy," he commented, "not only the Dutch, but many other princes as well will seek the chance to smash our plans." He was doing all he could to restrain the imperial court, for, as he gloomily prognosticated once again, "its example would lead to strange consequences."[8] Lionne was not cast down by the news that Lisola was going to The Hague. De

[1] Pomponne to Gravel, March 12, 1669, *ibid.*, fo. 86.
[2] Lionne to Pomponne, March 28, April 5, 1669, Bib. Ars., MS 4712, fos. 44, 46.
[3] Grémonville to Pomponne, March 31, 1669, *ibid.*, MS 4713, fos. 5–6.
[4] Grémonville to Pomponne, May 19, 1669, *ibid.*, fo. 22.
[5] Grémonville to Pomponne, June 30, 1669, *ibid.*, fo. 30.
[6] Grémonville to Pomponne, May 26, June 9, 1669, *ibid.*, fos. 24, 26.
[7] Lionne to Pomponne, June 7, 1669, *ibid.*, MS 4712, fo. 74.
[8] Grémonville to Pomponne, July 21, 28, 1669, *ibid.*, MS 4713, fos. 36, 38.

Witt's pride would puff up, and Van Beuningen's even more, he predicted, but Pomponne need have no worry, "for the king will discover means to assure that expansion of this alliance will cause him neither fear nor harm."[1]

Grémonville soon persuaded the emperor to limit the powers which had been granted to Lisola, and he breathed more easily. Something might come up to spoil Lisola's scheme, he thought, perhaps Pomponne's reports on his "mad proposings."[2]

Pomponne kept close watch on Lisola's activities at The Hague. He noted his involvement in the negotiations over Spain's subsidy to Sweden, and learned that he still lacked definite orders concerning imperial entry into the league.[3] Grémonville meanwhile became more confident that Lisola "would make more noise than he would do harm." He was compelling Lisola "to bite his nails to the quick," Grémonville boasted. But he also warned Pomponne repeatedly that French policy must become less aggressive. "If we are to dispel this great combination," he wrote, "everything depends on our not giving so much reason to fear us."[4] He did not seem to realize that his admonitions, if followed, could only mean ultimately the abandonment of Louis' plans for punishing and perhaps destroying the Dutch republic.

In mid-December, 1669, Grémonville was shaken by the dismissal of prince Auersperg, the best friend of France among the imperial ministers. But he did not lose hope that he could prevent an imperial decision to accept Lisola's scheme.[5] The next month, however, showed that he had failed. Lisola's importunings proved stronger than Grémonville's warnings and urgings. The emperor sent to Lisola his long-awaited orders to negotiate with the Triple Alliance regarding "everything which concerns the guarantee of peace," as Pomponne wrote to Louis XIV, but subject to the completion of the "concert of the Triple Alliance." Lisola at once informed the States General and Temple.[6]

Lisola pleaded with De Witt to conclude the affair at once, while the German princes were still sympathetic. He could not answer for their future attitude, he admitted. "Let us strike, I beg you, while the iron is hot." In March, he was still urging De Witt to act. "This is

[1] Lionne to Pomponne, Aug. 7, 1669, *ibid.*, MS 4712, fo. 103.

[2] Grémonville to Pomponne, Sept. 15, 22, 29, 1669, *ibid.*, MS 4713, fos. 52, 54, 56.

[3] Pomponne to Louis XIV, Oct. 3, 1669, Arch. étr., Holl., vol. 89, fos. 381, 384.

[4] Grémonville to Pomponne, Oct. 3, 13, Nov. 17, 1669, Bib. Ars., MS 4713, fos. 58, 62, 74.

[5] Grémonville to Pomponne, Dec. 15, 22, 1669, *ibid.*, fos. 80–81, 82.

[6] Pomponne to Louis XIV, Jan. 30, 1670, Arch. étr., Holl., vol. 90, fo. 42; Onno Klopp, *Der Fall des Hauses Stuarts* (Vienna, 1875–88), I, 259; Pribram, p. 480.

more important to you than to anyone else, for it is you who are under the greatest threat," he wrote.[1]

Soon after, De Witt instructed Johan Boreel, the Dutch envoy in London, to begin efforts to gain English support for the proposal. He observed "with sorrow" that Temple was "so cold and scrupulous" that he would not join in drawing up a draft embodying Lisola's proposal. This struck De Witt as "most strange." Boreel was told to inform the English government that it was impossible to believe that Temple had received such orders from Charles II. Boreel was to add a request that Temple be given explicit instructions to be more than a spectator in this "salutary work," and to help speed it in every way.[2] Pomponne, in a talk with Temple, also observed that the English ambassador "does not share the baron's ardor."[3] Nor did the imperial court, for that matter. One of the principal ministers at Vienna "laughed loudly" at Lisola's boasts, and assured Grémonville that the emperor would not join the Triple Alliance, but was only concerned with stilling the clamorous importunities of the Spanish ambassador.[4]

Pomponne considered De Witt's policy in this affair to be quite distinct from Lisola's. The grand pensionary did not want the emperor of the German princes brought into the Triple Alliance as full-fledged members. The more interests and opinions there were within the league, the more difficult would it be to control it and keep it united, he admitted to Pomponne. Instead he favored having all such prospective allies confine themselves to providing separate guarantees under the provisions of the treaty of Aix-la-Chapelle. Though Pomponne saw the "great hopes" which the Dutch placed on some such conjunction of "the larger part of the empire" with the Triple Alliance, he espied in De Witt's policy a deeper purpose—to maintain the superiority of the Triple Alliance, with other states no more than its "accessories."[5] Louis XIV hoped that De Witt's purpose ran no further than this.[6]

Late in March, Lisola formally presented his proposal to the ministers of the Triple Alliance at The Hague. The emperor, the principal

[1] Lisola to De Witt, Feb. 7, March 7, R. Fruin and N. Japikse, eds., *Brieven aan Johan de Witt*, ("Werken uitgegeven door het Historisch Genootschap te Utrecht," 3rd ser., nos. 42, 44) (Amsterdam, 1919–22), II, 486–98. Cf. Pomponne to Gravel, Feb. 3, 1670, Arch, étr., Holl., vol. 90, fo. 48.

[2] De Witt to Boreel, March 14, 1670, *Brieven van De Witt*, IV, 69–71.

[3] Pomponne to Louis XIV, March 20, 1670, Arch. étr., Holl., vol. 90, fos. 103–04.

[4] Grémonville to Pomponne, March 9, 1670, Bib. Ars., MS 4713, fo. 102.

[5] Pomponne to Louis XIV, March 6, 13, 1670, Arch. étr., Holl., vol. 90, fos. 89–90, 94.

[6] Louis XIV to Pomponne, March 14, 1670, Bib. Ars., MS 4712, fo. 213.

electors and princes of the empire, would enter into the guarantee of the treaty of Aix-la-Chapelle. In return, the Triple Alliance, originally intended only for the Low Countries, would promise to defend the German princes. The representatives of the Triple Alliance at once rejected this scheme. Only an exact neutrality, such as befitted guarantors, was acceptable, they told Lisola. Pomponne thought that the imperial diplomat, in his wily way, had deliberately courted rejection, in order to cover up the unpleasant fact that he had not received the full powers he had proclaimed were on their way from Vienna.[1] Louis XIV, too, believed that Lisola was acting on his own, as was usual with him. "A rebuff does not frighten him and a rejected proposal merely serves to make him put forward another on the morrow no more acceptable than the first," the king told Pomponne.[2] In Vienna, Grémonville obtained a promise that Lisola would not get his coveted powers, and hoped that the imperial court would stand by its word. He cheerily forecast that Lisola "would in the end become the dupe of the great comedy" being played at The Hague. He warned Pomponne against interfering with Lisola's negotiations: "Let him play out his rôle to its conclusion."[3]

Pomponne finally asked the grand pensionary what he sought to achieve in Germany. Only the guarantee to Spain, and to the guarantors if they were attacked by reason of the guarantee, De Witt replied. Then the United Provinces will be involved "in most of the wars which might arise in Europe," Pomponne commented. Any quarrel could be laid to this pretext. This danger was not real, De Witt said. The Dutch "would always be able to tell apart quarrels truly arising from the guarantee and those having another origin." Only the emperor was strong enough not to need the support of the Triple Alliance, and the allies did not wish to fight the Turk in Hungary and Austria. This last remark by De Witt caught Lionne's attention as he read Pomponne's dispatch, and he marked it off to be brought to Grémonville's attention.[4]

In April, Lisola made little progress. De Witt worked out with him a draft treaty embodying the principle presented to Pomponne of a parallel German league to give a guarantee to Spain. Lisola, lacking powers to conclude his negotiation, was able merely to send this

[1] Pomponne to Louis XIV, March 27, 1670, Arch. étr., Holl., vol. 90, fos. 107–08.
[2] Louis XIV to Pomponne, April 4, 1670, Bib. Ars., MS 4712, fo. 232; cf. Pomponne to Gravel, April 14, 1670, Arch. étr., Holl., vol. 90, fo. 135.
[3] Grémonville to Pomponne, March 30, April 6, 1670, Bib. Ars., MS 4713, fos. 110, 114.
[4] Pomponne to Louis XIV, and Lionne's marginal notation, April 3, 1670, Arch. étr., Holl., vol. 90, fo. 115.

proposal to Vienna. The Dutch were ready to go ahead with it if Leopold approved it.[1] Louis XIV, exuding confidence now that a treaty of offensive-defensive alliance with England seemed so close, took Pomponne's report lightly. The emperor would move less quickly than Lisola, the king told Pomponne.[2] Grémonville, indeed, thought that Lisola, by pushing through to conclusion an affair which he did not have power to decide, might create "the reef on which he will founder."[3] Pomponne confirmed these judgments. When Lisola received orders to hold his negotiation in abeyance, Pomponne looked for hostility against him at The Hague to grow quickly. Gamarra, his colleague, was already annoyed by his vanity, and Temple and De Witt both admitted to Pomponne that Lisola thought somewhat too much of himself.[4]

Grémonville gleefully informed Pomponne that Lisola's powers had in fact been "emasculated."[5] Lionne admitted to him that he had known for three weeks that Lisola's powers would be suspended, but he had waited to rejoice until "the thing had been done."[6]

Whatever the emperor finally decided to do about the Triple Alliance, Pomponne knew that there were princes in and near the Holy Roman Empire who were almost certain to remain friends of the Dutch, while others could be counted among their probable foes. The friends included the ducal house of Brunswick-Lüneburg, the elector of Mainz and the duke of Lorraine; the foes were the bishop of Münster and the archbishop-elector of Cologne. Where the elector of Brandenburg would take his stand, no one could safely say. Because many of these princes sent envoys to The Hague to negotiate with the States General and to confer with other ministers of the Triple Alliance, Pomponne observed, judged and reported these lesser diplomatic doings as carefully as those of the great powers, though occasionally a note of ennui slipped into his dispatches.

The dukes of Brunswick had not waited for the Dutch to come to them. Attracted by the glint of potential subsidies, they had asked to become members of the league. The English and Swedish envoys at The Hague refused to discuss the matter without instructions, and the Dutch made it clear that they had no intention of paying for the alliance of Brunswick at the rate promised to Sweden.[7] But the danger of such rebuffs became obvious when friends of the Dutch sent word

[1] Pomponne to Louis XIV, April 10, 1670, *ibid.*, fo. 130.
[2] Louis XIV to Pomponne, April 18, 1670, Bib. Ars., MS 4712, fo. 247.
[3] Grémonville to Pomponne, April 20, 1670, *ibid.*, MS 4713, fo. 118.
[4] Pomponne to Louis XIV, April 24, 1670, Arch. étr., Holl., vol. 90, fo. 153.
[5] Grémonville to Pomponne, April 27, 1670, Bib. Ars., MS 4713, fo. 120.
[6] Lionne to Pomponne, May 2, 1670, MS 4712, fo. 257.
[7] Wicquefort to Lionne, Nov. 1, 8, 1668, Arch. étr., Holl., vol. 88, fos. 273–74.

that the dukes would accept French offers if the States General did not somehow meet their demands.[1]

Pomponne soberly reported that the total amount of assistance the Dutch would like from the House of Brunswick consisted of 5,000 infantry and 3,000 horse. They would pay 30,000 crowns monthly for them, after hostilities began. The Lüneburgers demanded 42,000 crowns.[2] This difficult over 12,000 crowns proved insurmountable. The dukes were jealous of the Swedes. Their minister in London, talking to his Venetian colleague, called the Dutch selfish.[3] But, as Pomponne remarked, "only in the last extremity do these people cease to be thrifty."[4]

From the beginning of his mission, Pomponne knew that the Dutch counted Johann Philipp von Schönborn, the archbishop-elector of Mainz, as a friend. Long a pillar of the French party in the empire, Schönborn went over to the opposite camp during the War of Devolution. Lionne blamed his "almost monstrous ingratitude" upon his desire to gain Austrian support for the election of a nephew as coadjutor and therefore successor. Pomponne, however, emphasized a political motivation; Schönborn, he wrote, "seemed troubled, like others, by the over-great power of France." Thus he acknowledged, if only indirectly, the force of Grémonville's criticism of Louis XIV's policy.[5] Lionne realized Mainz's importance as a potential partner of the United Provinces, and did not minimize Schönborn's readiness to take the initiative, as did Gravel.[6] When the elector first proposed a defensive league to the States General, De Witt, though pleased, thought it wise to avoid a definite stand: why provoke Louis XIV just when Pomponne was coming to The Hague?[7] Consequently, Pomponne found little to report about relations between the two states until the departure of Gerard Hamel Bruynincx to take up his new post of minister resident at Vienna early in 1670. Hamel Bruynincx was well received by Schönborn when he stopped at Mainz, encouraging the States General to "conceive great hopes for Germany."[8]

[1] Wicquefort to Lionne, Jan. 24, 1669, *ibid.*, vol. 89, fo. 22.
[2] Pomponne to Lionne, March 21, 1669, *ibid.*, fo. 101.
[3] Mocenigo to Doge and Senate, July 12, 1669, *Calendar of State Papers, Venice*, XXXVI, 76.
[4] Pomponne to Lionne, July 18, 1669, Arch. étr., Holl., vol. 89, fo. 291.
[5] Pomponne, *Relation de Hollande*, p. 121; Lionne to Pomponne, July 24, 1669, Bib. Ars., MS 4712, fo. 94.
[6] Lionne to Pomponne, July 24, 1669, *ibid.*, fo. 94; Pomponne to Gravel, March 12, 1669, Gravel to Pomponne, April 8, 1669, Arch. étr., Holl., vol. 89, fos. 86, 121.
[7] Lefèvre-Pontalis, II, 10; Antal, I, xv.
[8] *Ibid.*, I, xiv–xxi; Wicquefort, *Histoire*, IV, 62–63; Pomponne to Louis XIV, Feb. 6, 1670, Arch. étr., Holl., vol. 90, fo. 54.

In February 1670, Dr. Johann Christoph Jodoci, a high official in Schönborn's administration, came to The Hague, though without regular credentials.[1] Jodoci saw Pomponne, however, on Schönborn's orders. He explained that his sole purpose was to persuade the States General not to decide against his master in a dispute with the elector palatine over Rhine shipping rights. Pomponne, "not wholly persuaded" that this was all there was to Jodoci's mission, "easily led" him into discussion of the Triple Alliance. Jodoci admitted he had also come to discover the exact status of the Triple Alliance; he understood it provided only for an equal guarantee to Spain and France. Pomponne at once "corrected his error," as the French envoy wrote to his royal master, lest Schönborn "be able to present my silence as a kind of approbation." Jodoci repeated his "great assurances" that Schönborn would never join any league displeasing to Louis XIV nor approve the Triple Alliance if it went beyond the simple guarantee of peace. Pomponne was more impressed by Jodoci's repeated interviews with Lisola. The ministers of the Triple Alliance were obviously counting Schönborn among those "who will follow the emperor" into the guarantee to Spain, he wrote.[2] Louis XIV shared Pomponne's judgment as to the true character of Jodoci's mission, but was even more confident about parrying Schönborn's thrusts than he was about preventing imperial entry into the league. "I shall carve out so much trouble for his master from his peers in the empire," the king wrote, that he would achieve nothing.[3]

Shortly thereafter, an envoy arrived from the archbishop of Trier to confer unofficially with Lisola and Kramprich regarding the Triple Alliance. Pomponne heard that he dropped hints that his master would be interested in Dutch subsidies. "If the sight of the wealth of this country brings the Germans here," Pomponne commented drily, "I foresee that their hopes will soon be withered by the drought they will find." Though Lisola used these arrivals to proclaim the success of his endeavors,[4] Louis XIV laughed at his boasts. The two most powerful electors, to say the least, would be among "my friends," the king assured Pomponne. Indeed, they might even win over those who were not.[5]

One ruler not likely to be won for France was duke Charles IV of

[1] This mission is not recorded in Bittner's *Repertorium* (p. 309).
[2] Pomponne to Louis XIV, Feb. 13, 20, to Gravel, Feb. 17, 1670, Arch. étr., Holl., vol. 90, fos. 63–64, 69–70, 72.
[3] Louis XIV to Pomponne, Feb. 21, 1670, Bib. Ars., MS 4712, fo. 196.
[4] Pomponne to Louis XIV, Feb. 27, 1670, Arch. étr., Holl., vol. 90, fos. 79–80.
[5] Louis XIV to Pomponne, March 7, 1670, Bib. Ars., MS 4712, fo. 207.

Lorraine, whose small sovereign state lay strategically between France and the empire, alongside Louis' contemplated route to the United Provinces through the bishopric of Liège. The duke was a vigorous and relentless warrior whose well-trained army felt a deep personal loyalty to him. Though repeatedly defeated by French arms, and several times driven from his duchy, Charles had regained his lands from Louis XIV on the promise to disarm and refrain from joining the enemies of France.

In January, 1669, Louis XIV decided to compel the Lorrainer to disband the regiments he had retained despite his pledge. Marshal Créqui entered Lorraine with a French army corps, bringing the duke to terms at once. Charles promised again to dismiss his forces, keeping only a bodyguard and the garrisons of several forts. But he had no intention of dismantling the army which gave him a voice in European affairs; some regiments moved south into Franche-Comté, others into Flanders, where they nominally entered the service of the king of Spain. Still other regiments "joined" the forces of friendly German princes. Whenever the occasion for their action should arise, the regiments of Lorraine could quickly reassemble under their own duke's banner.[1] Lionne had informed De Witt of Créqui's mission, and the grand pensionary answered through Wicquefort, their intermediary before Pomponne's arrival at The Hague, that though the king's action was "just and legitimate," the "repose of Christendom" was important too.[2]

Pomponne took the initiative in raising the question of Lorraine with the grand pensionary. De Witt denied the report that duke Charles had asked to be admitted into the Triple Alliance or that the States General had proposed his membership.[3]

In January, 1670, the Dutch were pleased to learn that the duke had sent a representative to Brussels to discuss his relationship with the Triple Alliance with the Constable of Castille. It was at this point that General Louvignies, a Spanish officer, entered the affair. Ostensibly sent by the constable to The Hague to work with Gamarra,[4] Louvignies was actually empowered, as Louis XIV learned in a report from Nancy, to negotiate on behalf of duke Charles for his entry into the Triple Alliance. The king's agitation was manifested in his dispatch to Pomponne. On the one hand, he instructed Pomponne to remind

[1] Pomponne, *Relation de Hollande*, pp. 75–76.
[2] Wicquefort to Lionne, Jan. 24, 1669, Arch. étr., Holl., vol. 89, fo. 21.
[3] Pomponne to Lionne, Feb. 28, 1669, *ibid.*, fo. 69.
[4] Pomponne to Louis XIV, Jan. 30, to Gravel, Feb. 3, 1670, *ibid.*, vol. 90, fos. 43–44, 48–49.

the councilor pensionary that the acceptance of the duke into the league "might well compel me, for the sake of my safety, to take measures at once against Lorraine which I would not dream of taking otherwise." On the other hand, he minimized the duke's importance: De Witt would be too prudent to involve his masters in the affairs of a prince "of such bad faith and fickleness that I could easily turn him against the States General a fortnight after he signed the Triple Alliance."[1]

Immediately after receiving this dispatch, Pomponne gave the king's warning to De Witt and took the opportunity to draw him out about Louvignies' mission. Like everyone else, said Pomponne, he knew that Louvignies had come on behalf of the duke of Lorraine. De Witt did not attempt a denial, but replied that he "knew as well as anyone how unsafe it was to trust" the duke's promises. The States General were only concerned with obtaining support for the guarantee of peace. De Witt might well be speaking the truth, Pomponne reflected, for the Dutch "could get little of advantage" from Lorraine, and in that case Louvignies would have no success at The Hague. From other sources Pomponne heard that the duke had offered to bring ten thousand men to the Triple Alliance upon payment of subsidies. The Dutch had put off the matter of subsidies by referring their payment to whatever state required assistance; but they were willing to include Lorraine in a reciprocal guarantee. Pomponne was uncertain whether this report or De Witt's assurance was true, but he tended to believe that the Dutch would not actually turn down the duke if he accepted their terms.[2] Pomponne soon learned that Louvignies did have full powers from duke Charles, who was willing to furnish ample troops to the Triple Alliance and undertake his own negotiations with Spain for payment; all he wanted was a guarantee for his present and future possessions, such as Spain had been given. De Witt and Van Beuningen were reported reluctant to risk war for the sake of the duke's military contribution.[3]

Finally the Dutch decided to subordinate the question of bringing Lorraine into the Triple Alliance to the more important one of obtaining the emperor as a member. Only then would it be safe to promise the duke assistance in his turn.[4]

Louis XIV scoffed at the duke's offer to assemble an army corps.

[1] Louis XIV to Pomponne, Jan. 31, 1670, Bib. Ars., MS 4712, fo. 184. Cf. Cuvelier, VI, 90.

[2] Pomponne to Louis XIV, Feb. 6, 1670, Arch. étr., Holl., vol. 90, fos. 51–54.

[3] Pomponne to Louis XIV, Feb. 13, to Gravel, Feb. 17, 1670, *ibid.*, fos. 62–63, 69.

[4] Pomponne to Louis XIV, Feb. 20, 1670, *ibid.*, fos. 71–72.

He assured Pomponne that he could easily prevent the duke from bringing together so little as five hundred horse. But De Witt should again be warned frankly that any further progress in this affair might compel the king to make Lorraine useless to the States General as an ally.[1]

Though the negotiation went no further for the moment, Louvignies remained at the Dutch capital, in close contact with Gamarra and Lisola. Pomponne heard that duke Charles was sending assistance to Louvignies in the person of François de Risaucourt, one of his most trusted councilors. Pomponne doubted that the States General would move far enough to require him to have further "explanations" with De Witt.[2]

The grand pensionary might turn down Louvignies in the end, Louis XIV admitted, but only thanks to his prudence and not to any good will "for what concerns me." De Witt would have acted otherwise, the king told Pomponne, if he had not feared to involve the States General "in an affair which might have taken them further than they wished to go." In any event, England and Sweden would resist bringing Lorraine into the Triple Alliance.[3] De Witt continued to deny that he had even seen, much less negotiated with, Louvignies. Perhaps, Pomponne explained to Louis XIV, Louvignies is waiting for Risaucourt, or Lisola may have thought it best to bring about the emperor's conjunction with the league before Lorraine's was pushed.[4] Another complication came before Pomponne when Grémonville informed him that his negotiations at Vienna with prince Charles of Lorraine, the duke's nephew and heir, might cause great changes. But the prince, encouraged by Austrian friendship, did not display proper subservience to His Most Christian Majesty, and nothing came of this démarche.[5]

In late March, Louis XIV informed Pomponne of an important report from Nancy. The duke was planning, in agreement with the electors of Mainz and Trier, to quarter a corps of some twelve or thirteen thousand foot and horse in the triangle between the Rhine, Meuse and Saar rivers, on the grounds of protecting the Rhineland. No doubt the duke will seek Dutch aid for this bold design, Louis wrote, but De Witt will hardly go into it. In any case, the safety of the Rhineland

[1] Louis XIV to Pomponne, Feb. 21, 1670, Bib. Ars., MS 4712, fo. 196.
[2] Pomponne to Louis XIV, Feb. 27, 1670, Arch. étr., Holl., vol. 90, fo. 80.
[3] Louis XIV to Pomponne, Feb. 28, 1670, Bib. Ars., MS 4712, fo. 202.
[4] Pomponne to Louis XIV, March 6, 1670, Arch. étr., Holl., vol. 90, fo. 90.
[5] Grémonville to Pomponne, March 9, 16, April 13, 1670, Bib. Ars., MS 4713, fos. 102, 106, 116.

rests on the treaties of Westphalia and needs no "novelty which would give me just cause for complaint," he concluded.[1]

Meanwhile Risaucourt arrived at The Hague, ostensibly to thank the States General for their mediation in the duke's quarrel with the elector palatine. His complaints against France made it clear, however, that he was really seeking measures against Louis XIV. He saw Gamarra and Lisola at once, Pomponne reported, "and will no doubt attempt to complete quickly what Louvignies had begun."[2] Lionne did not think that Risaucourt would succeed, but assured Pomponne that the king would take strong measures if the Dutch supported the duke's "caprices."[3]

Risaucourt proved no more persuasive than Louvignies, even though Lisola acted as his spokesman. Temple and Appelboom pleaded their lack of authority to act, and Pomponne thought that De Witt was unwilling to embroil his masters with France over the question of Lorraine.[4] This was what Lionne expected. The duke's plans, he jeered, "coming from as good and steady a head as his, are destroyed almost as soon as they are exposed to the air." Pomponne need not negotiate with De Witt on this matter, but simply inform him that Louis XIV knew why Risaucourt was at The Hague and did not take his mission seriously.[5]

Pomponne took the occasion of these instructions to discuss with De Witt the Dutch negotiations with the duke of Lorraine and the princes of the empire. He twitted the grand pensionary on his own greater sincerity: it was he, not De Witt, who told what Risaucourt was actually seeking. De Witt, however, denied that Risaucourt had taken such an initiative. His denial turned out to be worse than an admission would have been, for he added that it was the States General which had proposed to Risaucourt that Lorraine enter the guarantee of the peace of Aix-la-Chapelle. If Pomponne told him of private treaties between Lorraine and France which barred such an arrangement, he would have the proposal withdrawn, the councilor pensionary declared. Pomponne knew only of the public treaties, but stressed "the obligations of a prince in part a vassal of Louis XIV not to arm against the king's wish and without his approval." De Witt revealed that the Dutch desired various princes to join in the guarantee—much the same ones, Denmark, Brandenburg, Brunswick-Lüneburg, Lorraine,

[1] Louis XIV to Pomponne, March 20, 1670, *ibid.*, MS 4712, fo. 218.
[2] Pomponne to Louis XIV, March 20, 1670, Arch. étr., Holl., vol. 90, fo. 103.
[3] Lionne to Pomponne, March 21, 1670, Bib. Ars., MS 4712, fo. 217.
[4] Pomponne to Louis XIV, March 27, 1670, Arch. étr., Holl., vol. 90, fo. 108.
[5] Lionne to Pomponne, March 28, 1670, Bib. Ars., MS 4712, fo. 222.

which more than a year before he had told Pomponne that the States General were seeking to bring into the league. These princes should retain their troops in their own territories, and therefore the reported plan to place a common corps in the Rhineland would not receive Dutch support.[1] Pomponne was sure that the States General would not accept the scheme put forward by duke Charles.[2]

Louis XIV agreed with Pomponne that Risaucourt would not succeed, but for a different reason. Even if De Witt were "imprudent" enough to accept duke Charles' proposal, the king informed Pomponne, "I can tell you in confidence, for your own satisfaction and not to repeat to anyone, that I have reason to believe that he would not easily carry England with him." Thus Pomponne should oppose Risaucourt's negotiations with nothing but "great scorn."[3] Nevertheless the king did not fail to list all the various provisions of treaties between Lorraine and France which barred the duke from taking part in any league hostile to France.[4]

Armed with this information, Pomponne debated the question further with the grand pensionary. Risaucourt had finally produced his credentials, and the States General named commissioners—"the same ones named for all that relates to the Triple Alliance," Pomponne observed—to negotiate with him. De Witt admitted the general limitations placed upon the duke by the treaties he had with France, but denied, as he had done all during the past year, that joining the guarantee of the treaty of Aix-la-Chapelle constituted participation in a league against France. Pomponne again affirmed, therefore, that the partiality of the Triple Alliance was apparent to all the world, and bluntly repeated his warning that the duke might lose his duchy if he entered the alliance. De Witt was "impressed by the vigor with which I spoke," Pomponne reported, and "could not dispute these principles." Nonetheless there was no reason to expect the Dutch to abandon their efforts to construct "all the leagues and all the combinations" possible for opposing the power of France.[5]

Late in April, Risaucourt, his official status being public, came to visit Pomponne. The Lorrainer claimed his mission was merely to thank the States General for their offer of mediation, but Pomponne would not be put off with this prevarication. Sardonically he assured his

[1] Pompone to Louis XIV, April 3, 1670, Arch. étr., Holl., vol. 90, fos. 113–15.
[2] Pomponne to Lionne, April 3, 1670, *ibid.*, fo. 119.
[3] Louis XIV to Pomponne, April 4, 1670, Bib. Ars., MS 4712, fo. 232.
[4] Louis XIV to Pompone, April 11, 1670, *ibid.*, fos. 238–39.
[5] Pomponne to Louis XIV, April 17, 24, 1670, Arch. étr., Holl., vol. 90, fos. 143–44, 153.

visitor that he believed him. He was convinced, Pomponne continued, that Risaucourt's prudent master was incapable of giving Louis XIV the slightest cause for suspicion, as for instance by joining an alliance which all Europe knew he distrusted with good reason, or by arming beyond the limits imposed by treaty. Risaucourt, protesting too much his master's respect for Louis XIV, was visibly "embarrassed by the firmness with which I spoke to him," Pomponne reported to the king. Several days later, Louvignies and Risaucourt departed from The Hague, having gained no more than Pomponne's transparent warning and the indication that the Dutch were not ready to face the "dangerous consequences" of accepting the duke into the Triple Alliance.[1]

Dutch relations with other princes and potentates in Europe need not detain us here. In some cases, as with Münster, all important French negotiations were conducted without Pomponne's participation. In others, as with Poland and Tuscany, there was little relationship to the fundamental problems with which Pomponne was centrally concerned. Our study thus far has increasingly shown the crucial part played by England in the development of both Dutch and French policy, and it is therefore to the origins of the Treaty of Dover, especially as Pomponne observed and commented upon them, that we must now turn.

[1] Pomponne to Louis XIV, May 1, 1670, *ibid.*, fos. 163–64.

CHAPTER IX

THE DOVER TREATY
May-June, 1670

The knowledge that Louis XIV was seeking the alliance of Charles II against the United Provinces lay quietly beneath the surface of Pomponne's activity at The Hague. He learned little and could say less about what was being done in London by Ruvigny and Croissy. He knew the general purpose of their missions, but not the details of their negotiations. References to their work in dispatches, especially from Lionne, amounted to little more than assurances that all was going well. In his conferences with De Witt, Pomponne shied away from discussion of this topic; he sought only to prove that the Dutch could not trust England and should regain the French king's friendship on his terms. To hint at more was dangerous, lest the Dutch be driven to accept even the hardest conditions from Charles II to keep him on their side.

From the very beginning, Pomponne was sceptical of English fidelity to the Triple Alliance. England's wounds from the recent war were still painful and not quite healed. The peace of Breda had compelled the English to forgo the harsh conditions they had hoped to impose the Dutch in trade and shipping. Trade to the Indies formed the principal subject of rivalry between the two nations, Pomponne observed. He doubted that Temple could ever negotiate it out of existence. "Holland should not have placed too great expectations of solid friendship in a reconciliation which necessity had imposed," Pomponne recalled later in his Relation.[1]

Less than half a year after the conclusion of the Triple Alliance, De Witt already recognized that England sought special advantage from it. Though still distrustful of English intentions, he urged upon Temple, and through him upon Charles II, the settlement of their quarrels upon the basis of "reasonable equality." The union of the

[1] Pomponne, *Relation de Hollande*, pp. 63–65.

English and Dutch states would then be "indissoluble and eternal," so that they would never have to fear any one.[1]

Charles' appointment of Temple as ambassador to The Hague in July, 1668, was proof, the new envoy told De Witt, that the king's intentions in the Triple Alliance were quite sincere.[2] When the grand pensionary received reports the following spring that Colbert de Croissy was winning Charles II with his blandishments, he put Temple's assurances to the test. During a personal, unofficial visit to the British envoy, De Witt repeated to him a tale he had just heard from Esaias von Pufendorf, the Swedish diplomat.[3] While at the French court, Pufendorf had been regaled with an account of Croissy's achievements by Turenne, including obvious hints that bribes from Louis XIV were being accepted in London. Turenne's transparent purpose was to persuade the Swedes to quit the Triple Alliance too.

According to his own account of the interview, Temple tried to look innocent under De Witt's close scrutiny. He already knew of the story, he said, and admitted that its circumstances were "very odd." But he fended off De Witt's unspoken query as to how this squared with his own assurances that Charles II was unbending in his loyalty to the Triple Alliance. Perhaps the story was not all it seemed, he pleaded. "There might be artifice in it, on several hands." Perhaps Croissy was exaggerating his own successes, or the French court might have put up the whole affair in order to bring the Swedes to its side. But more he would not say, except to repeat his own promise that if the ministry did not live up to his expectations of fidelity to the Triple Alliance, he would not take any part in their betrayal. Scant satisfaction for De Witt!

The Hollander countered with a smile and words of assurance. He had been very suspicious when he had first become councilor pensionary of Holland, but "he had cured himself of that characteristic." In any event, he concluded, he would continue to build his policy upon the basis of the Triple Alliance and would encourage the States General to do so, at least until it was clear that the English had changed their position.

Temple, faced with the collapse of the entire program he favored, wrote a letter telling of his anxiety to Bridgman, the Lord Keeper and

[1] De Witt to Temple, June 4, to Van Beuningen, June 7, 1668, *Brieven van De Witt*, III, 413, 434–36.

[2] De Witt to Temple, July 6, 1668, De Witt, *Correspondance française*, p. 300; Temple to De Witt, June 18, 1668, *Brieven aan De Witt*, II, 399.

[3] Brother of Samuel von Pufendorf, the great German historian who also served in the Swedish diplomatic corps.

member of the government whom he most trusted. The subject was so delicate, he told Bridgman, that he hardly knew how to handle it and could trust it only to him.[1] Later that year, Temple made bold enough to press Arlington on the matter of English disunity and the steadiness of British fidelity to the alliance.[2]

The real situation in England was neatly summed up by Denzil Holles, the English diplomat, in a talk with Mocenigo, the Venetian ambassador in London. Unless the Dutch abandoned all effort to play with France, or decided to give complete satisfaction to England, some quarrel between the Netherlands and Britain was to be foreseen.[3] Mocenigo put the situation even more sharply. Charles II, having very little in his treasury, would not for the sake of others commit himself to the performance of his obligations under the Triple Alliance. This was the crux of the matter, since it did not look as if parliament could be persuaded to grant large funds for the performance of such tasks. Nonetheless, in the hope that parliament might loosen its purse strings, Charles would probably not advertise in any way a shift from the Triple Alliance, Mocenigo concluded.[4]

Pomponne gave close attention to all reports of Van Beuningen's planned trip to London.[5] Important as was the dispute between England and the United Provinces over trade to the Indies, Pomponne discounted this as the true purpose of his mission. Its source was actually "the interest which this state takes in sustaining the leagues it has formed, for it believes that should they fall, the danger it would face would be greater than any other." Some possible joint action against French trade might also be proposed, he thought. The anxieties of the Dutch had been heightened by the obvious incapacities of Johan Boreel, their ambassador at London, and by reports that Arlington, on whose proclivities in favor of the Triple Alliance they had counted until then, was shifting toward France. They expected that Van Beuningen would be able to "strengthen all that has been weakened there, and brighten a flame which it has been feared was dying out."[6]

Lionne's anxiety regarding Van Beuningen's journey increased when

[1] Temple to Bridgman, April 24, 1669, Temple, II, 39–43.

[2] Temple to Arlington, Sept. 2, 1669, *ibid.*, p. 67.

[3] Mocenigo to Doge and Senate, Sept. 27, 1669, *Calendar of State Papers, Venice*, XXXVI, 108.

[4] Mocenigo to Doge and Senate, Oct. 14, Nov. 1, Dec. 13, 27, 1669, *ibid.*, pp. 110, 124, 140, 144.

[5] Pomponne to Lionne, March 28, 1669, Arch. étr., Holl., vol. 89, fo. 109; Pomponne, *Relation de Hollande*, pp. 125–26.

[6] Pomponne to Louis XIV, March 28, 1669, Arch. étr., Holl., vol. 89, fos. 114–15; Pomponne, *Relation de Hollande*, pp. 125–26.

word came to him that Arlington, instead of shifting away from the Dutch, was standing by Temple. Lionne's indignation burst out in a dispatch to Pomponne, in which he blamed Arlington for England's rôle in the Triple Alliance and denounced him for being "as incapable of affairs as he lacks diligence in their conduct." Yet Lionne recognized that England, by means of the Triple Alliance, had "placed the States, as it were, in a kind of dependence, due to their fear of doing anything which might break or loosen the bonds of this union." Lionne decided to urge Charles II to increase his demands upon the United Provinces. The result, he told Pomponne, would be either to weaken and to humble the States General at once, or to sharpen their disagreement with England and thus provide the basis for weakening or disrupting the Triple Alliance.[1] It was this growing dependence upon England which made De Witt and "the most enlightened within the state," in Pomponne's words, regret the loss of Louis XIV's friendship and feel so strongly the importance of regaining it.[2]

On April 25, 1670, the States General at last decided to send Van Beuningen to England to serve alongside Boreel. It was a necessary though long delayed move. Boreel, on whose reports De Witt had been compelled to rely in large part, underestimated from the beginning the peril represented by Croissy's activity.[3] Later, when Croissy's negotiations were in the final stages, Boreel passed on to The Hague, without criticism, the assurances given him by the English ministers that the French envoy was still making no progress, and that Charles II would remain loyal to the Triple Alliance.[4]

Van Beuningen refused to leave for England until the prince of Orange had been named to the Council of State. De Witt pleaded with him at a meeting of the States General to delay no longer, because the duchess of Orleans was sailing from Dover to meet her brother earlier than had been expected. Van Beuningen replied savagely: If De Witt thought the matter so urgent, let him go himself; as for Van Beuningen, he saw no reason for rushing. The grand pensionary, stung out of his usual placatory mood, accused him of striving to please England by serving the prince of Orange.[5]

It was late May before Van Beuningen's instructions were drawn up, and not until June 1 that he finally set sail—but the Dover conference

[1] Lionne to Pomponne, April 26, 1669, Bib. Ars., MS 4712, fo. 54.
[2] Pomponne to Lionne, May 2, 1669, Arch. étr., Holl., vol. 89, fo. 165.
[3] Cf. Meerman to De Witt, June 22, 1668, De Witt, *Brieven*, IV, 822.
[4] Boreel to De Witt, Feb. 11, March 1, April 26, May 24, 27, 31, June 3, 7, 14, 1670, *Brieven aan De Witt*, II, 460–72; cf Mocenigo to Doge and Senate, May 2, 1670, *Calendar of State Papers, Venice*, XXXVI, 185–86.
[5] Pomponne to Louis XIV, June 5, 1670, Arch. étr., Holl., vol. 90, fo. 210.

was then already completed.[1] Arlington gave the French assurances that every effort would be made to nullify his influence.[2] To Temple, who urged that Van Beuningen be welcomed and supported, Arlington replied with soft thanks and a harsh warning. If Van Beuningen came to outwit the English, he told Temple, "to lead us out of our own measures into some of his, he may be deceived."[3]

Pomponne left on his own journey southward before Van Beuningen sailed for England. He reached Courtrai, in French Flanders, the day before the king arrived, and accompanied the royal party to Lille, where it remained for several days. In private audience with Pomponne, the king expressed satisfaction with the way he had conducted his mission. After discussing the state of affairs in the United Provinces, the king instructed him to tell what he knew to the duchess of Orleans, to aid her in her conferences with Charles II.

Just before Madame (to use the duchess' particular title of respect) set sail for Dover, Pomponne had a long interview with her at Courtrai. She knew not only that Pomponne's instructions were to avoid serious negotiations with the Dutch, merely deceiving them with idle talk, but also that the king planned to "give effect to his resentment" against the Dutch. She expressed indignation at Temple's ill-concealed hostility to France. Temple would not be long in a position to harm France while serving as her brother's envoy, she assured Pomponne. Although he had not been told the full reasons for Madame's trip to England, Pomponne easily drew the conclusion that her purpose was not restricted to "the simple pleasure of seeing the king, her brother." His guess was soon confirmed.

The evening before Louis XIV departed from Lille, he sent for Pomponne. Late that night, Berni roused Pomponne from his bed without warning. With every precaution for secrecy he took him to the Hôtel de Ville, where Louis had his lodgings. There Pomponne waited, out of sight, until all other visitors had gone. Then he was introduced into the royal bedchamber, where the king, garbed in a dressing gown, awaited him. Louis declared to Pomponne that the revelations which he was about to make demonstrated his confidence in him, but he reiterated the importance of secrecy. He then related in detail the course of events leading up to the Dover conference, from

[1] Fruin and Japikse commentary, *Brieven van De Witt*, IV, 67–68; Pomponne, *Relation de Hollande*, pp. 125, 133; Pomponne at Lille to Lionne, May 26, 1670, Arch. étr., Holl., vol. 90, fo. 208.

[2] Dijk, p. 74; Mignet, III, 180–82.

[3] Temple to Arlington, May 15, 1670, Temple, II, 108–11; Arlington to Temple, May 16/26, 1670, Arlington, pp. 433–34.

the secret mission of Lord Arundell to Madame on behalf of Charles II until a recent agreement on treaty provisions to which Madame needed to add only the final touches.[1]

This episode in Anglo-French diplomatic history has been repeatedly and intensively studied and appears to hold few if any secrets any longer. We may therefore easily reconstruct the probable shape of the account of the negotiations as Louis XIV gave it to Pomponne.

In April 1668, just before the Breda peace was concluded, Charles II proposed to Ruvigny, the French ambassador in London, that a "good liaison" between himself and the King of France might be arranged. He had in mind a treaty "gentleman to gentleman," he explained. When France made such proposals in the past, Ruvigny replied, they were rejected; only a frank statement of his intentions by Charles would overcome French mistrust. Actually Ruvigny was optimistic, and requested permission to return to France at his own discretion if "a great secret" were entrusted to him.[2]

The French monarch and his foreign minister did not see eye to eye on Charles' proposals. Louis, convinced that Charles was sincere now, became enthusiastic; Lionne confided to Ruvigny that he remained dubious because Charles' statements did not jibe with the actions of his government. Ruvigny received permission to return at his own discretion.[3]

Then the first real difficulty cropped up. Before the alliance could be made, Arlington intimated, the long-pending negotiations for a trade treaty would have to be concluded on terms favorable to English merchants. The French rejoinder was blunt: let the alliance be made and the trade agreement will follow in due course. The French were wary. If the trade pact were signed first, Arlington could stall off the proposal for alliance without difficulty. Louis' distrust was aroused. He ordered Ruvigny to make sure that the strictest secrecy was observed, lest the Dutch hear of the discussions.[4]

Ruvigny returned to France in July. He gave Louis XIV a memorandum summarizing the situation, in which he noted Charles' shilly-shallying and his dependence upon parliament; among his advisers, the dukes of York and Buckingham favored the negotiation, while Arlington was hostile. Thus far Charles had only proposed that the two kings act in the future after mutual consultation—an innocuous

[1] Pomponne, *Relation de Hollande*, pp. 129–31.
[2] Mignet, III, 8–11.
[3] Lionne to Ruvigny, May 30, 1668, *ibid.*, p. 11.
[4] Ruvigny to Lionne, June 11, Lionne to Ruvigny, June 31, 1668, *ibid.*, pp. 12–13.

liaison, indeed. Charles wished to have the French take the initiative in affair.

It was at this juncture that the duchess of Orleans began to play a part. When Colbert de Croissy was about to go to London as the new French ambassador, she wrote to her brother, Charles II, to assure him of Louis' good intentions and his desire for a closer union of policy. Charles, in reply, expressed his pleasure at this news; he hoped that Croissy would bring the necessary powers to promote the treaty. He also urged his sister to persuade Louis to abandon his distrust of Arlington, who would do his master's bidding and seek only his interest and the welfare of England.[1]

French suspicions were not lulled, as Croissy's instructions showed. He was told to get to the bottom of Charles' real intentions. He was to inform him that Louis XIV had accepted the peace of Aix-la-Chapelle in order to relieve Charles of his obligations to the Dutch under the Triple Alliance. The two monarchs, both having erred in the past by joining with the States General, should now combine against them. Louis was ready to undertake the initiative in discussions for an alliance, provided Charles made it the basis of his foreign policy without consideration for others powers. Having made these points, Croissy must await further developments. Arlington might be won over or at least neutralized, perhaps by a bribe. But absolute secrecy was a *sine qua non*. If Charles refused to assent to it, Croissy should thereafter talk only in empty generalities; if he promised secrecy and violated his pledge, Louis was ready to disavow all that had been said with a show of indignation.

By entering an alliance with Charles II, Louis would lose the advantage of a treaty with the Dutch for partition of the Spanish Netherlands when the king of Spain died. Charles should be assured that such negotiations with the Dutch would be delayed until it was known how talks in London were progressing. He could also be told that a trade treaty would follow an alliance in due course.[2]

Croissy's mission began inauspiciously. Part of Pomponne's scepticism toward Charles II must have been based on Louis' recital of his evasiveness. Croissy heard, for instance, that Temple was given instructions to support the Triple Alliance strongly. Charles' intention was obvious: to compel France to pay a higher price for his alliance.[3] Louis became more suspicious, and as a result, readier to consider

[1] *Ibid.*, pp. 18–19.
[2] J. J. Jusserand, ed., *Recueil des Instructions...*, *Angleterre*, II (Paris, 1929), 54–92.
[3] Croissy to Louis XIV, Aug. 20, 1668, Mignet, III, 48–49.

Dutch proposals. If the Dutch took the right steps, he informed Croissy, he was ready to change his attitude toward the States General.[1] This was, as we have seen, the attitude he still held when Pomponne went to The Hague six months later.

The year 1669 was a confused year in the negotiations. The conversion of the duke of York to Catholicism aided the prospects for the French alliance, but the merchants of England, especially, remained hostile to any rapprochement with France.[2] The French court remained sceptical of success. An accord between Arlington and Buckingham, which would be necessary, appeared unlikely.[3]

Suddenly the situation improved. Charles and his brother James paid a surprise visit to Croissy at the French embassy; the monarch whispered to Croissy that soon they would have the pleasure of bringing the affair to a conclusion.[4] Turenne, who had been reading the dispatches from Croissy, still distrusted the English. Arlington, whose political position was weak, was maintaining his policy of favoring the Dutch and the Spaniards; even Charles himself was less friendly than he pretended.[5]

Soon after, Charles wrote to his sister that he would like to "play some nasty tricks" upon the Dutch, but he wanted to know just how far Louis XIV was willing to go in breaking with the United Provinces.[6] The negotiation was then transferred to France. Lords Arundell and Saint-Albans spoke for Charles and Madame for Louis XIV. Croissy, who had proved too brusque for Charles' taste, was kept busy by spurious negotiations with Arlington and Buckingham. The necessity of avoiding the normal channels of communication slowed up the negotiation.[7] Arlington, like Croissy, was kept in the dark for a time. Croissy was brought into the full negotiations later in the year.[8]

Croissy, by now reconciled with Arlington, resumed conduct of the negotiations. He was confronted in particular by the problem of the order in which Charles' public conversion to Catholicism and the declaration of war upon the Dutch would take place. The French preferred that the war be declared first. Louis XIV insisted that he

[1] Louis XIV to Croissy, Sept. 8, 1668, *ibid.*, pp. 48–49.
[2] *Ibid.*, pp. 63, 67; Feiling, p. 290.
[3] Lionne to Croissy, Feb. 16, 1669, Mignet, III, 69.
[4] Croissy to Louis XIV, March 7, 1669, *ibid.*, p. 71.
[5] Picavet, *Les dernières années de Turenne*, pp. 300–02. Cf., however, an undated letter of Turenne to Lionne about this time, voicing suspicion that Arlington was feigning friendship for the Dutch. Picavet, *Documents biographiques sur Turenne (1611–1675)* (Lille, 1914), pp. 134–35.
[6] Charles II to duchess of Orleans, June 6, 7, 1669, Mignet, III, 89–92.
[7] *Ibid.*, pp. 94–98.
[8] *Ibid.*, p. 100.

would begin hostilities only at the very same time as Charles II.[1] This was a clear indication that the French monarch felt less than total confidence in English fidelity to him. He would take no chance of Charles' suddenly discovering the advantages of neutrality just when his principal rivals had begun war with each other. Louis knew only too well, from his own policy during the second Anglo-Dutch war, how tempting such a gambit was. Louis' wariness could only have been strengthened by word from Croissy that Arlington might press for the priority of the declaration of "Catholicity" (as the public conversion was called).

The first draft of the alliance treaty aroused Croissy's indignation. It included not only the priority for this declaration of Catholicity, but subsidy payments totalling five hundred thousand pounds. The English would receive command of the mouth of the river Scheldt in the form of cession of Walcheren island, Sluis and Cadzand, and some compensation would be given to the prince of Orange in view of the planned destruction of the republican state. Louis XIV would decide the date of war only after Charles had declared his conversion, provided that civil war did not ensue in England. In the event of such an outbreak, France must furnish Charles with assistance.[2]

Charles II became more tractable when he discovered that parliament would not grant all the funds he sought. Shortly before Christmas he prorogued the two houses till February 14 and began more intensive efforts to reach an accord with Louis XIV. Meanwhile, in interviews with Arlington, Croissy sharply criticized the draft treaty. In subsequent interviews with Charles, Croissy found him less demanding than the document presented in his name.[3]

Once more New Year's came and the negotiation had not been completed. Louis XIV now wrote cagily concerning Charles' sincerity. He continued, nonetheless, to hope that his cousin would not trick him. If he did so, Louis assured Croissy, his own excellent position would enable him to find consolation. He did not need to act and could put off till a better time the achievement of his glory and just ambition. He could wait until the English came to reason; indeed, he might even defeat the Dutch on land, without English naval assistance. More explicit instructions followed: Croissy must concentrate on reducing the English demands for subsidies.[5] Louis increased his offer

[1] Croissy to Louis XIV, Nov. 13, Louis XIV to Croissy, Nov. 24, 1669, *ibid.*, pp. 104–07.
[2] *Ibid.*, pp. 117–23.
[3] *Ibid.*, pp. 116–38.
[4] Louis XIV to Croissy, Jan. 4, 1670, *ibid.*, pp. 136–37.
[5] Louis XIV to Croissy, Jan. 29, 1670, *ibid.*, p. 138.

however, but warned he would not pay beyond a certain amount, because funds were also needed for the German princes who had to be won over.[1]

Several important features of the forthcoming treaty were soon settled. The declaration of war was set for the following year, 1671. Provision was made for collaboration if the Spanish succession came open. Subsidies of 3,000,000 *livres* annually would be paid to Charles. Louis even overrode Colbert's objection to paying the subsidy in specie instead of by letter of change.[2]

This, or something like it, was the story unfolded by Louis XIV to Pomponne. He warned him to tell no one of what had been revealed to him. In France only Madame, Le Tellier, Lionne and Colbert had been informed. (Turenne was aware of developments, but not fully informed.) It was important for Pomponne to know what was happening, in order to guide his conduct at The Hague, to enable him to evade proposals and to deceive the penetration of De Witt and the distrust of the States General.

Pomponne left the monarch's chamber and returned to his own lodgings, still unrecognized by any one. On the following day, he received final orders from Louis XIV, and departed from Lille at the same time as the king, stopping en route to visit the fortifications being constructed at Ath and Tournai.[3]

Meanwhile at Dover, Madame worked out with Charles II and his intimate advisers the few minor questions still remaining to be settled. She urged priority for the declaration of war over the announcement of "Catholicity," and Charles accepted. He had become increasingly concerned with the difficulties involved in a religious revolution and was more eager for war against the United Provinces.[4]

The treaty itself provided for the chief problems in war upon the Dutch. Charles would receive two million *livres* for announcing his conversion to Roman Catholicism. The Triple Alliance and the treaty of Aix-la-Chapelle would continue in effect so far as they applied to Spain: Louis would not attack the Low Countries. If the French king obtained new rights to the Spanish succession, Charles would support him in making them good. In war upon the States General, the French would attack by land with the aid of six thousand English troops. The English would lead the naval onslaught, with fifty of their own ships

[1] Louis XIV to Croissy, Feb. 16, 1670, *ibid.*, pp. 147–50.
[2] *Ibid.*, pp. 171–75; Colbert, II[1], ccxxvii–ccxxviii.
[3] Pomponne, *Relation de Hollande*, pp. 130–31, 146; Pomponne to Lionne, May 26, June 5, 1670, Arch. étr., Holl., vol. 90, fos. 208, 213.
[4] Mignet, III, 178–86.

and thirty under the command of the duke of York. In partition of the conquered territory, England would receive Walcheren, Sluis and Cadzand, as had been demanded, and France most of the remainder of the republic's territory. A subsequent arrangement would be made for the interests of the prince of Orange. A trade treaty would be concluded promptly.[1]

The treaty was signed on June 1. Two weeks later the instruments of ratification, in the monarchs' own hands, were exchanged.[2]

An extraordinary bit of diplomatic double-dealing ensued. The perpetrators of the duplicity were the two kings and the ministers of Charles II who had been entrusted with the secret of the negotiations, including the declaration of Catholicity. The victims were those English ministers who had been deftly kept outside the discussions—especially the duke of Buckingham. It was necessary to involve them in the performance of the provisions of the Dover treaty, so Buckingham was sent to France early in August, and later in the year, to conduct negotiations for an alliance; he thought he was being seriously employed, while the French ministers went through the show of debating with him provisions long since worked out. At the end of the year he signed a treaty virtually duplicating the Dover accord, except for its silence regarding the matter of religion. The subsidy provided in the original treaty on that account was disguised as an extra payment for the first year of war. In addition, Goeree and Voorne, islands controlling the mouths of the Meuse and Rhine, were to pass into English hands after conquest; the declaration of war was put off till 1672, and the commander of the English auxiliary corps was to have precedence over all French lieutenant generals. This shadow treaty was ratified in January, 1671.[3]

[1] *Ibid.*, pp. 186–99; Pomponne, *Relation de Hollande*, pp. 135–36.
[2] Mignet, III, p. 200.
[3] *Ibid.*, pp. 258–65.

CHAPTER X

UNEASY CALM
June–August, 1670

By June 3, 1670, Pomponne was back at The Hague,[1] where he waited for word that all had gone as planned at Dover. First came Lionne's hurried report that the "treaty of commerce"—a simple term of camouflage—had been concluded, then, a week later, Louis XIV's confirmation: "The things of which I spoke to you during the final night at Lille have since been accomplished, to the last letter of my desires."[2] Pomponne was confident that before long he would see "false policies confounded and great ingratitude punished." Though Madame's success "will cost me my employment," he wrote to Lionne, "I will gain by losing." The Dutch embassy had become an unbearable financial burden: it was "only for rich men."[3]

Pomponne expected that he would need all his wiles to deceive and lull the Dutch. To his surprise, he found it was a task that scarcely needed doing. There was not a suspicion among them that Charles II had played the republic false—such "utter tranquility" was hard for Pomponne to believe. Even the grave illness of Carlos II of Spain—that other Charles—caused them few jitters. For, as Pomponne reported to his master, "they still place great reliance upon their ties with England." To keep France out of the Low Countries, Britain would "act with like zeal and equal ardor to their own," they believed.[4]

This false confidence was mostly Van Beuningen's doing. He had been sent to England to discover whether Charles II was negotiating with France, and to inspire in him by his "skill and eloquence" fear of her growing might. Yet he let himself be taken in almost as easily as Boreel. His inability to penetrate the secrecy about the treaty of Dover

[1] Pomponne, *Relation de Hollande*, p. 131.
[2] Lionne to Pomponne, June 6, Louis XIV to Pomponne, June 13, 1670, Bib. Ars., MS 4712, fos. 264, 267.
[3] Pomponne to Louis XIV and Lionne, June 19, 1670, Arch étr., Holl., vol. 90, fos. 222, 227.
[4] Pomponne to Louis XIV, June 12, 1670, *ibid.*, fo. 216.

may be excused, but his failure to discount false assurances or to denounce them when he began to doubt them, must be called wrong judgment and devious politics. Because De Witt was sceptical about the English alliance, he must prove its firmness. He could not call Charles' loyalty into question lest he weaken the alliance between his own "middle party" and the supporters of prince William, the king's nephew. De Witt's angry accusation before the States General that Van Beuningen curried favor with England in order to please the prince had hit true.[1]

Pomponne knew how much the policies and attitudes of De Witt were at variance from Van Beuningen's. Thanks to the diligence of Bernarts, he received copies of Van Beuningen's instructions and dispatches from London. He was amused and comforted to see how the Hollander fell victim to the easy assurances of the English. But before long Van Beuningen learned that there was reason for anxiety, that several of the leading English ministers had "powerfully supported" the duchess of Orleans and Croissy in their efforts to destroy the Triple Alliance and form a league between England and France. Yet he drew a conclusion favorable to his domestic policy: because every effort must be used to prevent England from breaking away, "he believed it absolutely necessary to satisfy the claims of the English." Pomponne's comment was sardonic: Van Beuningen's letter "must have brought home to the States General how, in turning away from France, they brought upon themselves the cruel necessity to accept from England whatever laws she wished to impose upon them."[2]

Perhaps the duchess of Orleans did make proposals to her royal brother at Dover, Van Beuningen informed his masters, but she did not succeed. "They will no doubt be right in taking him at his word," Pomponne wrote ironically. Even though, a week later, Van Beuningen was no longer so sure that she had failed, the Dutch leaders at home did not share these apprehensions with the general public. As Pomponne put it, they did not wish "to create a bad opinion of the liaisons they have formed." But they could try to blackmail Charles II. Van Beuningen sought to frighten the English with a report that Estrades, then visiting in the Netherlands, had brought proposals from Louis XIV for a renewal of friendship, and that the Dutch would pay his price if Charles did not stand firmly by them. "I feel confident,"

[1] Cf. De Witt to Van Beuningen, Aug. 29, 1670, *Brieven van De Witt*, IV, 82.

[2] Pomponne to Louis XIV, June 5, 12, 19, to Lionne, June 5, 1670, Arch, étr., Holl., vol. 90, fos. 210–11, 213, 217, 225.

Pomponne commented, "that it will not be easy to make London believe this."[1]

The visit of Estrades, who paraded his own understanding of the Dutch, caused Pomponne some embarrassment. Wicquefort, in his weekly news sheet distributed far and wide in Europe, reported a sharp conflict of views on French policy toward the States General between the two diplomats, the former and present ambassadors to The Hague. By Wicquefort's account, Estrades, during two long interviews with De Witt, "let it be understood that M. de Pomponne does great disservice here, and that, in order to prove his skill, he wishes to create a belief that domestic disunity will ruin this state and that France will have an easy time with her. As long as affairs are in his hands. they cannot be expected to make progress." Yet when Estrades spoke to Pieter de Groot, who was pessimistic about his chances for success as the new Dutch ambassador to France, he gave no indication of a difference of views with Pomponne. He assured De Groot that the French court would receive him with highest personal regard, but that there was little hope for his mission unless the States General modified their policy toward France.

In writing on this episode to Lionne, Pomponne carefully assumed that his predecessor had not spoken as Wicquefort reported. He turned his sarcasm upon Wicquefort, though he did not minimize the influence of his "venom." If Wicquefort is to be believed, Pomponne said, "I am a very bad Dutchman and not at all fit to persuade the king that he should be satisfied with the States. No doubt the crime is great, but the real misdeed is not to be in Wicquefort's good graces."[2] Pay no attention to what you may hear about Estrades' journey, Lionne replied. As for "our gallant fellow, Wicquefort," his news letters merit only contempt.[3]

The complacent confidence of the French leaders was suddenly shattered by the death of the duchess of Orleans, soon after her return from England in mid-June. After drinking iced chicory water, she became violently ill on the afternoon of June 29, and died in great pain the next morning at Saint-Cloud, near Paris. It was four days before the first official notice was sent to Pomponne, who learned the dire news first from reports by way of England and Sedan. Lionne alluded to rumors that she had been poisoned by her angry husband, and sent Pomponne a memorandum dealing with the results of her autopsy.

[1] Pomponne to Louis XIV, June 26, July 3, 1670, *ibid.*, fos. 230–31, 240–41.

[2] Pomponne to Lionne, July 3, 1670, *ibid.*, fo. 244; Wicquefort, *Histoire*, IV, 25, 247–48.

[3] Lionne to Pomponne, July 11, 1670, Bib. Ars., MS 4712, fo. 286.

There was obvious fear behind Lionne's letter: would Charles II remain faithful to the accord made at Dover now that his sister was dead and the ugliest suspicions ran wild?

Louis XIV did not expect the Dutch to share his sorrow, and Pomponne soon reported that "ridiculous rumors" were rife among them. Lionne's fear was their hope. Pomponne betrayed his own anxiety in the remark that there were both "general and particular" reasons to mourn for Madame. Lionne reassured him: despite Van Beuningen's intimations that her demise was "unnatural," London was not turning against the Dover treaty. The storm in England had completely passed; if anything, the understanding with France was closer than before.[1]

Pomponne could scarcely conceal his surprise at this result. To his delight, too, the Dutch were worse dupes than ever. Van Beuningen believed that the duchess' death had caused England to turn away from France, and the Dutch were "in full repose" again. It was a good result, Pomponne mused: the secret of Dover would be safer and the Dutch would be more stiff-necked about conceding any advantages in the Indies trade to their British competitors.[2]

De Witt, too, presented less of a problem to Pomponne than might have been expected. The "vigor and perseverance" of his diplomacy were missing, as Japikse, his most recent biographer, remarks. Japikse suggests that De Witt trusted other men's promises too much and was reluctant to give subsidies in order to obtain allies. Yet the grand pensionary had never before naïvely counted upon the veracity of rulers and ministers of state, and subsidized allies were notoriously unreliable. Other historians have blamed the shortcomings of Dutch diplomatic organization, but the councilor pensionary had made do with it before.[3] Pomponne's simpler explanation is that De Witt could not act otherwise. He could not do without the English alliance, which created great difficulties for him in domestic politics and relations with France alike.

The growing influence of prince William was the gravest threat to De Witt's authority and power in the state. While Pomponne had been away in Flanders, the prince had been elected to the Council of State

[1] Louis XIV to Pomponne, memorandum on death of duchess of Orleans, July 4, Lionne to Pomponne, July 4, 11, 18, 1670, *ibid.*, fos. 280–84, 286, 288; Pomponne to Louis XIV and Lionne, July 10, 17, 1670, Arch. étr., Holl., vol. 90, fos. 249, 251, 254, 258.

[2] Pomponne to Louis XIV, July 24, 1670, *ibid.*, fo. 262; Pomponne, *Relation de Hollande*, pp. 136–37. Cf. Van Beuningen to De Witt, July 19, 26, 1670, *Brieven aan De Witt*, II, 473–74; Wicquefort, *Histoire*, IV, 98–99, 164–65; Fruin note, *Brieven van De Witt*, IV, 61–62.

[3] Japikse, *Johan de Witt*, pp. 303–04; Wicquefort, *Histoire*, IV, 26; Blok, V, 251; *Brieven van De Witt*, IV, 58, 61–62.

with both deliberative and conclusive votes. William's assumption of his first post of responsibility was more important as a political triumph over the grand pensionary than for the inherent powers of the position. "The party hostile to De Witt"—the "middle party" led by Van Beuningen and Valckenier—contributed as much to the prince's victory as his own supporters, Pomponne observed. He noted the twisted political motives at work: "The city of Amsterdam, with Van Beuningen at its head, acted as much to oppose the one as to assist the other." In the angry debate in the States of Holland, De Witt had flung arguments of republican principle at his adversaries: If this was the first step towards giving the prince the power his father had held, they should remember the danger the republic had faced from William II. (Years later, when writing his Relation, Pomponne betrayed his sympathy for De Witt, or at least his aversion for the stand of the "middle" party: "The last enterprise of the late prince of Orange, it might have been thought, would have compelled [Amsterdam] to show little favor to his son.")

When De Witt saw that the majority in the States General was against him, "he did gracefully what he would not do willingly." He brushed aside minor difficulties and the prince was elected a councilor of State on May 31; two days later he took his seat. Several limitations were placed upon him: one, that he could not take part in discussions concerning matters affecting his relatives to the fourth degree; two, when he reached the age of twenty-three he would be named captain and admiral general only for annual terms and when needed.

What was France's interest in the affair? The problem was posed at once when persons "particularly attached" to prince William, and therefore presumably acting with his assent, suggested to Pomponne that the prince would be pleased to receive official congratulations from Louis XIV. The only advantage Pomponne could see for France was that to do so would "make this prince even more important in this country than he is," thus sharpening the conflict between the prince's party and De Witt's. "In the present state of affairs here, this could only be good for us," Pomponne concluded.[1]

Louis XIV had no doubts that the prince's advancement was in his interest. He instructed Pomponne to pay William the desired compliments, "assuring him of my perfect pleasure in this event." Encourage the prince with these words: "I foresee that it will be only the first step," Pomponne was told. Soon he would re-establish the authority his fathers had held in the state, "toward which I shall be

[1] Pomponne to Louis XIV and Lionne, June 5, 1670, Arch. étr., Holl., vol. 90, fos. 209–10; Pomponne, *Relation de Hollande*, pp. 132–34; Dijk, p. 76.

most happy to have the opportunity to contribute." The king would express his thanks to the States General if William so desired. The limitation on questions concerning relatives to the fourth degree definitely involved himself, Louis told Pomponne, since he was the prince's second cousin. (William's maternal grandmother, Henrietta Maria, was Louis' aunt.) This was only another act of injustice to be held against De Witt as soon as he "found difficulty in maintaining the despotic government he wishes to exercise." These instructions and remarks Louis put in a letter obviously intended to be shown to the prince. In a separate dispatch to Pomponne, he explained that there were "secret reasons of greater force which you cannot mention to the interested party (William III) which must arouse in me all the good feelings I instruct you to display towards him."[1] "He can be useful to Your Majesty at a later time." In this simple phrase Pomponne summed up what the king implied.

On June 18, Pomponne conveyed the royal congratulations to the prince of Orange in a formal visit, amidst "all the ceremonies of an audience, though we had banished them from all our ordinary meetings." William was effusive in expressing his "joy, respect and gratitude." The following day, he paid a ceremonial visit to Pomponne in return. Though the prince was obliged to act with circumspection in the present situation of the United Provinces, Pomponne declared, he could rely on Louis' good will. William seemed "much touched."[2]

The prince's prestige "grows visibly," Pomponne reported. Amsterdam, to oppose the grand pensionary, "shows this prince greater favor from day to day." Amsterdam and Haarlem invited him to festive receptions in his honor. Pomponne also reported with amusement that "weak minds" were making much of an accident in Delft the day after the prince was elected to the Council of State. A symbolic hat on a figure representing freedom, part of a group surrounding the statue of William the Silent, was found on the ground. Events would show, Pomponne sententiously concluded, whether this augury "shall remain in oblivion or have its place in history."[3]

An exchange of letters between the prince and the king, written in their own hands, followed. Louis sent further instructions to Pomponne: Assure the prince "that in whatever concerns the interests of his house and his personal satisfaction, he will find in me no less ardor in advancing them, and no less fondness and friendship, than the king

[1] Louis XIV to Pomponne, June 13, 1670, Bib. Ars., MS 4712, fos. 267–68.
[2] Pomponne to Louis XIV, June 19, 1670, Arch. étr., Holl., vol. 90, fos. 222–26.
[3] Pomponne to Louis XIV, June 26, 1670, *ibid.*, fos. 231–32.

of Great Britain, his uncle, has for him." If William informed him in confidence how he could give "effective proof of this truth," he would consult with Charles II to achieve some "more solid results of the protection we would give him."[1] The price of aid, therefore, was plain: acceptance of the joint protectorate of his English uncle and his French cousin. It does not seem to have occured to the king of France that a mere prince of Orange might find this too high a price to pay.

When Pomponne brought the king's letter to William, another effusive exchange of compliments and thanks took place. The ambassador plied the prince with assurances of Louis' good intentions, leaving him to judge the time and circumstance for calling upon them. As usual, William responded with words of gratitude and respect. When the interview was over, it was Pomponne who had made promises for his master, while the prince had not given his word to anything more precise than another letter of thanks to Louis XIV. "I do not doubt," Pomponne concluded, "that being prudent, he will turn this to very good account."[2] The prince's letter to the king went so far as to promise that he would match his forebears' zeal on behalf of France, whenever Heaven would provide the opportunity to give proof of his word.[3]

A promise written in a boyish hand to which the man would give unexpected meaning! The irony of history was only revealed years later. At the moment, the primary importance of the prince's advancement lay in De Witt's discomfiture and the possibility that the prince would become the tool of France.

The French envoy saw relatively little of the grand pensionary in these months. At first De Witt had been away in Groningen, then in mid-June he came to see Pomponne. He wished to know, of course, how the king received his latest proposal for cantonment of the Low Countries. In a long speech, Pomponne repeated what he had been saying ever since this scheme came before him: public tranquility was safely established on Louis' promises and generosity; whenever Carlos II died, Pomponne would receive the necessary powers to negotiate with De Witt regarding the future of the Low Countries. The councilor pensionary, though "perhaps he did not find all he had desired in my discourse," wrote Pomponne, did not argue these points at any length. But Pomponne did not believe he was really satisfied, for he had failed to "impose upon Your Majesty by proposals which in fact would result only in the advantage of the States General."[4]

[1] Louis XIV to Pomponne, June 27, 1670, Bib. Ars., MS 4712, fo. 277.
[2] Pomponne to Louis XIV, July, 3, 1670, Arch. étr., Holl., vol. 90, fos. 239–40.
[3] Prince of Orange to Louis XIV (holograph), July 3, 1670, *ibid.*, fos. 248–49.
[4] Pomponne to Louis XIV, June 19, 1670, *ibid.*, fos. 223–25.

Pomponne's interviews with De Witt became less frequent, and were confined to secondary matters. When the ambassador decided, in his dispatch of July 24, to use the occasion of the visit of the prince of Tarento to The Hague, to analyze De Witt's general position more thoroughly and profoundly, there was no change in the grand pensionary's views to be considered.

Henri Charles de la Trémoïlle, prince of Tarento,[1] was a member of the leading Huguenot family of La Trémoïlle, closely related to the prince of Orange. Brought up a staunch Calvinist, he had served in the armies of the States General from youth, rising to the rank of lieutenant general of cavalry and governor of 's-Hertogenbosch (Bois-le-Duc). Now he had returned from a stay in France to resign his offices, ostensibly on the grounds of family needs, but actually because he was following Turenne's example in converting to Catholicism, and wished to withdraw from the services of the States General before the anticipated break with France.[2]

De Witt and his associates poured out their feelings to this old friend, who dutifully repeated their words to the French envoy. The councilor pensionary plied him with the same arguments he had used with Pomponne: "Always the same conviction that this state needs to keep Your Majesty's good graces, the same intentions to do what is needed to regain them. These good intentions and these measures never go beyond letting things stay as they are, that is, remaining still bound to the Triple Alliance and trying to persuade Your Majesty that it is as much to his advantage as to Spain's, with the furthest they can go being to take steps for the time when the king of Spain dies." Pomponne, weary of these stale arguments, knew why De Witt could not devise new ones. As the grand pensionary's friends explained, De Witt wanted French support, but not at the price of the Triple Alliance. He would not "destroy, by his own act," this barrier to the expansion of France in the Low Countries which he had created. "I see some here, still adhering to an old policy," Pomponne continued, "who believe that Your Majesty's interest in these provinces is misunderstood if the pensionary's party is not supported against another which is naturally united to England. But these folk are not as well informed as Your Majesty and do not know his plans. Perhaps they do not understand either how sharply we feel their ingratitude."

Nothing significant could therefore be expected from Pieter de

[1] A title assumed to maintain the claim of the La Trémoïlle family to possession of the Italian port.

[2] Pomponne, *Relation de Hollande*, pp. 140–42; L. Sylvius (Lambert van den Bos), *Historien onses Tyds...*, I (Amsterdam, 1685), 114.

Groot, the new ambassador, when he arrived in Paris. De Groot's draft instructions, a copy of which Bernarts procured for Pomponne, revealed that he would bring not new overtures but new complaints over the French tariffs, and an old argument in defense of Dutch intentions in the Triple Alliance.[1]

There seemed to be no more significant negotiating left for Pomponne, and even as an observer he had less to do. Lionne told him to disregard even the most boastful claims that came from Van Beuningen in London. There was no reason for any anxiety. "If I could bring you into my study," Lionne assured his friend, "I could show you proof so conclusive that you would not have the slightest remaining doubt."[2] He did not need such proof, Pomponne replied. "All these negotiations cause me no concern, knowing what Your Majesty has told me with greater assurance," he had already written to the king. Not that Van Beuningen any longer believed all he wrote about Charles II's fidelity to the Triple Alliance. Pomponne learned that he had sent a private letter to De Witt telling of the true state of his negotiation and urging that the Dutch East India company seek a compromise with its English rival.[3]

A deep quiet settled over The Hague. There was little to do, Pomponne reported, the note of boredom clear in his dispatches.[4] Boreel returned home for a visit, bringing renewed assurances that Charles II was standing by his alliance with the republic. De Witt did not quite believe him, although he did not know how far England had gone with France, Pomponne wrote. The grand pensionary visited Pomponne several days before De Groot left for Paris, and confirmed that his friend shared his own feelings toward France.[5] De Groot's departure was badly timed. Lionne believed that "the maxims preached by Van Beuningen are his masters' true sentiments, not those that De Witt gives you."[6] Van Beuningen, though unable to conceal all his suspicions, continued to affirm Charles' good intentions toward the States General. The calm he inspired in the Netherlands was "perhaps not a bad result," Pomponne observed. At the end of August, Van Beuningen, having made no progress in his negotiation, requested that he

[1] Pomponne to Louis XIV, July 24, 1670, Arch. étr., Holl., vol. 90, fos. 264–66.
[2] Lionne to Pomponne, Aug. 1, 1670, Bib. Ars., MS 4712, fo. 296.
[3] Pomponne to Louis XIV, July 31, to Lionne, Aug. 7, 1670, Arch. étr., Holl., vol. 90, fos. 271–73, 281.
[4] Pomponne to Lionne, Aug. 21, 1670, *ibid.*, fo. 294.
[5] Pomponne to Louis XIV, Aug. 7, 1670, *ibid.*, fos. 278–80.
[6] Lionne to Pomponne, Aug. 8, 1670, Bib. Ars., MS 4712, fo. 300.

be allowed to return. Pomponne was unperturbed: there was no sign that he "had discovered anything it was not desired that he should know."[1]

[1] Pomponne to Louis XIV, Aug. 14, 21, 1670, Arch. étr., Holl., vol. 90, fos. 285–86, 292.

CHAPTER XI

STORM OVER LORRAINE
September, 1670—January, 1671

During the night of August 25, an express courier from Paris galloped into The Hague with troubling news for the States General. A French army was marching toward the frontier of the Spanish Netherlands. The prince of Tarento had announced his resignation from his offices under the States General.

The news was kept secret till the next day, when the arrival of the regular mail courier made it known to all. "Never," wrote Pomponne, "was the world more suddenly shaken from deeper repose." The Dutch debated the news on the public squares and in the halls of government. A decision to reduce the armed forces was rescinded at once.

That very afternoon De Witt went to see Pomponne. "It was the first and only time," Pomponne later recalled in his Relation, "that I found some embarrassment in the mind and face of this minister, who was always the master of himself and kept his poise amid the greatest and most difficult affairs."

He was most surprised, De Witt said, by a report that the French troop movement had English approval, that France was sending four million francs to London to subsidize troop levies and equipping of warships, and that "these united forces were to divide the Low Countries." The report was difficult to believe, he said, for the king of France could not possibly wish to bring into the Low Countries, on the mainland of Europe, "a nation which France and her neighbors must strongly seek to keep apart from the rest of the world."

Pomponne replied calmly, though untruthfully, that nothing he knew substantiated this report. The pensionary admitted that Van Beuningen's dispatches confirmed Pomponne's assurance; orders were being sent to the Amsterdammer to remain in London, however. As for the resignation of the prince of Tarento, Pomponne passed it off as resulting from his conversion to Catholicism. "I tried in this way to draw him out of his anxiety," Pomponne reported to the king, "but, although it was less than in others, as much due to his own firmness as to what I had said, I saw clearly enough that it had not wholly vanished."

The French ambassador reminded his visitor of the moral of what was happening. Since the Dutch had turned against France, theirs was a star of trouble. They should have been able to count on French support; instead, they found cause for fear in any movement of the king's troops. Nor did they trust their new allies, either England or Sweden.

"All this is true," De Witt replied, "but what else can be done?"

Pomponne answered only that the Triple Alliance was a poor replacement for the friendship of France which they had deliberately abandoned.

The Dutch expected him to leave at any moment, Pomponne informed Lionne. "At least they send me on the journey in good weather. It would be very uncomfortable later in the year."[1]

The destination of the troops marching from the camp of Saint-Sébastien, near Paris, was not Flanders at all, as Lionne informed Pomponne in a dispatch he was instructed to decipher himself. The army, under marshal Créqui, was moving northward in order "to put down a false scent." At Verberie it would turn east, cross Champagne into Lorraine, and drive duke Charles from his duchy. If negotiations with prince Charles at Vienna had succeeded, he would be established on his uncle's throne. Until the news became public, Pomponne would remain silent; then he should announce that he had already been informed of the action against Lorraine and would soon make the king's reasons known.[2]

The secret was not Pomponne's to keep, however, for the news of the invasion reached The Hague on September 2, by the same mail as Lionne's dispatch. The duke rushed off a letter to the States General beseeching their aid.[3] Relief that the Low Countries were not the target of the French army[4] was weakened by concern for the loss of

[1] Pomponne to Louis XIV and Lionne, Aug. 28, 1670, Arch. étr., Holl., vol. 90, fos. 296–300; Pomponne, *Relation de Hollande*, pp. 139–43.

[2] Lionne to Pomponne, Aug. 29, 1670, Bib. Ars., MS 4712, fo. 312.

[3] Dijk, p. 78.

[4] Pieter de Groot met the French army near Senlis, less than thirty miles from Paris. Members of his party asked French officers their destination. Holland, they replied, some adding, to begin the siege of Maastricht. According to Pomponne, the officers, knowing the Dutch ambassador was in the carriage, gave this answer in jest. Pomponne accepted the story current in France that De Groot, taking the remarks seriously, and fearing that the army was indeed marching toward his homeland, had immediately informed his masters of what he had seen and heard. (Pomponne, *Relation de Hollande*, pp. 140–41.) The first letter in the published correspondence of De Groot to De Witt from France is dated at least five days later, September 4, from Paris. In it he did report that the officers had said the army was "op de Hollanders gemunt" (meant for the Dutch)

Lorraine, Pomponne observed. Immediately after the news was received, De Witt and a delegation from the States General paid a surprise dinner-hour visit to Temple. De Witt told the English ambassador that it was "a matter of so great importance, that all parties to the triple alliance ought to concern themselves in it, as wholly destructive to those ends of conserving the Spanish monarchy; yet they (the States General) should not, nor indeed, could not, proceed to any resolutions thereupon, without knowing those of his majesty (Charles II), and being assured of his vigorous conjunction."[1]

The following day De Witt went to see Pomponne again. Louis XIV should not have acted against the duke before he had been given an opportunity to make good his fault, De Witt argued. He had always discounted rumors that the king intended to wage war upon the States General because he had not asked them to repair any faults of theirs, De Witt went on. Pomponne let this delicate issue pass, merely defending the king's action in Lorraine.

Van Beuningen, ordered to ask Charles II for an explanation of the reports of a secret treaty between France and England, received solemn reassurance that the king remained faithful to the treaties of Breda and The Hague (the Triple Alliance). The Dutch were somewhat reassured, De Witt less than others. The councilor pensionary warned Van Beuningen to expect little from England. Yet he himself did not fathom the full depth of English-French understanding. The worst he expected was that, in the event of war between France and the United Provinces, England would fail to aid the Dutch but do them no positive harm. Years later, Pomponne expressed in his Relation his surprise that, "having been informed so nearly correctly of our ties with this prince," the Dutch "apparently did not give these reports the attention they deserved and remained quite tranquil about (Charles') friendship until the declaration of war provided violent proof of his collaboration with the king."[2]

and was going to Maastricht. He added only that it was certain that the French court was very indignant with the United Provinces, and warned against giving any reasons for offense. (*Brieven aan De Witt*, II, 481). De Groot wrote a fuller account of the episode to Wicquefort. The reply of the French officers he had considered to be "ingenuous," but said it reflected their sentiments. "I was not all at alarmed thereby, having too great confidence in the king's justice and the lateness of the season, which did not permit the beginning of a war of such character." Since this is the account given to Wicquefort, his intimate friend, in confidence, it has the ring of truth. (De Groot to Wicquefort, Sept. 12, 1670, De Groot, p. 13.)

[1] Temple to Arlington, Sept. 2, to Bridgman, September (no day indicated), 1670, Temple, II, 158–59, 163.

[2] Pomponne to Louis XIV, Sept. 4, 1670, Arch. étr., Holl., vol. 90, fos. 303–06; De Witt to Van Beuningen, Sept. 12, Oct. 3, to Van Beuningen and Boreel, Sept. 26, 1670, *Brieven van De Witt*, IV, 86, 89–90; Pomponne, *Relation de Hollande*, p. 142.

Shortly thereafter, Pomponne received orders to present formally to the States General the king's explanation of his action against the duke of Lorraine. Special emphasis was put upon the duke's plans to persuade Spain and the United Provinces to break the peace of Aix-la-Chapelle. Pomponne should assure the States General that only the person of duke Charles, not his duchy, was the object of French action. In a separate letter, the king confirmed his intention of placing "another prince" of the house of Lorraine on the ducal throne.[1] This was the point of chief interest to De Witt, to whom the French arguments were mere "*generalia.*" He continued to deny that he had heard of any plan to place a joint army between "the Sambre and Meuse rivers." The States General, he added, had not given any promise to support the duke. This was probably true, Pomponne judged, since he found among some Dutchmen a "ridiculous" belief that if they had given the duke such a pledge of aid, he would have been protected against French attack.[2]

De Witt's denial of knowledge about the plan put forward by the duke of Lorraine to quarter troops in the Rhine-Saar-Meuse triangle astonished Louis XIV. It was incredible effrontery, for the king had received a copy of the proposal as drawn up by De Witt with Louvignies and Risaucourt; traitors in the duke's service had transmitted a copy of the draft to Paris. However, if Pomponne had actually said "between the Sambre and Meuse rivers," as his dispatch read, De Witt was guilty only of "mental evasion." The king concluded that he would not bother justifying to De Witt his action in Lorraine. If the rest of Christendom approved, he would be satisfied.[3] Pomponne replied that De Witt had actually mentioned the Rhine and Saar rivers; the slip had been his own. De Witt's lie would have surprised him if he did not believe that the grand pensionary included lying occasionally "among his duties to his country."[4]

Public discussion continued as to what the invasion indicated for the future. Franche-Comté was now without direct communication with the Spanish Netherlands, it was noted; the Triple Alliance could not send it succor in case of need. But the Dutch were most afraid that, like the duke, they might face the king's armies without warning. At De Witt's urging, they were turning very seriously toward rearming

[1] Louis XIV to Pomponne, Sept. 5, 1670, Bib. Ars., MS 4712, fos. 317–18.

[2] Pomponne to Louis XIV, Sept. 11, 1670, Arch. étr., Holl., vol. 90, fos. 309–10; De Witt to Van Beuningen, Sept. 9, 1670, *Brieven van De Witt*, IV, 85–86.

[3] Louis XIV to Pomponne, Sept. 12, Lionne to Pomponne, Sept. 26, 1670, Bib. Ars., MS 4712, fos. 323–24, 330.

[4] Pomponne to Louis XIV, Sept. 18, to Lionne, Oct. 16, 1670, Arch. étr., Holl., vol. 90, fos. 318, 359.

themselves, though there was resistance to making the great expenditures involved. Finally, Pomponne reported, there was deep perturbation among the more thoughtful because of the duke of Buckingham's visit to France and Van Beuningen's failure to achieve any settlement of the dispute over trade to the Indies. The English demand that they be admitted to equal rights in trading with the native princes placed a pretty puzzle before the Dutch:

> It can be boldly concluded that either this state will be ruined, or it will not be able to avoid being embroiled with England. It cannot concede free trade and still retain the wealth it draws from it. If they were still compelled to spend the large sums required to maintain the Indies while these were opened to other nations, they would become a burden upon them. This is very well understood here and perturbs the most enlightened, who see clearly the peril in falling out with England when they act so badly with France, and foresee certain ruination if they become accustomed to accepting the laws which (England) wishes to impose upon them.

Amplifying these ideas to Lionne, Pomponne touched upon a crucial problem. Buckingham's visit was a good sign, he wrote. If the duke "does rightly know the feelings of his nation," and the English will not relax their demands on trade to the Indies, then "the most certain and unlucky horoscope can be drawn for Holland... By all appearances the star of the States General is beginning to decline strongly."[1] Thus, for a moment, Pomponne realized that the English people might play an independent rôle which could influence the relations between France and the Dutch republic. But he relied—with what justification later events would show—upon the interest of English merchants in destroying their Dutch competitors to overwhelm their own compunctions about the expansion of French power on land and at sea.

Perhaps no single event more brought home to the Dutch how England had been estranged from them than the recall of Sir William Temple—except perhaps the later news that he was being replaced by Sir George Downing, who had already displayed his "fitness to pick a quarrel," as Croissy called it,[2] while English ambassador to the States General on the eve of the second Anglo-Dutch war. Officially Temple was called back to London only temporarily, in order to discuss with Charles II his negotiations with Lisola regarding imperial entry into the league. Actually, the time had come to take negotiations

[1] Pomponne to Louis XIV and Lionne, Sept. 18, 1670, *ibid.*, fos. 314–16, 318.
[2] Croissy to Louis XIV, Oct. 2, 1670, Mignet, III, 229.

with the Dutch out of his hands, as had been promised to the French.[1]

De Witt, informed by Temple of his forthcoming journey across the North Sea, saw in it the result of the "coldness" which had come upon Anglo-Dutch relations after the duchess of Orleans went to Dover. De Witt became "very pensive upon the news of it," Temple noted. All the circumstances of the preceding months, De Witt said, were "enough to awake a suspicious man." Temple knew, he added, "how his majesty (Charles II) had engaged these States in those common measures, and even prevailed with them to make a sacrifice of the ancient kindness and alliance this State had always before with France... though they might have had what terms they pleased from them for the dividing of Flanders." For that reason, De Witt averred, "he could never think it possible for any nation, or court itself, to quit so certain a point of interest and great a point of honour, as must be forfeited by our breaking our alliances with this State, or entering into any with France, whose greatness had occasioned our measures for our own as well as our neighbour's defence." Temple was at a loss for a way to convey an assurance he did not feel. He said he too believed such a change to be impossible, but added that if it came, he would have no part of it. At which De Witt "smiled, and said, I was in the right, that, in the mean time, he would try to cure himself and others of all suspicions upon my journey."[2]

Pomponne reported that Temple informed only De Witt, but neither his fellow-ambassadors nor the States General, of his orders to return to London. "As not much good is expected from England," Pomponne wrote, "the general opinion is that this journey is a harbinger of evil." The Dutch, "by dint of talking about a treaty between Your Majesty and the king of Great Britain," he added, "are beginning to become wholly convinced that there is one." He observed that the Dutch continued with their rearmament, expecting that the French army now in Lorraine might be at the gates of Maastricht, "which would be both his easiest and his most important conquest," in the spring. Lisola meanwhile informed the States General that the emperor would like to come into the Triple Alliance for the guarantee of the treaty of Aix-la-Chapelle. The Dutch were pleased, Pomponne reported, but expected little to come of this request in view of England's general attitude.[3]

[1] Pomponne, *Relation de Hollande*, p. 146; Arlington to Temple, Sept. 1-11, 1670, Arlington, p. 452.

[2] Temple to Bridgman, September (no day indicated), 1670, Temple, II, 161–64. Wicquefort's assertion that the Dutch placed great hopes on Temple's good offices in London (*Histoire*, IV, 104) seems to be refuted by this letter, at least as it applies to De Witt.

[3] Pomponne to Louis XIV, Sept. 25, 1670, Arch. étr., Holl., vol. 90, fos. 321–23, 325.

On September 26, almost a month after the invasion of Lorraine, Louis XIV sent Pomponne a long, formal statement of justification, citing each of the treaty provisions which the duke was accused of breaking. Pomponne was instructed to defend the king's action before the States General, emphasizing that duke Charles had been guilty under both feudal and international law. "As my vassal for the duchy of Bar, he committed the crime of felony against his lord, and as sovereign he failed in all the obligations with regard to me which he had accepted by our treaties," the king wrote. Lionne added that two French intendants, Choisy and Aubéville, had in fact made formal complaint to the duke about his various infractions.[1]

This explanation was found satisfactory by De Witt and Ghent, president for the week of the States General, when Pomponne had extended interviews with them to present the king's arguments. The grand pensionary did not endeavor to contest most of these points, but continued to deny that he had discussed the project of a joint army corps with Risaucourt. Again he showed most interest in the king's promise not to retain Lorraine for himself.

"Although I gave him no reason to do so," wrote Pomponne, De Witt used this occasion to return to the conflict of interests between France and the Netherlands over the Low Countries. It would be desirable, the councilor pensionary declared, that Pomponne have power to negotiate regarding the future status of the Spanish provinces in Belgium for the event either of the death of Carlos II or of Spanish aggression. He admitted Pomponne's oft-repeated charge that the States General would assist Spain in any war for their defense, just or unjust, and that they therefore had to apprehend the king's resentment. That was the very reason why the two states should take steps to destroy the grounds for this dispute between them, and to create a situation in which "the States General would not fear France and France would have no anxiety concerning the States General." When Pomponne avoided responding to this lead, De Witt did not continue. Pomponne thought he had brought up the question "to see if I would act on it, as he might perhaps have desired in view of the difficulties of this state."

Dutch plans for arming were becoming substantial. There was talk of equipping sixty warships and increasing the army from forty to seventy thousand. De Ruyter discussed with deputies from the admiralties measures to protect Dutch shipping in the Mediterranean in

[1] Louis XIV and Lionne to Pomponne, statement on seizure of Lorraine, Sept. 26, 1670, Bib. Ars., MS 4712, fos. 330–39.

the event of war, landing operations on the coast of France, and what should be done if England joined France against them. The financial question was the great difficulty; the other provinces were not as willing as Holland to accept new taxes. The decline in trade, industry and revenues from the land made difficult the re-establishment of the finances after the recent war with England.

Prince William finally acceded to numerous requests from Charles II to visit him, Pomponne reported. Having little hope of obtaining payment for the sums due him, "he has shown no great inclination for this trip."[1]

Créqui's troops in Lorraine moved faster in conquering the duchy than deliberations at The Hague concerning measures to aid the duke, Pomponne informed the king. The States of Holland debated whether the Triple Alliance could be involved by a chain of obligations leading back through the treaty of Aix-la-Chapelle to the treaty of the Pyrenees, by which the duchy had earlier been restored to duke Charles. In reality, the scheme was intended to provide "an infallible means for discovering his (Charles II's) real intentions," Pomponne observed. The Dutch also proposed that the Triple Alliance be backed by all the armed forces of its members if need be. They were also ready to conclude an offensive and defensive alliance with England, Pomponne reported, with the same purpose of compelling Charles II to make his position clear.

Dutch suspicions now extended to Spain. It was feared that Madrid might make its own private settlement with France. This was one reason Hieronymus van Beverningk was being hurried to Spain after accepting appointment as ambassador. It was hoped that he would arouse the Spaniards to a more vigorous defense of the Low Countries and resist the machinations of France. Beverningk, who was close to the "middle party," was characterized by Pomponne as "without contradiction one of the most competent men in the government, preferred by many to De Witt. It is true that he usually is not equal to him all day long, and often loses with his morning sobriety the worth and skill he possessed till dinner time."

The struggle between De Witt and Amsterdam continued within the States of Holland over the issue of rearming, Pomponne reported. There was agreement on the need to rearm, but not on how it should be done. De Witt favored new taxes, Amsterdam opposed them. Many families would withdraw abroad, her representatives said; the

[1] Pomponne to Louis XIV, Oct. 2, 1670, Arch. étr., Holl., vol. 90, fos. 327–33; Louis XIV to Pomponne, Oct. 3, 1670, Bib. Ars., MS 4712 fo. 338.

reduction in interest would harm individuals and the low cost of credit money would encourage merchants to take greater risks than they should. The "most convenient and innocent" means of financing military expenditures was by loans, as during the war of independence against Spain; for "these loans enriched the people, who gave with pleasure funds on whose interest they lived." Amsterdam also demanded that new troops be used to form additional companies rather than to expand those existing, and that within the provinces each city appoint the officers of the companies it paid; this would give Amsterdam control of about one-quarter of all Dutch troops, Pomponne emphasized.

The States General meanwhile not only approved the journey of the prince of Orange to England, but asked him to plead their case with his uncle, Charles II. William visited Pomponne to repeat his respects for Louis XIV, and received from the envoy renewed assurances that the French monarch would match the English king's "desire to oblige him."

The campaign against espionage was intensified. Harsher punishment was decreed for those who violated secrets of state. The result was that secretaries "and other folk who peddle news" compensated for the increased danger by raising "the price of their wares," Pomponne reported. He asked that more money be sent to Bernarts to enable him to meet the higher cost of his "intelligences."[1] When, after almost a month, no money had yet come for Bernarts, Pomponne asked Lionne to obtain for him the sixty or eighty pistoles—less than a thousand francs—which he needed. Pomponne emphasized how much he needed Bernarts, who had threatened to quit French service if he did not receive additional funds. "You know," Pomponne told Lionne, "that a person of this kind is absolutely indispensable in this country, where everything is kept secret and everything becomes known, though only by these obscure and hidden ways." "Many things will no doubt occur here this winter which it will be important to know," he pleaded, "and I should fear doing less well if this means failed me. The sum is little and will be most usefully spent for His Majesty's service."[2] The full amount requested was granted, bringing Bernarts' pension, out of which he paid his informants, to 2,000 francs annually.[3]

By mid-October, the belief that spring would bring war with France was "a fear neither doubted nor concealed," wrote Pomponne. De Groot

[1] Pomponne to Louis XIV, Oct. 9, 1670, Arch. étr., Holl., vol. 90, fos. 340–47.
[2] Pomponne to Lionne, Nov. 6, 1670, *ibid.*, fos. 377–78.
[3] Colbert to Pomponne, Nov. 21, 1670, Bib. Ars., MS 4586, fos. 151–52.

reported on Louis XIV's war preparations and his efforts to win the electors of Cologne and Brandenburg, the duke of Pfalz-Neuburg and the bishop of Münster. The crisis over Lorraine continued. The Dutch hoped that the duke's "good favor" at Vienna would bring him the aid of the empire; Gamarra gave the States General a memorandum in the duke's defense. In general, the Dutch would prefer a general war to one whose full weight would fall upon themselves alone, Pomponne declared. De Witt admitted to him not only that the Dutch were arming, but that if his opinion were followed, they would continue with even greater vigor. They had no intention of starting war, the councilor pensionary said, but must be ready to sustain one if it came.

With all the military preparations under way here and in England, Pomponne twitted him, Europe might think that some "grand design" was under way on their side. De Witt replied philosophically: the spirit of republics, especially the United Netherlands, which is founded on trade, is directed only towards self-preservation and the maintenance of peace; it is characteristic of princes and monarchs to engage in conquests. Therefore Dutch levies could not be suspected, for the republic needed at least 100,000 men for its frontier garrisons and a field force. Pomponne replied, less philosophically but more subtly, that however little ambition republics might have, they could be involved in war by princes to whom they were joined, and no doubt there were some such to solicit their aid for a cause other than their own defense. De Witt "avoided a reply on what he well knew I meant regarding Spain and the Lorraine affair." They had to act because the might of France was so close, De Witt insisted.

Military preparations were continuing. The Rhinegrave, who was governor of Maastricht, reported to the Council of State on the needs of his command. The economic difficulties of the land made it difficult to collect increased taxes; Amsterdam's proposal to borrow the needed money would probably have to be accepted.

As for the prince of Orange, he would soon leave for England. A proposal to the States General to authorize him to join Boreel and Van Beuningen in their negotiations was rejected by the province of Holland, "which feared this would be the start of giving him a greater part in affairs." Though De Witt distrusted Charles II, Pomponne added, he had confidence in Temple. "The pensionary, by the power he has acquired over his mind, will have disposed him to act as he wishes."

At the same time, Pomponne learned, De Groot was ordered to spend money freely to discover the king's plans and the state of his armed forces. Pomponne anticipated that the coastal regions of France would receive particular attention, "for they have always boasted of the success they would have in landings on our coast in the event of war. By all appearances, there is no greater mistake they can make."[1]

Maastricht, the great fortress at the southeastern tip of the country, became the first matter of attention. Only a few miles north of the bishopric of Liège, it commanded one of the most important routes between France and the lower Rhineland. The Rhinegrave returned to Maastricht, Pomponne reported, accompanied by commissioners charged with strengthening its fortifications and bringing in adequate stores. Fresh troops were going to 's-Hertogenbosch, Breda and Bergen-op-Zoom as well. "In a word," wrote the French ambassador, "every preparation apparently is being taken here for war."

More troubling for Pomponne was a report of a project which had been received at The Hague from England. There were boasts from "persons in the state" that it would prove as great a surprise as the Triple Alliance had been three years before. Pomponne's inquiries indicated it concerned plans for troop levies by the Triple Alliance powers and the expansion of the league for the guarantee to Spain into a offensive-defensive alliance. Pomponne was surprised and not a little worried, although he took comfort in Lionne's reassurances; he did not know whether it actually originated with Charles II or with Temple and the Dutch ambassadors in London. "For myself," Pomponne declared, "I wish to believe that nothing has changed in that court."

Hotheads in the United Provinces, Pomponne reported, favored taking the initiative for war, with England and Sweden, the emperor and Spain as the allies of the republic. The French tariff restrictions against Dutch trade were making peace prove more ruinous than war. General war would destroy the budding French enterprises in manufactures, shipping and trade, without hurting the Dutch, who would completely recapture control of them as soon as peace returned. This opinion was held by all, Pomponne reported, but many objected that the allies could not be counted upon, and that the republic might face the anger of France, alone and defenseless.[2]

Lionne treated with disdain the report that England and the United Provinces were negotiating for a closer treaty of alliance. "On the supposition, which you make with even greater right than before, that what was confided to you at Lille is true," Lionne declared, "there is nothing to fear from all of De Witt's negotiations, present or future, in

[1] Pomponne to Louis XIV, Oct. 16, 1670, Arch. étr., Holl., vol. 90, fos. 353–57.

[2] Pomponne to Louis XIV, Oct. 23, 1670, *ibid.*, fos. 361–63; Pomponne, *Relation de Hollande*, p. 147; De Witt to Van Beuningen, Oct. 31, 1670, *Brieven van De Witt*, IV, 103–04.

all the courts, either to enlarge the Triple Alliance or to bring about a concert and union of several princes to embrace the cause of the duke of Lorraine."[1] In reply, Pomponne wrote to the king, "I shall henceforth remain quite unperturbed by rumors which could shake the assurances Your Majesty wished to give me."

The duke of Lorraine continued to seek Dutch assistance. He sent Risaucourt to The Hague again, accompanied by the marquis de Gerbevillers, former governor of Nancy. They conferred first with Lisola and Gamarra, and then with De Witt. The States General instructed its ambassadors in London to support the plea which Gerbevillers was bringing to Charles II. Pomponne was more interested by a report that a representative "from the emperor and the empire," Count Windisch-Grätz, was going to France on the duke's behalf. Pomponne's last item of news was that the prince of Orange had at last departed for England.[2]

The States General will obtain little satisfaction for the duke of Lorraine in London, the king replied. If anything were done, it would be to save appearances and with Louis' approval. As for an envoy from the emperor, he would not be moved from his course if one came. The duke of Lorraine would be foolish to expect help from that side. If things continued as they were, Louis added, he might decided to keep Lorraine, "despite my first intention."[3] Lionne was more sarcastic. Windisch-Grätz's visit "will embarrass the king as little as events in China," he assured Pomponne.[4]

De Witt used the occasion of an audience of Pieter de Groot with Louis XIV to renew his plea for a settlement. Pomponne reminded him that it was his masters who had failed to show the necessary "uprightness, courage, moderation and good will" to achieve that result. De Witt replied by a long speech in defense of their conduct which contained "the same things heard so often before." To Pomponne's assertion that Dutch partiality was proved by their declaration that they would prevent the Low Countries from ever falling into the hands of Louis XIV, De Witt replied that he personally considered the guarantee to Spain to cover only the event of aggression against her. If Louis were attacked or the Low Countries came to him by legitimate inheritance, he would seek to persuade the States General to support

1 Lionne to Pomponne, Oct. 31, 1670, Bib. Ars., MS 4712, fos. 345–46.

2 Pomponne to Louis XIV, Oct. 30, Nov. 6, 1670, Arch. étr., Holl., vol. 90, fos. 368, 374–76; Grémonville to Pomponne, Oct. 19, 26, Nov. 2, 1670, Bib. Ars., MS 4713, fos. 177, 181, 189.

3 Louis XIV to Pomponne, Nov. 14, 1670, Bib. Ars., MS 4712, fo. 352.

4 Lionne to Pomponne, Nov. 21, 1670, *ibid.*, fo. 355.

the king; if he failed, he "would withdraw from public affairs rather than consent to such injustice." Pomponne avoided the hint that their negotiations should be reopened.

He was more interested in the growing dissension within the republic. Van Beuningen was due to return in three weeks, though he had had no success in settling the dispute over trade to the Indies. As for the prince of Orange, his opponents feared he would come back with enhanced prestige and that the king of England would demand his appointment as captain general. It was proving easier to decide on rearming than to find the money to pay for it; the increases in fleet and army strength might be less than planned.[1] The king was not impressed by De Witt's promise to retire if the Dutch refused to act justly toward France. "These are fine words, subject to captious interpretation of the term 'legitimate,'" the king told Pomponne. The councilor pensionary was trying to lead Pomponne into negotiations "which it will always be wise to avoid in the state in which you know affairs to be."[2]

Beverningk at last sailed for Spain, having assured Pomponne in a farewell visit that he would work for peace. "This means, actually, that he will ask them to pay closer attention to the Low Countries," wrote Pomponne. Spain was becoming "the first ally" of the republic. "It would have been difficult in earlier times to imagine the States General going so far as to become dependent again on their former enemies." This "reversal of principles" might have "dangerous consequences" for them. One weapon Beverningk might use against the Spaniards, Pomponne surmised, was a threat to dismember the Low Countries. The States General would accept a lesser portion than was provided in the proposal of 1663 if this were done.[3]

In mid-December 1670, Pomponne was informed that the king was planning another springtime visit to Flanders in 1671. He would be accompanied by the court and a corps of 30,000 troops, and expected to stay for four or five months. The plan would be made public at once, so that the necessary preparations would not frighten Spain, England or the emperor. The only reason for the journey would be to speed various works of fortification, but the Dutch would no doubt take great alarm. "This will be to the good," Lionne commented, because they—and the Spaniards too—would make useless outlays on measures for defense in 1671, a year before they would be needed.

[1] Pomponne to Louis XIV, Nov. 27, 1670, Arch. étr., Holl., vol. 90, fos. 392–95.
[2] Louis XIV to Pomponne, Dec. 5, 1670, Bib. Ars, MS 4712, fo. 364.
[3] Pomponne to Lionne, Nov. 27, to Louis XIV, Dec. 4, 11, 1670, Arch. étr., Holl., vol. 90, fos. 397, 404, 407.

"We would not have done this if everything had been in order and ready on all sides for the other affair, which, as you know, we were forced to put off to the following year," Lionne explained.[1]

Dutch speculations as to the "true" purpose of the king's journey varied—the official reason was not believed, of course. Some thought it was war on themselves, others more numerous thought it was a means of pressure upon Spain to come to an agreement in the Lille conference. The States General decided to increase infantry companies to a strength of 100 men, cavalry to 80. This would add twelve or thirteen thousand men to the army, and more would be recruited later. The problem of finances continued. Lisola, still working to realize his political dream, meanwhile announced that he had received a letter from Leopold I to send to Charles II, in which the emperor indicated his desire to be taken into the league. He was forwarding it to London, and in the Netherlands there was hope that their alliances would be strengthened to the east. Van Beuningen's return was put off again until the king of England gave an answer to the emperor's request.[2] Bernarts obtained for Pomponne copies of draft treaties prepared by Lisola and De Witt providing for imperial entry into the league and alliances with unnamed princes of the empire.[3]

Without Lionne's warning, Pomponne admitted, he too might have thought war was coming in the spring. "I would have seen with joy and hope for His Majesty's glory what is envisaged here with sorrow and fear." He confided his personal feelings to his friend and superior. His mission was becoming empty and he would not regret its end, though he knew he would have to stay at The Hague for some months longer now. Almost no one visited or talked with him. He could be of little further use. He reminded Lionne that he had been out of France as an ambassador for five years. His private affairs were in turmoil, and he was needed at home to set them right. He hoped this mission would not last more than another year. Lionne must advise him; he would obey the king's wishes, "but in truth six years in the embassies demand more strength than I possess."[4]

The Christmas season brought the Lorraine affair to a virtual end with the ineffectual and ignominious visit of Windisch-Grätz to France. When, at his first audience, he asked Louis XIV for a commissioner with whom to negotiate regarding Lorraine, the king replied that he

[1] Lionne to Pomponne, Dec. 12, 1670, Bib. Ars., MS 4712, fo. 367.
[2] Pomponne to Louis XIV, Dec. 18, 1670, Arch. étr., Holl., vol. 90, fos. 417–19.
[3] Pomponne to Louis XIV, Dec. 25, 1670, *ibid.*, fos. 423–25.
[4] Pomponne to Lionne, Dec. 18, 1670, *ibid.*, fos. 420–21.

would be his own commissioner. This answer "flustered" Windisch-Grätz, Lionne told Pomponne.

When they met again, the king's answer to the imperial representative was curt and decisive. In view of widespread rumors that Windisch-Grätz came to press for restitution of Lorraine, the king declared that "he will never return this state at the request of anyone, for his honor is involved." He had intended to restore Lorraine to the ducal house, but the action of both duke and prince of Lorraine in refusing to make any amends and in seeking foreign assistance compelled him to delay a decision on this matter.

As for Pomponne's desire to bring his mission to a close and to see to his own affairs, the king seemed favorably inclined when Lionne read him what Pomponne had written. "We must think now how we will be able to bring him to some action as soon as possible," Lionne concluded.[1]

[1] Lionne to Pomponne, Dec. 26, 1670, Jan. 2, 1671, Bib. Ars., MS 4712, fos. 377–79, 381–83; Grémonville to Pomponne, Nov. 9, 16, Dec. 14, 1670, *ibid.*, MS 4713, fos. 191, 193.

CHAPTER XII

WHO WILL BELL THE CAT?
January-April, 1671

As the New Year began, Pomponne hoped at last for a respite from his ambassadorial career—"unless His Majesty orders otherwise," he told Lionne, "for as soon as I know his will, all other reasons become silent." His mission at The Hague had become burdensome and "useless." Even his friends no longer came to see him, "as if it were suspicious to converse with me." He put himself at Lionne's command, "to determine, if you please, my fate."[1]

The ordinary business of his embassy did not cease, and Pomponne continued dutifully to report on events in the Netherlands. Van Beuningen returned from London on December 28 to paint so comforting a picture of the situation in England that "great calm" reigned in the land. He vouched for Charles II's friendship and fidelity. To be sure, His Britannic Majesty was not as bitterly opposed to France as were his people, yet "their general disposition will always triumph over his own." Croissy's announcement that Louis XIV was going to Flanders in the spring had caused a furor in England; parliament enthusiastically voted a grant of 800,000 pounds to prepare a fleet for sea. The emperor's request to join the Triple Alliance had been well received in London, Van Beuningen declared, and Temple would soon be back at The Hague to sign the treaty which Lisola had so long urged. Van Beuningen admitted that he had settled only the minor dispute over Surinam, but was confident that his arguments had persuaded the English that they had no reason to complain against the Dutch East India Company.

The prince of Orange received Van Beuningen's special praise. William's mere presence in England had aided the republic's cause, he proclaimed. The passions of a few individuals hostile to the prince—"obviously the pensionary and his friends," Pomponne commented—

[1] Pomponne to Lionne, Jan. 1, 1671, Arch. étr., Holl., vol. 91, fos. 15–16.

could only harm the state; their policy must be abandoned. "We see therefore the preparation of a division which will in time apparently become favorable to the prince of Orange," Pomponne noted.

Even when he visited the French ambassador, Van Beuningen kept his bold self-assurance. He hinted "obscurely" that he knew what had been accomplished by the duchess of Orleans at Dover and the duke of Buckingham in France; their measures, he intimated, had either been put aside or would not endure. England would not fail to stand beside the United Provinces to prevent France from seizing the Low Countries, he predicted.

The Dutch took it for granted that the army which would accompany Louis XIV to Flanders "would not remain idle," yet they were not stricken by panic fears, Pomponne reported. They no longer feared England; they counted on the emperor to join their league. There was little talk of Lorraine any more.[1] Pomponne saw this calm as Van Beuningen's doing. "Himself deceived by the sentiments which he thought he had found in the king of England," Pomponne commented in his Relation, "he deluded his masters and inspired in them great confidence in that prince, when by the secret measures he had taken with the king (Louis XIV), they had never had more reason to fear him."

The Dutch discussed the prospect of war with more intrepidity. An open break with France might be better than a secret war in trade and wasted spending on an idle army and navy. Why not take the initiative for war instead of waiting for it? Pomponne derided this bold talk. True, the Dutch "lack almost nothing but companions to risk the outcome of so perilous an undertaking." But where was the "considerable party" without which they would never act?[2]

Van Beuningen's joy over the parliamentary grant to Charles II caused Lionne sardonic amusement. "The poor dupe," he vaunted, "will be in a great rage when he sees the dénouement of the comedy in which he has played a most villainous part." Louis XIV, too, mocked Van Beuningen's "fine portrait" of the situation in England. If there was any change, it was only for the better. Charles II might take certain steps such as approving the entry of the emperor into the Triple Alliance, in order to quell suspicions about his relations with France, but Pomponne should not be thrown off by them. "When our other design will begin to be enacted," Louis assured him, "all these ap-

[1] Cf., however, De Witt's remark that he had not expected much from Windisch-Grätz's mission because of the "faint-heartedness" of emperor and empire. De Witt to De Groot, Jan. 1, 1671, *Brieven van De Witt*, IV, 150.

[2] Pomponne to Louis XIV and Lionne, Jan. 1, 8, 1671, Arch. étr., Holl., vol. 91, fos. 11–13, 22–27; Pomponne, *Relation de Hollande*, pp. 154–55.

parently contrary measures will cease."[1] Pomponne was grateful for these reassurances. "I was beginning to see things only darkly and in another shape," he confided to Lionne.[2]

In his dispatch of January 9, Lionne informed Pomponne that the council of ministers would accompany Louis XIV to Flanders. He suggested that Pomponne request permission to come to Flanders to see the king, as he had done the previous year. This was "almost the most pleasant news" he could receive, Pomponne replied. The conflict with France over the tariff was becoming more heated, he added; perhaps, even before the king began his journey, "ambassadors will be among the wares no longer in commerce." He did not really expect the Dutch to start war, though: "Van Beuningen may be as wrong about this as about everything else."[3]

Lionne was not dismayed by the thought that the Dutch might begin hostilities. Let them do it, he told his friend. It would be only to the king's advantage. He doubted whether they would take the risk. He was reminded of the council of rats at which it was decided to bell the cat. "The decision was good and useful, but who dared be first to attach the bell?" he inquired. In the same jesting mood, he expressed regret that he could not spend a quarter hour at The Hague "to laugh with you as loud as I could" over Van Beuningen's belief that he "has worked wonders in England." Nonetheless, Lionne continued, "If you can put a match to the train of powder between him and De Witt, I am sure you will not miss the opportunity."[4]

Pomponne found the fable only too apt. "I think I shall never be able to write you seriously about deliberations in this country or elsewhere to prevent or halt the purposes they attribute to France," he told Lionne. "La Fontaine's verses will always come to mind, and I will expect to see many rats, bells in their hands, losing their resolution as soon as it comes to attaching them." Lionne would be even more amused if he could see Van Beuningen strutting about The Hague, pleased with himself for having made the English court do his will. "I had this pleasure only a few days ago," Pomponne wrote, telling how Van Beuningen had come to pay him "most ironic compliments on the way in which that country has turned in our favor." Yet Van Beuningen's very exaggeration of his triumph made Pomponne suspicious. "Perhaps

[1] Louis XIV and Lionne to Pomponne, Jan. 9, 1671, Bib. Ars., MS 4712, fos. 386, 389.

[2] Pomponne to Lionne, Jan. 15, 1671, Arch. étr., Holl., vol. 91, fo. 33.

[3] Lionne to Pomponne, Jan. 9, 1671, Bib. Ars., MS 4712, fo. 386; Pomponne to Lionne, Jan. 15, 1671, Arch. étr., Holl., vol. 91, fo. 33.

[4] Lionne to Pomponne, Jan. 16, 1671, Bib. Ars., MS 4712, fos. 389–90.

he is not as much deceived as he pretends. Perhaps it is to serve his own purpose that he has inspired in all Amsterdam the confident belief that England will be ready with thirty thousand men and a powerful fleet whenever there will be a falling-out with France," he wrote. His suspicions were shared by De Witt, who thought Van Beuningen "not as positive" or "as satisfied" as he had been before his journey to England.[1]

Domestic broils became "the most important business of the state," Pomponne reported. Valckenier, leader of the "middle party," was being opposed for re-election as burgomaster of Amsterdam by Hooft, who had De Witt's covert support. Valckenier's defeat would mean a setback for the prince of Orange. "In no other land do these factions for private interests play so great a rôle," Pomponne commented. "Almost as much attention is given to winning the vote of a single town as to the greatest affairs of Europe."[2]

Louis XIV now showed the Dutch studied discourtesy. He quickly accepted an Anglo-Swedish request to prolong the Lille conference on the "dependencies" dispute, due to expire on January 29, for another year. He had no intention of seeking war with Spain during 1671. But he pointedly acted at the instance of England and Sweden only, to demonstrate that the States General had "no share in the merit" of influencing him.[3] The Dutch concealed their humiliation at these "unfavorable distinctions" between themselves and other powers, but were disturbed at the thought that only the Low Countries were safeguarded by the king's promise. De Witt and his colleagues were not without bitterness that the repose of the Spanish Netherlands should imply a threat to the United Provinces. Expecting to be attacked in the spring, the Dutch continued their military preparations. Officers named to command the new levies were ordered to report to The Hague.[4]

The king kept Pomponne informed of major developments in England, though only for his "personal knowledge." Charles II would not accept the emperor into the Triple Alliance; he would assent only to a simple guarantee of the treaty of Aix-la-Chapelle. Like the Swedes, he rejected proposals for reciprocal assistance. Temple would not return

[1] Pomponne to Lionne, Jan. 22, 1671, Arch. étr., Holl., vol. 91, fos. 44–45; De Witt to De Groot, Jan. 29, 1671, *Brieven van De Witt*, IV, 154.

[2] Pomponne to Louis XIV, Jan. 15, 1671, Arch. étr., Holl., vol. 91, fos. 30–32.

[3] Louis XIV to Pomponne, Jan. 16, 21, 1671, memorandum on Louis' reply to Montagu and Ekeblad, Jan. 19, 1671, Bib. Ars., MS 4712, fos. 391–94.

[4] Pomponne to Louis XIV, Jan. 22, 29, 1671, Arch. étr., Holl., vol. 91, fos. 37–38, 51–53.

to The Hague, but "some other person whom De Witt will not easily control."[1]

The Dutch became suspicious again of secret agreements between England and France. There were many, Pomponne reported, who now said that when Charles II made his alliance with the States General, he "had had in mind more the re-establishment of the prince of Orange than the common welfare of the allies." In Amsterdam Hooft was elected burgomaster, an event of "great consequence," Pomponne emphasized. The prince of Orange was as much the loser as Valckenier. De Witt would oppose William's promotion even more strongly than before. Charles II would be roused to greater indignation, and "true accord" between the States General and England would be impossible. The advantage to France was obvious. Louis XIV agreed with this judgment, but also stressed the "bitterness and division" which would result among the governing circles of the republic. "Thus," he declared, "from whatever way it is considered, I find it only good and helpful to my interests."[2]

"Good and helpful," however, only if Charles II were his ally, not the States General. This was the king's choice, confirmed by the treaty of Dover, Pomponne knew quite well—he also knew that new circumstances change old decisions. Was apparent readiness on the part of the grand pensionary to give up his policy of leagues against France actually such a new circumstance? The train of events started by a minor incident in the States General in February caused Pomponne to treat this as a real and immediate question.

Several deputies, wondering why the States General had not received any dispatches from its ambassador in London for more than a month, accused Boreel of negligence. A deputy from the province of Holland rose to his defense. De Witt, he said, had received a letter from Boreel only the night before. There was an outcry of indignation: a minister who serves the whole state should not write to a single province. The innocent tale-bearer was sent to bring the letter, which was then read before the States General.

In it Boreel revealed that Arlington's refusal to consider bringing the emperor into the Triple Alliance had shocked him out of easy acceptance of English assurances of friendship. The growing coldness in Britain was indisputable, he admitted. He warned that the States General could expect only talk from England if they were attacked;

[1] Louis XIV to Pomponne, Jan. 30, 1671, Bib. Ars., MS 4712, fo. 399. Cf. Boreel to De Witt, Jan. 17, 31, 1671, *Brieven aan De Witt*, II, 555–57, 559–65.

[2] Pomponne to Louis XIV, Feb. 5, 1671, Arch. étr., Holl., vol. 91, fos. 57–60; Louis XIV to Pomponne, Feb. 13, 1671, Bib. Ars., MS 4712, fo. 407.

if any aid came, it would be delayed until it was of no use. These views would have been more embarrassing to Van Beuningen than to De Witt, except that Boreel, reflecting the former's influence, believed that it was possible to recapture England's friendship. The means indicated in his letters of January 24 and 27 must be employed, Boreel urged De Witt.[1]

Pomponne admired the grand pensionary's skill in handling the crisis. "This affair would have given difficulty to one less firm than De Witt or less assured of the province of Holland," he wrote. He pacified his critics without telling them exactly what Boreel had written in the earlier letters.

To many, however, this reticence was proof that Boreel had urged action on behalf of the prince of Orange. De Witt, on the contrary, "prefers the greatest dangers to the re-establishment of this prince, especially upon the recommendation of the king of England. He is said to believe that the republic would receive a double yoke, in the person of a leader who could rise from the post of captain general to all those his fathers had filled, and in the fact that he would receive this post from the hand of a suspect crown." The prince of Orange, De Witt's adherents declared, must look for his preferment, which he might expect in time, only to the "affection" of the Dutch people and their gratitude to his house. William "does himself harm," they warned, "if by a longer sojourn in England he seems to place his confidence in the support of that crown."

Some of the prince's party agreed that he hurt his cause by seeking his uncle's assistance. Others, however, believed that "he must profit by the favorable circumstance" of Dutch dependence upon Charles' good will.

For himself, Pomponne said, "I see that the pensionary, compelled either to accept this prince with England's sponsorship, or to run the danger of losing the friendship of that crown, will choose instead to return to Your Majesty and place in his hands, under whatever conditions he wishes to require, the fortune of this state and the preservation of the republic." Not for a long time had Pomponne seen the Dutch so favorable to France, so ready to accept Louis' terms if he would give them. The Dutch admitted to him that the Triple Alliance had "fallen." The States General, they told him, were utterly dependent upon Louis' will, "and the Low Countries were left without defense when events would bring a legitimate right over them to Your Majesty."

[1] There are no letters corresponding to Pomponne's description in *Brieven aan De Witt*, II, 458–61, but only a small number of Boreel's dispatches were preserved.

De Witt's friends were denouncing Van Beuningen as the source of the misunderstanding with France; he was, they said, the real author of the Triple Alliance, "which De Witt did no more than continue."

A grave choice lay before Louis XIV. If he wished to prevent an Anglo-Dutch accord, to take more of the Low Countries, to humble the Dutch, he could do so now without war. Pomponne realized this:

> I listen to these various reasonings and confine myself to learning the sentiments of the various sides without allowing my own to be detected. There can remain no question whatever that De Witt is deeply troubled because he can place so little reliance upon England, and I do not doubt that he would even prefer the most extreme solutions to seeing the prince of Orange re-established by the hands of England. But, since he sees little likelihood of being able to establish an advantageous rapprochement with Your Majesty, I believe that he will be reduced to the expedient of doing something for the prince of Orange, apparently by the sole action of the States General, perhaps even giving him the post of captain general, though with such restrictions as to deprive him of that principal part of authority which would make him feared.[1]

Lionne received this dispatch in Paris while the king was away at Versailles "for his pleasures." The possibility that the Dutch might turn back to France under these conditions was "a matter for much consideration," he declared. He hoped that the "painful consequences" of their estrangement would not stop at this point.[2]

After the king heard Pomponne's dispatch, he admitted that it was a "curious account." Could Pomponne discover what Boreel had proposed in those earlier letters? It was probably the advancement of the prince of Orange. De Witt, already stunned by England's rejection of his reciprocal defense project, would be in even greater difficulties. The king spelled out the moral of the tale. Spain "will perhaps have its security while the United Provinces, which sought to procure it for others, will not have their own. This is where roundabout roads lead when one no longer follows the old and fundamental maxims of a state."

"Whatever De Witt proposes to his masters," Louis declared, "I cannot receive any imaginable harm thereby." If he did nothing for the prince, Charles II would be more bitter against him and the Orangists might create a great division in the state. If De Witt did something for the prince, William would profit while the king of

[1] Pomponne to Louis XIV, Feb. 12, 1671, Arch. étr., Holl., vol. 91, fos. 67–71. Only the briefest excerpts from this significant dispatch are given by Mignet (III, 629).

[2] Lionne to Pomponne, Feb. 20, 1671, Bib. Ars., MS 4712, fo. 411.

England would not allow this "forced condescendence" to change his decisions "already taken for other, greater purposes."

The means by which De Witt might seek to regain his friendship and protection could be "dangerous and harmful" to his interests, the king continued. This was true even if the Dutch were acting sincerely, "which will always remain very dubious as long as they retain some hope of a new bond and union with England." Even if the States General were to propose joint conquest of the Spanish Netherlands in all sincerity, "I would neither wish nor be able to accept." Keeping the king of England as France's ally was the overriding question: "I must act, and you too where you are, so that I avoid giving any imaginable cause for suspicion to the king of England; on the contrary, I must take great care to persuade him (as is true) that whatever advantages the United Provinces could offer me today, they would not be able to make me fail to observe the slightest of the promises which we took together against these provinces."

Pomponne must therefore act with extreme caution. If any proposals along the lines indicated were made to him, he must not become involved in any negotiation, saying no more than that he was pleased they were recognizing their mistakes but that he could no begin such talks without a power to treat, which he did not have. If they insisted, he should tell them to have De Groot present their proposals directly to the king. "As for yourself," Louis warned, "you will never have any itch to negotiate concerning anything, except when I shall order you specifically to do so." He must not fall into any trap.[1]

"What hope still remains of regaining (England's) friendship lies wholly on the side of parliament and no longer on that of the court," Pomponne reported. The best way to win back England was thought to be "to establish close ties between this state and the English nation." Therefore the Dutch were pleased to hear of a conflict between Charles II and the House of Commons. They "base their main hopes on the aversion to France which they claim to be natural in the people of England, and on whatever may strike down the authority of the king there." It was proposed in the States of Holland that parliament be asked to ratify the treaties between the two states, especially the Triple Alliance. Compelling arguments would be placed before the English: the "reason of state which is common to them" demands "a close and mutual friendship between two powers already bound to each other as neighbors, by religion and by like interest in trade"; Britain and the Netherlands, once united, could "lay down the law

[1] Louis XIV to Pomponne, Feb. 27, 1671, *ibid.*, fos. 414–16.

for all the seas and share between themselves alone the advantages of shipping." It was presumed that if parliament accepted and ratified these treaties, the ministers of Charles II "could not undo them and they would be able to do nothing thereafter without similar approbation." It was proposed to send Van Beuningen back to London to make contact with the English opposition. "All these reasonings do not extend beyond mere talk until this hour," Pomponne reported. "What is certain is that no more reliance is placed on the court of England."

The Dutch were turning towards Germany for their friends. They still sought a league of imperial princes—Mainz, Trier, the emperor—with the United Provinces; with Brandenburg and Brunswick-Lüneburg already bound to them by treaty, they believed they would be safe. The proposal was very new and still very secret. "We must expect De Witt to neglect nothing for its success," Pomponne wrote. Lisola would no doubt support it.[1]

Lionne, delighted with Van Beuningen's humbling in Amsterdam, was not disturbed by De Witt's plans to find allies in Germany to replace the English. For one thing, the Dutch were still expecting England merely to remain neutral; for another, "they have no knowledge either of the means the king can use to bring some princes of Germany into his design and to intimidate the others." Charles II had said nothing to Croissy about sending an embassy to The Hague on behalf of the prince of Orange. If he decided to do so, which Lionne doubted, "an ambassador as skillful as yourself will discover, perhaps, means to arouse the party of the prince of Orange for his interest, and to create in the state a great division which might perhaps place it in a danger no less great than that of declared war."

As for the question of Pomponne's going to Flanders, it would be unwise to press the issue at the moment, Lionne declared. Pomponne should request permission for the journey after the king reached Dunkirk.[2]

Louis XIV treated the Dutch debate about turning to the English nation for friendship as a matter of importance though not of anxiety. Pomponne, he assumed, had informed Croissy directly, so that Charles II would have time to "apply the remedies necessary for this illness, which nonetheless does not, in my view, seem much to be feared." He was not concerned about De Witt's endeavors to win German allies.[3]

Pomponne continued to report that De Witt was ready to return to his first maxims: he was less afraid of seeing France on the frontiers

[1] Pomponne to Louis XIV, Feb. 19, 1671, Arch. étr., Holl., vol. 91, fos. 75–78.
[2] Lionne to Pomponne, Feb. 27, 1671, Bib. Ars., MS 4712, fos. 413, 420.
[3] Louis XIV to Pomponne, Feb. 27, 1671, *ibid.*, fo. 418.

of the Netherlands than of "receiving a kind of master from a great and naturally suspect power"; the peril from without would be uncertain, that within the country close at hand. The Dutch would choose the lesser of two evils, and "seek in the protection of Your Majesty the safety of the republic against the hostile designs of a crown and the advancement of a connection which they apprehend."

These were sensible views, held by "the most intelligent" men in the state, Pomponne said. They corresponded with the interest of the party in the Netherlands "which can do most." Nonetheless, until De Witt came to see him on February 24, he had treated these arguments as mere talk.

The tariff dispute was the topic of this interview. De Witt "turned over the question of trade from top to bottom," Pomponne wrote, a little wearily still, two days later. The grand pensionary pleaded for a compromise, but Pomponne left him no hope. As he was about to leave, De Witt turned back. Realizing apparently that the Frenchman would give him no lead for introducing the political question, De Witt decided to speak what was on his mind anyway. A compromise over the tariff could be the first step to a better understanding in general, he said. He recalled that he had repeatedly proposed that France and the United Provinces act together to eliminate the cause of their quarrel—the "cantonment" scheme again. Neither of the events which would make it possible had occurred, Pomponne replied. Spain had not attacked France and was not likely to do so; Carlos II was alive, but if he died, Pomponne would receive the necessary powers to negotiate with De Witt. "I could easily see that he had hoped for more immediate measures," wrote Pomponne to the king. At last De Witt left, "saying he had done all that was in him to do, and that he would be satisfied that he need not reproach himself as concerns an interest which he knew to be the first of this state, and believed was of some importance to France."

Pomponne analyzed the implications of this interview. He believed that it confirmed the views attributed to De Witt, who had seen his mistake and wished to correct it. On the other hand, there might be "craftiness and guile" at work. De Witt's real purpose might be to make it appear he was achieving a settlement with France, and thus compel England to return to her alliance with the republic. Whatever his intentions, Pomponne's evasive answers had not helped him. Louis XIV, the envoy wrote, "may judge himself, with his great prudence, what were De Witt's true feelings on this occasion."[1]

[1] Pomponne to Louis XIV, Feb. 26, 1671, Arch. étr., Holl., vol. 91, fos. 84–86.

The grand pensionary's long discourses were all in vain. There was no need, the king told Pomponne, to give any reply to De Witt or enter into any discussions with him. Louis wondered how De Witt would take Pomponne's silence and if he would elaborate his views further. It would not matter; whatever proposals he made, "you must not exceed what I told you of my intentions."[1]

"I will follow, Sire, with the exact obedience to which I am bound, the orders which Your Majesty does me the honor to give me on this subject." Thus Pomponne accepted the royal command which effectively ended his rôle as a negotiator at The Hague. His tasks as an observer continued unchanged.

The Dutch, he reported, were trying to discover whether the chill in England resulted from secret measures with Louis XIV. They counted upon "the natural aversion of that nation for ours," but "neglect nothing to bring the court back to their side."

Boreel's letters of late January which had caused the uproar in the States General were produced, but amid such close secrecy that it had been impossible to discover just what his proposals had been. The affair was placed in the hands of a small committee, "or rather of De Witt, who is its principal member." There were rumors, nonetheless, that he had hinted at action on behalf of the prince of Orange. It was also probable that he had proposed bribes to several of the English ministers.

The prince of Orange returned from England, "overwhelmed," Pomponne reported, by his uncle's cordiality and overjoyed at receiving a large part of the debt due him. His prestige in the Netherlands had risen, though his opponents argued against entrusting military authority to him while he had the "almost certain protection of a foreign power." Yet there seemed no way to leave him without employment if war came, nor to get the people and the troops to accept anyone else as their commander. Therefore, said Pomponne, he continued to expect that William would be named captain general, though with less complete authority than his fathers had held.[2]

Thus, at the time, Pomponne gave no indication he knew of any tension between Charles II and prince William. In his Relation, however, though he repeated that the king of England was "filled with friendship" for his nephew, he gave a more informed and candid evaluation of what had happened to the prince in England.

William, he wrote, had been interested in making the journey not

[1] Louis XIV to Pomponne, March 9, 1671, Bib. Ars., MS 4712, fo. 421.
[2] Pomponne to Louis XIV, March 5, 1671, Arch. étr., Holl., vol. 91, fos. 95–98.

merely to do as his uncle asked, but also because "it was important to him to be seen by peoples who considered him to be, after the daughters of the duke of York, the nearest heir to the crown." The visit ran a less friendly course than had been anticipated, observed Pomponne. The "humors" of the two men were unlike. Charles, "free, open and familiar, was given over wholly to pleasures, particularly to those of the table and of women, with, one might say, some manner of debauchery." The prince, on the contrary, was "concerned with glory, serious and reticent, without the slightest semblance of vice." He took part in the festivities held by his uncle "only so far as he was compelled to by his desire to please." By his "modest and restrained conduct," he seemed to condemn these affairs, and thus gave "extreme pleasure" to those Englishmen who praised a character opposite to their king's. "But," added Pomponne, "what touched the people even more was his assiduous and exact fulfillment of his religious duties and his demonstration of a great zeal for Protestantism." Thus, when William returned home almost two months later, Charles saw him go with little regret, but the English people looked to him with affection.[1]

Lionne's attention continued to be given to the Dutch scheme of turning the "natural aversion" of the English people for France into a weapon against Charles II. He did not deny the existence of Gallophobia in England but expected that Charles would be able to defeat Dutch machinations.[2]

In Pomponne's dispatch of March 12, the "most considerable news" was of Dutch troop levies. Officers for the new forces were paid only for six months, after which they would be released if they were not needed any longer. The Dutch were counting on the dispute between Münster and Lüneburg over the town of Höxter to keep the bishop, von Galen, occupied; their mediators would really work to prevent a settlement and to prolong the controversy, Pomponne decided.

He enclosed a copy of the letter sent by the States General to Charles II on March 4 asking for extension of the Triple Alliance into a general defensive treaty. "Everything here turns on whether England is to be trusted or not," he wrote.[3] Louis XIV, who was being kept informed of Dutch proposals in England by Charles II, assured Pomponne he was not troubled about this appeal.[4]

[1] Pomponne, *Relation de Hollande*, pp. 149–50. Cf. Burnet, *History*, II, 450; Sir John Dalrymple, *Memoirs of Great Britain and Ireland...* (London, 1790), I, 122.

[2] Lionne to Pomponne, March 13, 1671, Bib. Ars., MS 4712, fo. 423.

[3] Pomponne to Louis XIV, March 12, copy of letter of States General to Charles II, March 4, 1671, Arch. étr., Holl., vol. 91, fos. 93–94, 106–08.

[4] Louis XIV to Pomponne, March 20, 1671, Bib. Ars., MS 4712, fo. 426.

De Groot in Paris meanwhile reported to De Witt that Pomponne's picture of conditions in the Netherlands had strengthened French hopes to make use of the prince of Orange. A high-placed Frenchman had come to him in strictest secrecy to give warning of what impended. Pomponne's description of "great perplexity in our land," of "great confusion in the government, disunity among the provinces, a great party in favor of the prince of Orange which might be able to win the upper hand," had confirmed the French in their hopes. De Groot's informant told him that Charles II and Louis XIV were planning "not simply to wage war upon our state, but to undermine its foundations and overthrow its entire constitution." They would leave a rump Dutch state for the prince of Orange in full sovereignty, and expected him to display due gratitude. Charles II was going to demand the prince's promotion; rejection would serve as a pretext for breaking with the Dutch. French negotiations in Germany were going well. De Groot's informant correctly described the French strategy for attack upon the republic: the principal assault along the Rhineland into the eastern provinces, an observing action along the frontiers of the Spanish Netherlands.

De Groot did not believe this report as a literal forecast of the immediate future. Yet he felt sure that the crowns of England and France were planning something against the Dutch. In any case, he told De Witt, it is good to be on one's guard, "*quia tela praevisa minus nocent*" (the weapon you see beforehand will do less hurt).[1]

De Witt was troubled by this report, but consoled himself with the belief that Charles II had promised only "not to budge" if France attacked a nation other than Spain.[2]

Though De Groot's warning did not fall into the hands of Bernarts' spies, Pomponne sensed anyway the change in the grand pensionary's attitude. De Witt seemed certain, he reported on March 19, that France had turned definitely against the Netherlands. Distrust of France was no longer hidden in the country. Most of Pomponne's former visitors stayed away and the few who still came to see him were almost treated as exiles or criminals in their own land. He found

[1] De Groot to De Witt, Feb. 27, 1671, *Brieven aan De Witt*, II, 542–46. Pomponne does not seem to have known of this or several other significant letters written by De Groot to De Witt in this period. Most important was one of January 30 reporting that Marshal Schomberg, the great Huguenot military leader in French service, had come to him to offer his services to the States General. Another, on February 20, reported that Frenchmen, Huguenots and Catholics alike, had expressed their sympathy with the Dutch. They were afraid that "the increase in the king's power meant an increase in their own servitude as well." *Ibid.*, pp. 538–40.

[2] De Witt to Boreel, March 6, 1671, *Brieven van De Witt*, IV, 189–92.

it difficult to believe that the Dutch would actually take the risk of starting war, but was comforted by the thought that the king had already thwarted their plans. "They can do nothing without being sure of England," he wrote, and though they were depending on parliamentary opposition to Charles II, he felt sure that they would not achieve any success by that tactic.

The Dutch were most active now in and near Germany. The new regiments were being encamped along the eastern borders. There were renewed discussions about a showdown with France instead of wasting the country's strength by eternal preparedness. The quarrel between the city of Cologne and the archbishop-elector, who was supported by France, might provide a convenient pretext for war.[1]

Louis XIV informed Pomponne that Charles II had received news of the Dutch plans to incite parliament against him. The English monarch was not perturbed; he would give a bad time, he promised, to any envoy who made contact with that assembly, and treat him as a rebel and enemy.[2]

The Dutch were encouraged when they discovered that they were able to raise troops in Germany without difficulty. There was talk of forming five new infantry regiments and three of cavalry. Thirty-six ships were ready to sail with the first good wind, and the admiralties had been ordered to prepare more vessels for sea. Thus, Pomponne commented, the Dutch hoped that military and naval preparation would turn aside the storm. There was talk, too, of naming the prince of Orange general of cavalry with a pension of 25,000 florins. This promotion might be designed as much to remove William from the Council of State, where he "acquires much authority," as to please England.[3]

In Germany, where the principal Dutch diplomatic effort was now concentrated, the emperor remained the key to general action. Louis XIV therefore carefully analyzed for Pomponne the reasons for his confidence that his plans, in which the lower Rhineland would serve as the pathway to the Dutch frontiers, would not be traversed. He believed that the emperor was really pleased by the obstacles placed by England in the way of his admission into the triple league. Leopold was trying to appease the Spaniards and still outcries against him in the empire. England might consent to his joining the league if the clause for reciprocal defense were removed. Leopold would not consent to

[1] Pomponne to Louis XIV, March 19, 1671, Arch. étr., Holl., vol. 91, fos. 112–16.
[2] Louis XIV to Pomponne, March 27, 1671, Bib. Ars., MS 4712, fo. 430.
[3] Pomponne to Louis XIV, March 26, 1671, Arch. étr., Holl., vol. 91, fos. 119–22.

that clause either, Louis thought, though he would probably leave to Charles II the burden of raising difficulties over it.[1]

The increasing boldness of Dutch talk of war and preparations on land and sea stirred Pomponne's anxiety. French plans, which assumed that the war would begin in 1672, might be too late. The Dutch were raising more troops. "Fear has changed into confidence, and far from fearing war (the Dutch) display much desire to wage it," Pomponne reported. It was admitted that there was

> nothing less suited than war to the form of this state, whose first interest is peace and the tranquility of trade it creates. But, faced with the alternatives of accepting slow and certain ruin or seeking more violent remedies to a malady to which they see themselves gradually falling victim, many here hold the opinion that it is better to trust somewhat to chance and discover, whatever the price, what will be the permanent state of affairs with France. There are no two opinions here about the impossibility of sustaining for long the present condition to which they see themselves reduced. The diminution of their trade and the expense of a powerful corps of troops which they cannot avoid because they are afraid of seeing Your Majesty with a large army every year in his new conquests, cannot endure for many years without exhausting the States. Many believe that they must use their forces before they are beaten down.

The Dutch were confident, Pomponne reported, that they could have 40,000 men under arms and that Spain would join them in the event of war, sending auxiliaries so as to avoid a breach of the treaty of Aix-la-Chapelle. They were also sure that the emperor and other German princes would assist them. They had not met the anticipated financial difficulties. Although the new taxes would begin to come in only during the autumn, the province of Holland had already borrowed four million pounds at three and one half per cent interest, and more lenders were ready with funds.[2]

The Dutch were forming two armed camps, one at Bergen-op-Zoom, in the southwest, the other in Overijssel, facing east. Each would receive 15,000 of the troops already raised and new levies would be distributed among them. Most of the newly hired officers and all their troops were foreigners, who were considered to be more reliable than

[1] Louis XIV to Pomponne, April 3, 1671, Bib. Ars., MS 4712, fo. 433.

[2] Cf. Wicquefort's judgment that the United Provinces could easily cope with the expenditures of a land war if no major naval campaigning was forced upon the country simultaneously. Wicquefort correspondence, Dec. 21, 1669, Wicquefort, *Histoire*, IV, 177, note 2.

the native soldiers "who have grown old in the idleness and sloth of garrison life."

The troops on the Brabant frontier, aided by Spanish auxiliaries, could begin a campaign in much greater strength than the French and exploit their advantage before Louis XIV could raise additional troops. "In their plans, they count no more upon England," Pomponne wrote, "supposing only that because the king of England will have difficulty in bringing parliament to favor war against either side, she will remain out of the action."

Pomponne reported these plans to the king "as a piece of reasoning which is taking firm shape among the leading persons in the government, though it has not yet come to a resolution." Such private talk often did become the sentiment of the States General, he warned. As for the confidence the Dutch displayed in the German princes and in the Spanish authorities, he asked the king to judge whether this matter required further reflection.[1]

Pomponne continued to doubt that either the Dutch or the Spaniards would actually begin war against France. "I cannot imagine that the States General of these provinces will dare commit itself to it," he told Lionne. He did not think that Spain would go back into a war in which "the main burden" would fall upon her. "The one thing certain" was the "hostility of the States General, who are no longer restrained except by their lack of power and the sight of the danger."[2]

"I would gladly give a most beautiful present to the person who brings me the good news that the States have wished to assume the quality of aggressors, a glory I would willingly leave to them," the king replied to Pomponne. Unfortunately, the Dutch preferred to be "brave only in speech and argument." It was much to be doubted that Spain would join them as auxiliaries. In fact, the government at Madrid had sent orders to the count of Monterey, the governor general in Brussels, to confine himself to the question of maintaining the treaty of Aix-la-Chapelle without becoming involved in other interests and leagues. Lionne pointed up the king's scorn for Dutch threats by offering Pomponne a choice of two expressions to apply to them: a Spanish saying, "*No es tan bravo el león como le pintan*" (The lion is not as fierce as he is painted), or Tasso's line, "*E gli mancò l'ardire in mezzo all'ira*" (And his fierceness left him in the middle of his wrath).[3]

[1] Pomponne to Louis XIV, April 2, 1671, Arch. étr., Holl., vol. 91, fos. 132–35.
[2] Pomponne to Lionne, April 2, 1671, *ibid.*, fo. 136.
[3] Louis XIV and Lionne to Pomponne, April 10, 1671, Bib. Ars., MS 4712, fos. 437, 438.

Pomponne found both expressions so apt the choice was difficult. Perhaps the Tasso was better, because he should like to see it enacted by the Dutch in their wrath; he would be indignant, Pomponne said, if they deprived him of the pleasure of seeing their fierceness leave them. In any case, he concluded, the two phrases summed up the situation better than many dispatches.[1]

The Dutch would not take the audacious step of which they talked so easily, Pomponne believed, unless they received a Spanish promise of assistance. According to Pomponne's informants, Monterey was willing to come in alongside the Dutch in an attack on French Flanders, but disagreed with them as to which of the two parties should be the aggressor and which maintain the "less odious quality of auxiliary." The Council of Madrid, which would make the decision, had not yet been heard from.

There could be little doubt of Dutch readiness to act, however. Pomponne was told that if the forthcoming assembly of the States of Holland voted for additional troop levies, he could assume that the States General would decide for war. He noted, too, Dutch confidence in their maritime supremacy. De Ruyter gave the States General assurances of victory over the French at sea, and promised to make successful landings on the French coast. His plans, according to Pomponne's informants, were to seize islands off Britanny, Poitou and Saintonge. Oléron was the most important of these because it controlled the mouths of the Loire, Garonne and Charente rivers. "But all these projects, easy to make when the need to apply them is distant, will assume another aspect when they must be reduced to action," Pomponne predicted. He was sure that French fortification construction and other measures would confound De Ruyter's plans and his masters' hopes.

Dutch confidence in England had vanished, Pomponne reported, because of Charles II's reply to Boreel on the proposal to extend the Triple Alliance into a broader reciprocal league. Charles' query as to what subsidies he could receive if he went to war on behalf of the States General destroyed the last shred of belief in his sincerity. Now the Dutch would ask him for a promise just to remain neutral in their quarrels with France, Pomponne heard. If they receive such a promise and gain Spain's assent to a break, "they declare quite openly that the armaments at sea and on land will not remain without use."[2]

If Dutch readiness to go to war as the only remedy against their

[1] Pomponne to Lionne, April 16, 1671, Arch. étr., Holl., vol. 91, fo. 160.
[2] Pomponne to Louis XIV, April 9, 1671, *ibid.*, fos. 139–42.

slow and inevitable ruin depended upon Spain, Louis XIV informed Pomponne, then their republic was in desperate straits, for Spain would not be so rash.[1]

The report sent by the king that Madrid was reluctant to go along with the Dutch only confirmed Pomponne in his scepticism as to Dutch temerity. "I see now the disappearance of their plans," he wrote. They would be less ready to act on De Ruyter's promise to take the islands off France and seize French vessels in the Charente with the same success that the Dutch had had in the "river of Chatham" (the Thames). Military preparations were continuing, but so were outcries against the huge expenditures. Some cities within Holland and several of the other provinces opposed a break with France because it would not only threaten public safety but would also exhaust the citizens and ruin trade. "Thus," Pomponne reported, "the pensionary and those who agree with him that the danger of war would be preferable to certain ruin in peacetime, find much repugnance to acceptance of their opinion."

De Witt made another desperate effort to involve Pomponne in discussion of the conflict. He warned the envoy that the States might be forced to take action which by themselves they would be incapable of doing, and asked for some means whereby to re-establish amity. Pomponne replied in his usual noncommittal way. It was only Dutch arming and efforts to establish leagues which gave cause to fear for peace, he said. He hardly needed to explain why Dutch fears were legitimate, the grand pensionary answered: France had obviously singled them out for attack.

"He made no mistake about how little reliance they should always have placed in England," Pomponne reported him as saying, for "that nation did not change at all." The French now could "make the test whether we found more firmness in the measures we took with them at present than this state has found in those which it thought it had established." He "let escape" some angry remarks about England, "which abandoned the Triple Alliance after it had formed it against France to make peace with Spain."

De Witt's ire against England and his desire for reconciliation with France were obvious, Pomponne wrote. Pomponne kept to his generalities. If anything, he augmented De Witt's fears by failing to assure him that the States General had no cause for apprehension. "But at least I did not fall into the artifices which he might intend to use in London to

[1] Louis XIV to Pomponne, April 17, 1671, Bib. Ars., MS 4712, fo. 444.

have it believed that he would return to negotiations with Your Majesty."[1]

The project for a Dutch attack in the springs of 1671 never went beyond mere discussion. At the time Pomponne did not paint its dangers for France as very great, though on occasion he dropped hints of concern to Lionne. When he summed up the episode a decade later in his Relation, he admitted frankly that France had run more peril than he liked. War then "might have been the best choice" for the Dutch, he wrote. French fortifications were incomplete, troops being raised abroad had not yet been assembled, the French fleet was not at sea, the coast was "stripped." England was not ready. But the advocates of immediate war did not prevail in the Netherlands, and the Dutch were "satisfied to wait and see what the designs of His Majesty would be."[2]

[1] Pomponne to Louis XIV, April 16, 1671, Arch. étr., Holl., vol. 91, fos. 151–59. Cf. De Witt to De Groot, April 30, May 1, 1671, *Brieven van De Witt*, IV, 164–65, 194–95.

[2] Pomponne, *Relation de Hollande*, p. 161.

CHAPTER XIII

MISSION COMPLETED
April—July, 1671

Though Lionne had told Pomponne to wait until the king's arrival at Dunkirk before asking permission to come to Flanders, he could not wholly conceal his restlessness. What he had had to report during the months gone by was interesting, sometimes important, but hardly enough to occupy his time and his mind.

Late in April, he wrote to Lionne that he would send his request for permission as soon as he learned that the king had left for Dunkirk.[1] The reminder was unnecessary. The very day after Pomponne wrote, Lionne sent him news that Louis had left, and would arrive at Dunkirk on May 3. Lionne himself would travel separately by a different route, reaching there the same day. The king commanded Pomponne to leave as soon as possible for Dunkirk; he wished to see him regarding "an important and urgent affair."[2]

Pomponne was puzzled. No question of Dutch affairs was so urgent that he required orders from the king. He obeyed, however, "with much pleasure." He left at once for Flushing, traveling incognito with his party in order to avoid the usual ceremonies in his honor. At one place in Zeeland, they came under suspicion as spies because they spoke French. The party was halted until Pomponne revealed his true character to the local magistrates. The next morning, he boarded a small coasting vessel, hoping to reach Dunkirk that same night. The wind went down, however, and they did not arrive until too late to land. At the first gleam of dawn, Pomponne hurried ashore and "gave to rest and sleep the time which remained until the hour when social intercourse and visits are renewed."[3]

As soon as Lionne was "in a state to see me," Pomponne called upon him. Lionne praised his punctuality but tried to evade telling him what

[1] Pomponne to Lionne, April 23, 1671, Arch. étr., Holl., vol. 91, fo. 168.
[2] Lionne to Pomponne, April 24, 1671, Bib. Ars., MS 4712, fo. 449.
[3] Pomponne, *Relation de Hollande*, pp. 161–62; Wicquefort correspondence, May 14, 1671, Wicquefort, *Histoire*, IV, 253, note 1.

the "urgent matter" was which had necessitated his immediate departure. Louis XIV wished to tell Pomponne himself, Lionne said. Finally the foreign minister relented under his friend's persistent questioning. The king wanted Pomponne to go back to Sweden, because he was "more informed than any one else" of the king's interests and plans, and "more capable than any other" person of persuading the Swedish government to do as the king wished. Pomponne was taken aback and grieved by this news. He implored Lionne to prevail upon the king to change his decision. His friend said it would be of no use; Louis insisted that Pomponne was needed at Stockholm. Thus, Pomponne wrote, "there remained for me no other decision than to obey cheerfully His Majesty's wish." He accompanied Lionne to the royal levée, where he was greeted favorably and told to return in the in the afternoon for a conference. Pomponne spent the morning in the company of the monarch as he inspected the fortifications under construction outside Dunkirk.[1]

That afternoon, Pomponne attended a meeting of the council; Le Tellier, Lionne and Colbert were with the king. A year ago, Louis said, he had disclosed to Pomponne his plans for waging war upon the Dutch republic. The war had been put off for a year so that fortification of the frontier places could be completed. One of the first requirements for so great an enterprise was to acquire allies and deprive the foe of them. The elector of Cologne and the bishop of Münster were already in the French camp; negotiations were under way with the elector of Brandenburg and the dukes of Brunswick-Lüneburg. It was especially important to win the alliance of Sweden. The French party in Stockholm was in a difficult position. He had therefore decided, the king continued, that Pomponne, who combined full knowledge of the French plans and familiarity with the Swedish court, should return to Stockholm. To ease the burden on him, Pomponne was given permission to leave whenever he concluded a treaty or decided that it was not possible to do so, without writing first to Paris.

At Louis' request, Pomponne presented his views on the situation in Sweden and his suggestions as the policy he should follow in Stockholm. He also reported on the situation in the United Provinces; the king was particularly interested in knowing exactly what De Witt thought and felt. Pomponne's proposed policy toward Sweden was approved, and Lionne asked him to prepare a draft of his instructions. According to Pomponne's brother, Lionne brought this draft, unchanged, to the king, who read it and told him that he had surpassed

[1] Pomponne, *Relation de Hollande*, p. 162; Arnauld, pp. 333–34.

himself. The foreign minister at once replied, "Your Majesty must not be deceived; it is M. de Pomponne who wrote it." "I am happy that you let me know," the king replied. "He is a man who can be used when the occasion arises."[1]

Despite Pomponne's confidence that Louis XIV "had not left him uninformed of anything of general affairs," he does not appear to have known of the sharp struggle which had just been waged among the king's advisers over the question of France's alliances. In any event, he wrote nothing in the Relation to indicate such knowledge.

Until the spring of 1671, the French war plan had assumed the active alliance of England, the neutrality of the emperor, an offensive alliance with some German princes, including the elector of Brandenburg. The German part of this program had been suggested by Wilhelm von Fürstenberg and supported by Lionne. Fürstenberg and his French colleagues in Germany had been unable to persuade Frederick William II to join the French alliance. As a result, this entire policy toward Germany had been under discussion just before the conference at Dunkirk. Lionne pressed for the original program, stressing that allies were needed within Germany to keep the United Provinces isolated from the rest of the empire. He admitted that the Germans were making exorbitant demands for subsidies, but thought that they would fall into line if paid a little extra money. By sending an ambassador to Stockholm, the king would give the German princes reason for fearing Swedish intervention against their flank if they opposed France. Louvois, on the contrary, considered the Germans of little value: their own armies would do little and might even interference with the smooth performance of the French army. The money for subsidies would be better spent on French troops; it would be cheaper, he said, to buy the neutrality of the Germans than their alliance.

Louis XIV settled on this latter approach. It was decided to ask the German princes, especially Frederick William, only to be neutral during a war against the United Provinces. Fürstenberg was warned to keep in mind that there was not enough money to pay for the Swedish and German alliances. "You must take as a basis that the king cannot do both these things together," Lionne told him.[2] The importance of winning Stockholm therefore made obvious the king's choice of Pomponne as the new ambassador to Stockholm.

While discussing with Lionne the state of French relations with England, Pomponne revealed his reluctance to trust Charles II or the

[1] Pomponne, *Relation de Hollande*, pp. 163–65; Arnauld, pp. 334–35.
[2] Pagès, *Le Grand Électeur*, pp. 258–60.

English nation. The clauses in the Dover treaty and the shadow treaty of December 31, 1670, providing for the cession of Walcheren, Goeree and Voorne islands, and the towns of Sluis and Cadzand, to England, troubled him. The consequences of this division of the anticipated spoils of conquest could be very dangerous from the point of view of French interests, he told Lionne. His friend responded with a laugh. "To tell you the truth, when we made the treaty, we did not give thought to the fact that Middelburg and Flushing are on Walcheren island," he admitted.

At the moment, there was nothing that could be done. Years later, Pomponne still considered that France had narrowly escaped a perilous position. "Even if the king had conquered the rest of Holland, it is my opinion that his conquests would have been disadvantageous if these lands had passed into the hands of the English," he wrote. Sluis and the islands would have opened to them "an easy road to conquest of Holland," England would have become "absolute mistress of the seas, and she would have had a foothold on the mainland in the best country in the world." This was something "France has always had much reason to prevent."[1] By thus using the very phrase which De Witt had spoken to him, Pomponne admitted that he agreed, more than he had said at that time, with the arguments the grand pensionary had presented about the danger of the rise of English power to French interests.

Pomponne remained with the king during the remainder of his stay at Dunkirk, and then accompanied him to Tournai. There, on June 8, Louis presented him with his instructions and publicly announced his recall from The Hague.[2] The next day, the king informed the States General that Honoré Courtin would replace Pomponne as ambassador, while Bernarts would be in charge of affairs at the French embassy until Courtin's arrival.[3]

Pomponne returned to The Hague less happy than he had left it. He was ill from the effects of the journey for several days after his arrival on June 18, and was not pleased at the thought of going again to Stockholm, "the end of the world." Bernarts was concerned for his own safety after Pomponne left, even though he would be acting for the king of France. He beseeched Pomponne to request Lionne for a royal letter of protection. He wished to be called not an agent, "which passes for very little in this country," but "ordinary secretary of the king's

[1] Pomponne, *Mémoires*, II, 484–85.
[2] Pomponne, *Relation de Hollande*, p. 165.
[3] Louis XIV to the States General, June 9, 1671, Arch. étr., Holl., vol. 91, fo. 180 (minute).

chamber, for which he has long had letters." Pomponne supported this request, and Lionne sent him the document at once.[1]

De Witt came to see Pomponne immediately after his return. He did not conceal his apprehension, which Pomponne took as double flattery, over his departure from The Hague and the mission he was undertaking at Stockholm. De Witt expanded upon his favorite theme again: the Dutch misfortune at having lost the good will of Louis XIV, the great desire of the States General, and of himself in particular, to re-establish themselves in his favor. His arguments were the same that Pomponne had heard so many times before. He asked the ambassador to make a report on this last-minute plea before he left The Hague, to which Pomponne assented. He assured the grand pensionary that he would be at Stockholm only long enough to renew the 1662 treaty of Fontainebleau, which was about to expire. He would then return to France to see to his personal affairs. The new treaty, said Pomponne, would only continue and strengthen the old friendship between the two countries. He also stressed the qualities of Courtin, his successor, whom the Dutch already knew as one of the negotiators at the Breda peace conference. De Witt "was scarcely convinced by what I told him," observed Pomponne. He told De Witt that he did not demand of him a belief he might not grant, and did not doubt that the grand pensionary used this permission.[2]

On June 30, Pomponne took official leave of the States General. He gave them assurances, "in truth, not very sincere," of the king's friendship. In the usual fashion he was conducted by two deputies of the States General to a distance of a league and a half outside The Hague. On his return to The Hague that evening, he was a private person.

The next day, De Witt paid him a final visit, like their first technically informal in character. He repeated his plea for an understanding between the two states, based on an agreement between the Triple Alliance powers and France for the event of the death of Carlos II or of hostilities initiated by Spain. If that were done, the Triple Alliance which Spain believed to have been formed in her favor might be turned against her. Pomponne again repeated his "gentle remonstrance" that it was up to the Dutch to remedy by improved conduct what they had spoiled by ill-advised action, and his belief "that time alone will bring back to their first principles alliances based on ancient and real in-

[1] Pomponne to Lionne, June 25, July 2, 1671, *ibid.*, fos. 202, 217; Lionne to Pomponne, July 1, 1671, Bib. Ars., MS 4712, fo. 451.

[2] Pomponne, *Relation de Hollande*, pp. 165–66; Pomponne to Lionne, June 18, to Louis XIV, June 25, 1671, Arch. étr., Holl., vol. 91, fos. 183, 196-97.

terests." Thus he sought to keep alive De Witt's hope that one day the Dutch might regain the friendship of Louis XIV. "But," concluded Pomponne in the penultimate sentence of his Relation, "although it appeared to me that he strongly desired it, a minister as enlightened as he could only with difficulty be deceived by general words when all that took place at our court had so little correspondence to them."[1]

The strength of De Witt's desire for reconciliation, even at this time when Pomponne believed he could scarcely be deceived, is demonstrated by the grand pensionary's endeavor to keep some kind of negotiation continuing with France. He distrusted Bernarts too profoundly to use him, and turned instead to Estrades, who had acted the part of a sincere friend of the United Provinces and of De Witt personally during his embassy at The Hague. The occasion for seeking out Estrades' intervention was provided by the journey of three deputies of the province of Holland to Sluis to install magistrates there. Two were the burgomasters of Purmerend and Alkmaar, the third was the pensionary of Medemblik, all towns in North Holland.

On the pretext of sight-seeing in Dunkirk, the group went to the French port town where Estrades was in command. The pensionary of Medemblik, in a private talk with Estrades, confided to him De Witt's hopes that he could come to The Hague for only a week, some time after Pomponne had departed, on the pretext of settling a dispute over maritime prizes. "There he would disclose to me a number of things which he cannot communicate to anyone," the Medembliker said. Estrades was trusted in the province of Holland, he continued. "They will always do whatever I suggest in the interests of the king, provided that he promises that the king will consider them his good friends and allies." They had only gone into the Triple Alliance "under compulsion" (*forcément*), but if De Witt could speak to him in person, the quarrel between France and the United Provinces could be settled.

Estrades' comment on this proposal revealed him as a crass and eager double-dealer. He suggested that, "if the king's affairs required," he go to The Hague, where he could discover the intentions of the States General and of the various parties, and contribute, "by means of my credit in the towns," to division among the Dutch. He was also interested in arranging private booty for the event of war; there were four merchants in Amsterdam and Rotterdam who were ready to assure him a share in prizes taken after the outbreak of war. It was

[1] Pomponne, *Relation de Hollande*, p. 169; Pomponne to Louis XIV, July 2, 1671, Arch. étr., Holl., vol. 91, fos. 214–16.

worth 100,000 crowns to him, he told Lionne. Did the foreign minister wish to join in this arrangement? he asked.

On the other hand, if the king decided not to go to war, he boasted that "the provinces of North Holland and Zeeland have such confidence in me that in a few days I can turn them to whatever the king will desire, provided that he shows some moderation in the trade question." De Witt, he said, would say to him things he would not say to anyone else.[1]

Lionne was willing to use De Witt's apparent confidence in Estrades in order to keep his illusions intact a little longer. The king, however, was more cautious. For one thing, he wanted Estrades to supervise the construction of fortified works at Dunkirk. For another, he insisted that the grand pensionary "make no distinction of persons" in presenting his views. Pomponne was still at The Hague, Courtin would be there soon, De Groot was at his court—any of these could serve. Louis therefore drew the conclusion that De Witt was only seeking to impress the English with the apparent eagerness of France to settle with the Dutch.[2]

Pomponne, informed by Lionne of the Medembliker's overture to Estrades, did not doubt that De Witt was behind the journey of the three deputies to Dunkirk. Though his embassy was over, he defended himself against Estrades' clear implication that he was not as capable as his predecessor. There was hardly anything easier than to reach an agreement with De Witt, he said. France need merely accept something less than the entire Spanish Netherlands, such as partition even before Carlos II died, and offer a compromise on the tariff question. Pomponne strongly opposed even seeming to negotiate against England. De Witt would certainly like to upset Charles II by engaging in talks for renewed friendship with France, "if he did not go even further in case of necessity." If the king gave any opening for such negotiation, Pomponne concluded, with a stab at Estrades' boastfulness, "I assure you that the choice of persons would matter little to De Witt."[3]

As soon as it became clear that Estrades would not make the trip to The Hague, the pensionary of Medemblik wrote to him that the things De Witt would have confided to him "will remain dead." He raised the bugbear of the Orangist party: "I wish that they would consider in France that we can be assured of England by acting for the prince of Orange, and that in doing so we shall be covered from that

[1] Estrades to Lionne, mémorandum by Estrades, June 22, 1671, *ibid.*, fos. 184–93.
[2] Lionne to Estrades, June 30, 1671, *ibid.*, fo. 208.
[3] Lionne at Ath to Pomponne, July 1, 1671, Bib. Ars., MS 4712, fo. 451; Pomponne to Lionne, July 8, 1671, Arch. étr., Holl., vol. 91, fos. 223–24.

side, and that precautions are being taken against whatever can disturb the internal peace of the States, and that in any case the parliament will not permit the king of England to act for the interests of France."[1]

Pomponne remained at The Hague, receiving and returning visits, and preparing for his own journey to Stockholm and his wife's to Paris. On July 9, he went to Amsterdam for the final preparations. He hired a ship of 500 tons burden to carry him to Sweden. On July 15, he went abroad and the next morning, in the simple final words of his Relation, he "sailed through the Vlie by a quite favorable wind."[2]

His mission was completed.

The next time Pomponne saw the territory of the United Provinces, he came in the train of an invading army. He was foreign minister of France, Lionne's successor in completing and executing the plans of war against the States General.

He never again saw De Witt. The grand pensionary died hideously on August 20, 1672, murdered with his brother Cornelius at The Hague. He was accused of betraying his country to France. Pomponne knew this as utter falsehood, and during the almost three decades of life still remaining to him, Pomponne seems always to have remembered De Witt not only as an "enlightened minister," but also as a man of worth whom he would have proudly called friend if political life had not made them enemies.

[1] Pensionary of Medemblik to Estrades (copy), June 26, 1671, *ibid.*, fos. 204–06.
[2] Pomponne, *Relation de Hollande*, p. 169.

CHAPTER XIV

TARIFFS—THE LESSER "WAR" 1667—1671

French and Dutch statesmen—Louis XIV, Lionne and Pomponne, De Witt and Van Beuningen alike—frankly called their dispute over the Spanish Netherlands the source of the conflict between their countries. Yet some historians have held doggedly to the belief that the true cause of the war of 1672 lay in Colbert's tariffs of 1664 and 1667.[1] They assumed that economic considerations dominated the thinking and actions of both statesmen and people in this controversy. As a result, they either failed to observe the contrary evidence, or arbitrarily interpreted it out of existence. The interest of French and Dutch leaders in economic matters is undeniable, however. The important question is the exact rôle they assigned to them.

Pomponne was well aware of the facts of economic life. Throughout his mission he paid close attention to the commercial struggle between France and the United Provinces. The long section in his Relation on the economic history of the republic is one of the most remarkable contemporary statements of its kind.[2]

Pomponne recognized that the commercial predominance of the

[1] The earliest expression of this view I have found is in the article "*Tarif*" in the *Encyclopédie méthodique, ou par ordre de matières*: *Finances* (Paris and Liège, 1784–87): "The seed of this war lay in the *tariff* of 1667. Except for this tariff, which embittered the Dutch and drove them in their resentment to every kind of misconduct against France, what interest would they have had to antagonize a king like Louis XIV, against whom they otherwise had no complaint, and from whom they had everything to fear?" (III, 682). Elphège Frémy, in his article, "Causes économiques de la guerre de Hollande (1664–1672)," (*Revue d'histoire diplomatique*, XXVIII–XXIX [1914–15], 523-51), says more simply: "...the determining motivation for the hostilities was the tariff of 1664." Henri Sée called the war "the direct consequence" of Colbert's mercantilism, and asserted it was "provoked above all by causes of an economic kind." ("Que faut-il penser de l'oeuvre économique de Colbert?", *Revue historique*, CLII [1926], 189; review of Elzinga, *Het voorspel*, in *ibid.*, CLIV [1927], 251–52; *Matérialisme historique et interprétation économique de l'histoire* [Paris, 1927], p. 117; *Science et philosophie de l'histoire* [Paris, 1928], pp. 489–90.) Charles W. Cole, the leading modern student of Colbert, accepted this view, though with hesitation. (*Colbert and a Century of French Mercantilism* [New York, 1939], I, 445.)

[2] Pomponne, *Relation de Hollande*, pp. 34–47.

republic rested upon the skill and assiduity with which the Dutch had developed their production, shipping and trade. Their near-monopoly in shipping and commerce only endured, however, until the nations among whom they bought and sold realized what was happening. "It seems that all Europe reawakened at the same time from the profound slumber into which Holland had cast them," Pomponne wrote. France held definite advantages in undertaking competition with the United Provinces. Her position, with ports on the Atlantic and the Mediterranean, was favorable. Though the newly formed companies for trading to the West Indies, the Baltic and the Levant required firm support, Pomponne thought that French skill and perseverance would in time overcome the Dutch advantages, their monetary reserves, low interest rates, large fleet, and great knowledge and boldness as seafarers.[1]

Shortly after he reached The Hague, Pomponne was instructed to write about trade matters to Colbert only, as a consequence of a redivision of responsibilities between him and Lionne. Colbert, who now had charge of the navy, galleys, overseas colonies, the East and West India companies, and trade and manufactures in general, asked Pomponne to keep him "exactly informed" on all important happenings relating to his area of responsibility.[2] Bernarts obtained for Pomponne as he had done for Estrades, copies of the debates and decisions on these matters not only of the various States, but also of the East and West India companies. Colbert gladly arranged a pension for him.[3]

In his dispatches to Colbert, Pomponne therefore reported in detail upon commercial developments and other matters under the jurisdiction of the great minister. The political significance of these events he analyzed more briefly, though clearly, in his correspondence with the king and Lionne.

De Witt, in his first conference with Pomponne, only "mentioned a word about trade in passing." He made a precise distinction. The Dutch, he said, required "tranquility" in order to "preserve the safety of their trade," but "their safety depended upon the barrier" of the Low Countries. He would discuss the question of trade another day more fully, he told Pomponne.[4]

A week later, Pomponne remarked that De Witt still had not returned to the problem. He did not think it necessary to call his atten-

[1] *Ibid.*, pp. 36–37, 44–45.
[2] Colbert to Pomponne, March 7, 1669, Bib. Ars., MS 4586, fo. 1; Lionne to Pomponne, March 15, 1669, *ibid.*, MS 4712, fo. 41.
[3] Colbert to Pomponne, March 15, 29, 1669, *ibid.*, MS 4586, fos. 3, 10.
[4] Pomponne to Louis XIV, Feb. 28, 1669, Arch. étr., Holl., vol. 89, fos. 58–67.

tion to it. The cities of the province of Holland, especially Amsterdam, complained loudly against French tariffs and were debating Van Beuningen's proposals to place higher tariffs in reprisal on French wine, brandy, salt and manufactures. Louis XIV, they cried, was trying "to ruin them by the ruin of their commerce."[1]

Almost two weeks passed before De Witt at last brought up the trade question. Pomponne wrote to the king merely that this matter would be a principal topic of debate in the States of Holland, and summarized his long interview with De Witt in a letter to Colbert, in order "not to abuse the honor I have of corresponding with Your Majesty." He made clear to Lionne, however, the general tenor of De Witt's arguments. "He claims that the duties we have placed upon their wares make it impossible for them to avoid doing without our goods."[2]

In his reply, Colbert emphasized that he was concerned to strike at the sources of Netherlands strength. The two-way trade between the United Provinces and the countries on the Baltic "is what produces their strength and the wealth of their people and sailors." Their principal import into the Baltic lands was French wine which they bought every autumn in the ports of southwest France, stored over the winter, and then sold, often watered or modified, in the spring; they returned with cargoes of wood, hemp, iron and other bulky commodities for use in shipbuilding. Since two-thirds of their wine purchases were for this Baltic trade, the effect of import duties on French wine would be to hurt themselves. Other nations, the English and perhaps even the French, would gladly take over this trade.

"I can assure you," Colbert informed Pomponne, that if the Dutch hamper French exports to their provinces, "they will be working much more for us than for themselves." He did not expect De Witt to "give justice easily" to Frenchmen in matters of trade.[3]

Van Beuningen's other proposals would only aid his own program for increasing industrial activity in France and expanding her shipping, Colbert maintained. The French would be enabled to put somewhat more than their present five or six hundred ships to work, nearer the "natural" number France ought to have.

Because the "question of trade is very delicate and difficult to decipher," he again urged Pomponne to keep him carefully informed on all matters concerning trade. He asked him to find out the number

[1] Pomponne to Louis XIV, March 7, 1669, *ibid.*, fos. 78–79. Cf. Wicquefort to Lionne, March 7, 1669, *ibid.*, fo. 83.
[2] Pomponne to Louis XIV and Lionne, March 14, 1669, *ibid.*, fos. 88, 90.
[3] Colbert to Pomponne, March 15, 1669, Bib. Ars., MS 4586, fos. 3–4.

of ships belonging to the States and to their subjects; how much wine, brandy and other French products they imported and re-exported; and their decisions concerning French cloth and fashion goods for men and women. These inquiries must be made with "skill and secrecy," showing no apparent interest on the part of the French ambassador in these topics. "It is even necessary to pretend to less knowledge than you possess in these matters, which the Dutch hold so close to their hearts."[1]

To Pomponne, the essential question was the economic resources of the Dutch state for waging war. These would be exhausted in a long war, especially because the sources of their strength, "which consist only in freedom of trade," would vanish during war at sea.[2] The safety of their trade and their state was linked. Both would be inevitably ruined, the Dutch felt, if the Low Countries, especially Antwerp, came under the king's rule.[3] For all of Colbert's concentration on economic matters, this was essentially his view too. "It is easy to see that De Witt uses feeble pretexts for preventing the States from giving satisfaction to the king in all things," he wrote Pomponne. The "whole question of trade," he stressed, "was not as important as other affairs of state."[4]

"As long as they (the Dutch) will be masters of commerce," he wrote, "their land and sea forces will always increase and will make them so powerful that they will be able to make themselves the arbiters of war in Europe and give such bounds as they please to justice and to all the purposes of kings."[5]

Although he repeatedly assured Pomponne that Dutch reprisals could only aid France, Colbert was pleased when it seemed that they would not take such steps.[6] He rebuffed Van Beuningen's complaints that France was violating her treaties in order to ruin Dutch trade. If any treaties had been broken, he said, the States would not have failed to complain. The king was "only giving his protection to his subjects in their trade, and there was no basis for complaining about this." The best thing to do was to "treat their fears as phantasms, on the grounds that it is impossible that the trade of this kingdom, weak

[1] Colbert to Pomponne, March 22, 1669, *ibid.*, fos. 5–8.
[2] Pomponne to Lionne, May 9, 1669, March 3, 1670, to Louis XIV, Dec. 19, 1669, Arch. étr., Holl., vol. 89, fos. 174, 448, vol. 90, fo. 97.
[3] Pomponne to Louis XIV, May 16, 1669, *ibid.*, fo. 192.
[4] Colbert to Pomponne, May 10, 1669, Bib. Ars., MS 4586, fos. 25–26.
[5] Colbert to French consuls abroad, March 15, 1669, Colbert, II², 453; Colbert, "Dissertation...," *ibid.*, VI, 264.
[6] Colbert to Pomponne, March 29, April 5, May 3, 31, 1669, Bib. Ars., MS 4586, fos. 10, 12, 23, 31.

as it is, with the lack of diligence and steadiness of the king's subjects in it, should ever cause any harm to so great and powerful a trade as that of the Dutch."[1] He recognized the immense strength and flexibility of the Dutch in commercial matters. Though they were bound to be affected by the efforts of all nations in recent years to increase their own share of trade, "they are quite right to say that they can sustain the loss they may suffer more easily than any other nation, and they can no doubt correctly hope that they will surmount all the difficulties and re-establish themselves afterward in the enjoyment of all their commerce."[2]

The return of the Dutch East Indies fleet with large cargoes, Colbert admitted to Pomponne, would "certainly give them great means to ruin the commerce which all other nations in Europe strive to have with those lands and place them above all apprehensions." He was not surprised, he said, but continued to hope that French establishments in both the East and West Indies would bring considerable advantage to the kingdom.[3]

When Dutch trade declined, Colbert was delighted. Pomponne might point out to De Witt and Van Beuningen, chagrined as they were over the rise of French trade, that the exchange rate had turned favorable to France.[4] In less than a month, Colbert became much discouraged. Trade had declined everywhere, he now reported, and the French were suffering badly. He found reason to hope for its re-establishment, but admitted that when it occurred "there is no power or diligence in the world which can prevent Holland from having almost all of it. All that can be done in the kingdom is to re-establish our manufactures somewhat, and although they relieve the subjects of the king, they can never do any harm to the great establishments of Holland."[5]

In the fall of 1669, De Witt made an effort to persuade Pomponne that Dutch popular unfriendliness toward France was rooted in the commercial restrictions. He urged that the situation be remedied before both countries were harmed. Pomponne replied that the Dutch would be unable to prevent the lands which desired French wine from obtaining it, and that the Dutch were already manufacturing many products which they formerly imported from France; thus, a ban on import of these products would be less of a blow to France than it seemed.[6]

[1] Colbert to Pomponne, June 7, 1669, *ibid.*, fos. 33–34.
[2] Colbert to Pomponne, July 5, 1669. *ibid.*, fo. 42.
[3] Colbert to Pomponne, July 12, 19, Aug. 7, 1669, *ibid.*, fos. 47, 51, 57.
[4] Colbert to Pomponne, Aug. 23, 1669, *ibid.*, fo. 59.
[5] Colbert to Pomponne, Sept. 13, 1669, *ibid.*, fo. 61.
[6] Pomponne to Colbert, Sept. 5, 1669, Frémy, pp. 536–37.

In a letter to Colbert, Pomponne summed up the real difficulty faced by the Dutch. In order to conduct reprisals against France, they would have to reorganize the character of Dutch trade; the establishment of new routes was precarious compared to the advantages they had found in French commerce till this time.[1] In a conference with Pomponne early in November, when the States of Holland were meeting to consider reprisals against France, De Witt told him that he would still be able to halt the discussion if he received an indication that Louis XIV would moderate the duties upon the Dutch, though with more advantage to French subjects than before. If the king insisted on depriving the Dutch of their subsistence in trade, they could not be prevented from taking defensive action along the same lines. "But he declared that he would be grieved to see them reduced to that step," Pomponne added.[2] De Witt's position on trade questions was like that which he had adopted toward France in general: to seek reconciliation, but to see to the Dutch defenses if Louis XIV was unyielding.

Colbert meanwhile continued to flaunt his optimism that he could easily counter Dutch reprisals, but he was not able to conceal a fear that they would take them. He was therefore relieved when he learned that Van Beuningen, the chief instigator of the reprisal scheme, was going to England. It was fortunate, Colbert told Pomponne, that Van Beuningen had not succeeded in winning adoption of his proposals, "because it would have made it necessary to turn aside in our present road" and seek to defend the trade of the kingdom.[3]

The way political factors overrode economic considerations even for Colbert was illustrated during the course of the negotiations with England during this period, leading up to the Dover conference. He refrained from sharpening the commercial struggle with England in order to make it easier to win her as an ally against the Dutch, just as political estrangement from the United Provinces permitted the unfolding of his policy of economic hostility toward that state.[4]

After the conclusion of the Dover treaty, Colbert became less concerned about the immediate economic consequences of possible Dutch reprisals against French imports. He began instead to place even

[1] Pomponne to Colbert, Oct. 3, 1669, *ibid.*, p. 538.
[2] Pomponne to Colbert, Nov. 8, 1669, *ibid.*, p. 540; cf. Japikse, *Johan de Witt*, p. 302.
[3] Colbert to Pomponne, Oct. 4, 10, Nov. 8, 25, Dec. 6, 13, 20, 1669, Jan. 17, Feb. 21, March 28, April 7, 18, 25, May 16, 1670, Bib. Ars., MS 4586, fos. 73–113 *passim*. Cf. De Witt to Jean Deutz, Jan. 19, 1670, *Brieven van De Witt*, IV, 26.
[4] Colbert to Croissy, May 23, 1670, Colbert, II[2], 528; Elzinga, *Het voorspel*, pp. 267–68; Geyl, *Geschiedenis*, II, 512–13, 516.

greater stress upon the necessity to weaken Dutch finances as much as possible, in view of the war in preparation against the republic.

When the Dutch East India company again brought in huge cargoes, Colbert admitted his surprise. The Dutch company was flooding the market in order, he believed, to smash its French rival while it could. The king's protection would undo the damage, he predicted. "You will see hereafter," he told Pomponne, "that we can do them at least as much harm as they can do us." There was no reason to change the French course of action.[1]

He was pleased by the arrival of a fully-laden French ship from the Indies, with another due soon after, and hoped that "with time, much patience, and all the protection and assistance of the king, our company will succeed."[2] In any case, he reminded Pomponne, it was the Dutch conflict with the English over the Indies which really endangered their commerce, not the brawl with France. The English demand to trade anywhere not under the absolute dominion of the Dutch East India company "will be more difficult for them to swallow than all our little difficulties."[3]

Pieter de Groot's departure meanwhile for Paris meant that Colbert's mercantilist theories would be confronted with the free-trade arguments which the Dutch employed, at least for European trade. Colbert was hardly ready to engage in serious intellectual debate with the Dutch ambassador, however. "I will merely say to you," he told Pomponne, "that the king has not been much shaken by the threats they have made till now and therefore I very much doubt that M. de Groot can oblige His Majesty to change his sentiments, so that we shall await patiently the harm they wish to do us." Lionne wrote in the same vein: "De Groot will have to be very eloquent to persuade the king to change any of the taxes he has placed on the wares of his country."[4]

In mid-September, noting that De Groot had not yet appeared at Saint-Germain to make his proposals concerning trade, Colbert did not "despair that the king will protect himself against the result of their hostility," even if they eventually decided upon the measures of reprisal which they had so long discussed.[5] Early in October, the States General sent De Groot a memorandum expounding their arguments on

[1] Colbert to Pomponne, July 4, 18, 25, Aug. 7, 1670, Bib. Ars., MS 4586, fos. 119, 123, 125, 127.

[2] Colbert to Pomponne, Oct. 2, 1670, *ibid.*, fo. 141. Cf. Temple, "Observations," I, 201.

[3] Colbert to Pomponne, Sept. 26, 1670, Bib. Ars., MS 4586, fo. 139.

[4] Colbert to Pomponne, Aug. 22, 1670, *ibid.*, fo. 131; Lionne to Pomponne, Aug. 22, 1670, *ibid.*, MS 4712, fo. 309.

[5] Colbert to Pomponne, Sept. 12, 1670, *ibid.*, MS 4586, fo. 137. Cf. Dijk, p. 82, note 3.

behalf of freedom of trade, upon the principle of international division of labor. If he were too ill to deliver the document in person, he was ordered to have Christiaan Rumpf, the secretary of the embassy, present it. It was not to be delayed.[1]

On October 10, De Groot at last brought the memorandum to Lionne, who permitted him to come to his study in a sedan chair because of his severe gout. De Groot painted a dire picture of the results of the tariff conflict for France. The king's subjects would suffer more than those of the States, and the king himself would lose customs revenues when trade slackened. Many French luxury goods, for which the province of Holland was an important market, would be replaced by goods made in the Netherlands. Lionne put on an air of innocence. He did not wish to give false hopes, he said. The only way to obtain reduction of the new tariff was to provide good arguments proving that France would lose more than she gained by it. It was Colbert who would have to be persuaded, Lionne made clear. On such matters, he told De Groot, the king relied upon Colbert's advice. Win Colbert to your argument, and no one else will stand against it, he assured him. De Groot was taken in. He thought Lionne a patient listener, easy to persuade, though aware that trade was not a matter on which he was well-informed.

Lionne doubted that the Dutch ambassador would find the arguments he needed to convince Colbert, and that minister, when Lionne told him of the interview, laughed at De Groot's confidence in his persuasive powers. Actually the Hollander was more dubious of them than he let Lionne think. In due time, he predicted in a letter to Wicquefort, Colbert will find out for himself how right I was.[2]

A month later Louis XIV received De Groot in official audience. De Groot told him that Lionne still had not given him any reply to his statement on the trade controversy. "Give me your memorandum," the king replied. He wished to read it himself, he said, and would have an answer made to it. Lionne, who admitted that De Groot spoke "very well," assured Pomponne nothing would come of his efforts.[3]

Finally, late in November, the States of Holland, recognizing the hopelessness of changing the French king's attitude by words, adopted

[1] Resolutions of States of Holland, Oct. 1, of States General, Oct. 2, 1670, Dijk, p. 83.

[2] Lionne to Pomponne, Oct. 17, 1670, Bib. Ars., MS 4712, fo. 343; memorandum of De Groot to Louis XIV, Oct. 10, 1670, Arch. étr., Holl., vol. 90, fos. 351–52; De Groot to Wicquefort, Oct. 17, Nov. 6, 1670, De Groot, pp. 17–19; De Groot to griffier Ruysch, Oct. 17, 1670, Dijk, pp. 137–41; Colbert to Pomponne, Oct, 31, 1670, Bib. Ars., MS MS 4586, fo. 149.

[3] Dijk, pp. 83–84; Lionne to Pomponne, Nov. 21, 1670, *ibid.*, MS 4712, fo. 355. Cf. Saint-Maurice, pp. 509–10.

the long-discussed measures of reprisal: a ban on foreign brandies; prohibitive import duties on French salt and manufactured goods. For the moment, French wines were not touched by the new tariffs.[1] Gelderland, Utrecht and Overijssel followed Holland's example, as did Friesland and Zeeland during the next two months. Groningen's decision was delayed by an internal political crisis, but the States General took action for the Union on January 2, 1671, without her approval.[2]

Opinions were divided in the Netherlands concerning the effects of the ban. The livelihood of many people would be endangered, wrote Pomponne, but all "flatter themselves that by the damage which will be done to France, a new agreement will be achieved and the interruption will not last for long."[3]

The French response was indignant. The ministers considered these reprisals only one more misdeed of the Dutch to be punished in the war against the United Provinces planned for the next spring. Colbert, who first heard of the action of the States of Holland by merchants' reports from The Hague and Rotterdam, expected little difficulty in repaying them in kind, especially since the ban on French brandy was a violation of the treaty of 1662. "They have grown accustomed, on other occasions of even greater importance, to putting little value on the obligations of their treaties," he wrote Pomponne. "What is bad for them is that I do not see the king willing to tolerate this as in the past, and I hope that you will shortly see that they will have every reason to regret beginning this skirmish."[4] Lionne gave De Groot a brusque answer to the memorandum of the States General. The king was observing his treaties, he said with obvious irony, and did not wish to change anything in the establishment of trade.[5]

On January 7, 1671, a decree in council was issued in France placing new duties upon imports of Dutch herring and spices. The king, "tired at last of all the threats they had repeated so often during the past two years," desired to give the Dutch "a sample of what he can do when he wishes to depart from the true and faithful execution of his treaties, as the States have so often done and still do by shameful chicanery," Colbert told Pomponne.[6]

De Witt came to Pomponne to plead for withdrawal of the decree. He

[1] Pomponne to Louis XIV, Nov. 20, 1670, Arch. étr., Holl., vol. 90, fo. 386.
[2] Dijk, pp. 84–88; Frémy, pp. 542–43 (where Groningen is incorrectly named instead of Zeeland).
[3] Pomponne to Colbert, Nov. 20, 1670, Frémy, pp. 542–43. Cf. Elzinga, p. 285.
[4] Colbert to Pomponne, Nov. 21, 1670, Bib. Ars., MS 4586, fo. 151.
[5] Lionne to Pomponne, Nov. 28, 1670, *ibid.*, MS 4712, fo. 359.
[6] Colbert to Pomponne, Jan. 8, 15, 1671, *ibid.*, MS 4586, fos. 163, 165.

would have the Dutch ordinances repealed at once if the king revoked the decree, he said. Pomponne observed with equanimity the grand pensionary's manifest concern for the weakening of the fisheries and the Indies trade, the two pillars of the republic. He shared the general fear that France would be able to do without all their wares and apply herself more strongly than ever to fishing, shipping and commerce. The wellsprings of Dutch wealth would dry up.[1]

The new decree violated treaty provisions for equal treatment of the subjects of both states, De Groot observed, "but no account is taken of the 1662 treaty any more, as if it had never been made." The boldness of France was due to Dutch weakness, he told Wicquefort. He quoted the proberb, "*Qui se fait brebis, le loup le mange*" (Act like a sheep and be eaten by the wolf).[2]

Colbert did not expect rapid benefits from the tariff conflict. "These results, though slow, will be felt in both countries," he told Pomponne. It was a sign of a much broader struggle, he indicated. "As for all the other grand dreams of Van Beuningen to prevent the progress of everything the king has undertaken," he continued, "I can assure you that for each step in this path that he takes, he will meet an equal number of counter-blows, like that of the decree in council, which will certainly cause him to fall back much further than he will advance." He added that the United Provinces would "long remember his baleful embassies, during which by his eloquence he aroused the little war which we are waging in trade, in which they have acted like the man who gambles 100,000 crowns against one who possesses absolutely nothing, that is, they have nothing to gain from us while we, who run no risk of loss because we have nothing, can win a great deal."

The importance of the whole affair, Colbert made clear, lay primarily in the weakening of the Dutch state on the eve of the French attack. "All the advantages which we think to gain over them in commerce would be almost useless if they continued to have the same abundance of money and the same ease of obtaining it for all the great expenditures they are considering." The difficulty for his own program, he realized, was that falling trade would reduce the revenues of the Dutch republic only in the long run.[3]

On February 29, De Witt came again to Pomponne to discourse

[1] Pomponne to Louis XIV, Jan. 15, 1671, Arch. étr., Holl., vol. 91, fo. 30; to Colbert, Jan 15, 1671, Frémy, p. 543. Cf. De Witt to De Groot, Jan. 15, 1671, *Brieven van De Witt* IV, 153.

[2] De Groot to Wicquefort, Jan. 9, 1671, De Groot, p. 24.

[3] Colbert to Pomponne, Jan. 29, Feb. 26, 1671, Bib. Ars., MS 4586, fos. 170–71, 179–80. Cf. De Groot to Fagel, Jan. 23, 1671, Dijk, p. 170.

upon the trade conflict. He played strongly on the theme that French subjects would be badly hurt. Pomponne merely mentioned the interview in his dispatch to the king, leaving the details for his letter to Colbert.[1] The minister replied that the grand pensionary might spare himself pity for the subjects of the king, who "loves his people more than does De Witt." The French nation had not complained and probably would not.[2]

This was the last important mention of the trade question in Pomponne's dispatches, though almost five months remained before he left the Netherlands. There is another major document coming from Colbert's hand, which relates to the economic conflict with the United Provinces. This is a memorandum of July 8, 1672, to which he gave the title, "Proposals on the advantages which may be drawn from tht States of Holland for increasing the trade of the realm."[3] In it Colbere suggested that France could reap advantage for her trade either by transferring part of the commerce of the United Provinces to French hands if the republic was incorporated into the monarchy, or by including favorable conditons for French merchants in the peace terms if the republic were permitted to remain independent.

He was, of course, skinning his bear too soon, for the war lasted another six years and his tariff of 1667 was one of the principal victims of the peace of Nijmegen. Perhaps the most significant about this document, however, is the date when he wrote it. The war had already been under way for three months. If his purpose in supporting the war against the United Provinces had been primarily to wrest trade from the hands of the Dutch, we might expect that this methodical statesman would have prepared such plans long in advance, in the period between 1668 and 1670 when the decision actually to wage war was made. We know of no such plans. Were the economic potentialities of military victory something of an afterthought even for Colbert?

Why then, it may be asked, should he have repeatedly used the term "war" to characterize economic competition between states. His use of the word, if deeply felt, was nonetheless metaphorical: economic conflict was "warlike" in the sharpness with which it was

[1] Pomponne to Louis XIV, Feb. 26, 1671, Arch. étr., Holl., vol. 91, fo. 84. Frémy (p. 546) erroneously gives the date of this interview as "early in March."

[2] Colbert to Pomponne, March 6, 1671, Bib. Ars., MS 4586, fo. 181. There were reports in the Netherlands that merchants in Bordeaux, Nantes, Rouen and other towns were complaining, though without result, about damage to their trade. Sylvius, I, 123. Perwich, an English agent in Paris, reported that "French merchants doe as generally complain as the foreigners." Perwich to Williamson, Nov. 29, 1670, Perwich, p. 120.

[3] Félix Joubleau, *Études sur Colbert*, (Paris, 1856), II, 421; Colbert, II[2], 658. The phrase, "States of Holland" clearly means the States General, not the States of the province of Holland.

waged, not in any inevitable appeal to arms. To him, "trade is a perpetual and *peaceful* war of the mind and of industriousness between all nations."[1] This was precisely how Pomponne looked at it, as we have seen.[2]

The economic conflict, though not the primary cause of the war of 1672, played an undeniably important part in the events leading up to it. First, the "little war" of tariffs exacerbated feelings already embittered by the dispute over the future of the Spanish Netherlands. It aroused the populace in the United Province by endangering their livelihood; it convinced De Witt of Louis XIV's implacability. Second, the French leaders were trying to strengthen their own sinews for war and enfeeble their opponents. *Pecunia nervus belli.* But the judgment can scarcely be disputed that the war would have come about on the sole issue of the Low Countries, even if Colbert had never lived and his tariffs had never existed.

[1] Colbert, VI, 269 (my italics. – H. H. R.).
[2] *Supra*, p. 185.

CONCLUSION

POMPONNE, LIONNE AND LOUIS XIV

We may smile at the absoluteness of Keith Feiling's judgment that Arnauld de Pomponne was the greatest of French envoys, and still appreciate the spirit which moved him to such exaggeration. Pomponne did embody, to a remarkable degree, the qualities of a great diplomat.

As a negotiator, he was persuasive, even-tempered, self-confident but never brutally self-assertive. He did not lose sight of the grand design of policy in the forest of petty affairs. The failure of his discussions with John de Witt to lead to a settlement of the dispute between France and the States General was the result of high policy on both sides, not of inadequacies of the two ministers.

As an observer, Pomponne performed with equal skill his never-ending tasks of reporting and evaluating. He did not construe his own ideas as reality, but looked about him with an honest, though not dispassionate, eye. He did not lead his masters astray to coddle his own vanity, and flattered the Sun King as little as any servant of Louis XIV could hope to. His dispatches, therefore, are a valuable source for understanding the history of the Dutch republic in the years immediately before the tragedy and glory of 1672. Least, though not unimportant, was his ability to put on the mask when it became his duty to conceal the intentions and attitudes of his master.

Pomponne's dispatches are models of their kind, clear in organization and style, with masses of secondary detail compressed into little while fundamental problems are spelled out for thoughtful analysis. Pomponne could catch the essential quality of a man or a situation in a few words, or describe their multifarious subtleties in extended periods.

Pomponne was never a good drudge. He accepted the quasi exile of an embassy not merely because he was an obedient servant of his king, but because he enjoyed the very difficulties of a complex and uncertain negotiation. Thus, though he performed his essential tasks with a skill sharpened by zeal and zest, he became restless when negotiation virtually ceased during the last third of his Dutch mission.

Pomponne's contemporaries were most vividly impressed by his probity. It was not that he never told a lie, for he practiced no absolute faithfulness to virginal truth. His honesty was a pattern of character more than a rigid rule of conduct. Prevarication was for him a last recourse, not a first step, in negotiation; to lie was almost to confess failure. He respected too much the intelligence of those with whom he negotiated to think that he could beguile them unless they had first deceived themselves. He preferred the difficult method of persuading by truth to the easier but dubious successes that rest on falsehood. Though he lied abroad for the good of his country, he remained an essentially honest man.

Fellow statesmen also praised Pomponne's moderation. This did not mean that he won their favor by easily sacrificing the interests of his own prince and state to those of other rulers. He was no simpleton to be led around by the nose. What Pomponne's contemporaries recognized was his acceptance of the fact and spirit of the European states system. By character and by intellectual conviction, he was ready to live in a world of many and varied interests. In seeking the advantage of France, he did not think it necessary systematically and needlessly to harm other states. He did not believe in insulting opponents. He was almost always fair.

Curious about people and respecting them as individuals, Pomponne had the gift of seeing his adversary's side of a question without making it his own. He was able, therefore, to describe more profoundly what he saw and to provide a sounder basis for policy.

Pomponne distinguished clearly between fundamental and secondary factors. Although he emphasized the interplay of private and general considerations in the development of policy, he put heavier stress on the basic urgencies and necessities of a land.

He never forgot that an ambassador is an agent, not a maker of policy. He followed precisely and dutifully the orders he received from king and foreign minister. But he did not therefore forgo his private judgment. He accepted, for instance, the king's program for punishing the Dutch, ultimately because he considered the Spanish Netherlands too valuable a prize to be abandoned without adequate compensation. But he was always distrustful of Charles II and the English nation, and would probably have preferred to make a settlement with John de Witt in order to keep England off the continent.

The fundamental method employed by Pomponne in his negotiations was to seek to persuade the leaders of the state to which he was accredited that it was to their true interest, as well as to France's, to adopt the policy he proposed. For this reason, he preferred De Witt's quiet firmness to Van Beuningen's practice of diplomacy by declamation. Pomponne's diplomatic method may be said to have rested on the principle of honesty in the broad sense of seventeenth-century *honnêteté:* a never-failing courtesy in the midst of the sharpest controversy, a decent regard for the opinions and interests of others as well as for one's own. If not all men could be his friends, he preferred not to make them needlessly his foes.

Pomponne, the diplomat, exemplifying the art of the ambassador in its classic age, contributed some essential elements to the making of French policy, but was not actually part of it during most of the period we have studied. The diplomatic preparation of the war of 1672 was the work of Hugues de Lionne (only rarely can we detect the separate attitudes of king and foreign minister), and it is this which we must now evaluate.

The vigor, breadth and resiliency of Lionne's diplomacy cannot be denied. The vast material resources of the French monarchy were matched by his tactical resourcefulness. When unforeseen difficulties arose, he quickly devised new solutions. The scope of his planning was breathtaking. In his mind, Portugal and Norway, the Sublime Porte and the Danish Sound, all became part of a single grand design.

Nonetheless, the French plans for war upon the Dutch republic were flawed from the beginning. Strategically the invasion was an enterprise bold to the point of foolhardiness. The whole operation was based on the calculation that swift success, though it required that every single element work exactly as planned, would be achieved, and thereby obviate the undoubted difficulties of a long war. To send an army thrusting through the Liège corridor all the way to the Rhineland was immensely risky. "Unreconciled enemies" in the Spanish Netherlands were given a tempting opportunity to cut off the French in the Rhineland and the United Provinces from their homeland. The war plans were even more dubious because the most difficult operation, the investment of Fortress Holland-Zeeland, came at the very end of an extended campaign.

The weaknesses in the French war plans were not only military in character, however. If anything, the political mistakes were more significant.

Louis XIV and Lionne tended to minimize the degree to which other powers felt threatened by the immensity of French power and the imminence of French hegemony. They were aware of such feelings, to be sure, but believed that by confronting the rulers of the European states with the donkey's choice between the carrot and the stick, they could make them obedient or at least harmless. But these princes, even though they often took French bribes and succumbed to French threats, did not want to become the donkeys of the French king. Pomponne recognized this attitude and did not equate it with inevitable unfriendliness to France; the king and foreign minister, on the other hand, were wont to disregard and to denigrate the passion of these rulers to preserve their sovereignty against the treat of French power. Grémonville's dispatches to Pomponne revealed, though indirectly, that the emperor was stirred by this fear; Pagès has shown in detail how this same feeling dominated the elector of Brandenburg; and Pomponne specifically referred to it as the guiding motivation in the defection of J. P. von Schönborn, the archbishop-elector of Mainz, from the French camp. This insensitivity on the part of Louis XIV to the interests and sensibilities of other states was later revealed in the motto which the king took for his own, *nec pluribus impar.* Could one imply any more clearly that it did not much matter whether other rulers were for him or against him?

Yet a lively prudence was also characteristic of Louis XIV. He tried to prepare every enterprise so thoroughly and carefully that there was no danger of failure. His bugbear was the combination of powers to oppose him, and he sought to prevent such leagues even before they formed. He feared the Triple Alliance as the hub around which might be built a vaster, all-European league against him. But his prudence, when linked to his selfishness, his failure to consider or respect the interests of others, caused him to choose brutal methods of action which repeatedly led precisely to the result he was seeking to avert. At best, this was a prudence of means, seldom of ends. He thought not about what he was seeking, but about how to attain it.

It is in this respect that his political character differed most sharply from Pomponne's. The ambassador warned the king and Lionne that the Dutch would wage war with great vigor and perseverance if it were forced upon them. The French leaders did not give sufficient weight to these words of caution. They preferred to rely on the expectation, partly engendered by Pomponne's reports, it is true, that the Dutch, stunned by the enormity of the French invasion, would be shaken from all will to resist by internal dissension or perhaps even civil war.

There was another major source of weakness in the French plans, in which Pomponne's responsibility was more definitely involved. A whole series of questions remained open and uncertain even when the war was launched. Spain and the empire had to remain neutral, at least for a considerable time, while the French armies conquered the northern Netherlands. Yet Pomponne had repeatedly reported that the Spaniards were more eager for war than were the Dutch. The Spanish authorities in the Low Countries did not have to read Lionne's letters to know that their neutrality assured them only of the Cyclops' favor, to be devoured last. How likely was it, then, that they would let their troops stand idly by when the French channel of communication through the Liège passageway was open to their attack? At the least break of luck against France, they could be expected to strike the French king's armies at this chink in their armor. As for the empire, its neutrality was predicated upon its territory not being used for attack upon the Dutch, and to do just this was the very heart of the French strategy.

Nor was French policy toward England based on a more solid calculation of the probabilities. The course of the negotiation for the Dover treaty had revealed the fragility of Charles II's rule; he had already been forced to sacrifice Clarendon, saved by flight to France from Strafford's fate, to the Anglican passions of the Cavalier parliament. His flirtation with Roman Catholicism could only increase his difficulties with a parliament upon which he obviously depended for funds. French policy required that England be safely in her camp, and relied upon Charles' promise as if he were an absolute monarch, like Louis himself; yet the British struggle over sovereignty was far from completed. The Dutch, as well aware of this as the French, correctly relied upon it to undo Charles' alliance with France. It was De Witt's misfortune that the English nation forced Charles out of the league with France only two years after the war began, to the benefit of William III, not himself. This was an age when wise statesmen did not bet on keeping a king of England tied to a policy which the majority of his nation—at least the political nation—did not approve. This was precisely the wager made by the French leaders.

Pomponne's responsibility was graver in misjudging the stamina which the Dutch state would display, especially in the first hard year of the war. He exaggerated the difficulties the States General would face in financing the war. Yet, towards the end of his mission, he did report that loans to pay for military preparations had been fully subscribed, with more funds available. In any case, Pomponne did not scoff at the spirit of the nation. He saw that it had weaknesses such as the slackness of the native soldiery, but emphasized the endurance, diligence and resourcefulness of the leaders of the republic; with the vast German reservoir of hireling troops nearby, the laxity of the indigenous forces was only a passing problem. In war the most dangerous weakness is loss of courage; Pomponne gave the king little reason to anticipate that either John de Witt or William of Orange—and one or the other would certainly lead the republic in its hour of need—would fail in this respect.

On the other hand, Pomponne, for all the subtlety and insight of his analysis of William III's character in his Relation, did not think through while at The Hague the implications of the prince's position in Dutch politics and in the French-Dutch-English triangle. The basic assumption of French policy, which so far as can be seen Pomponne continued to share in the years before the outbreak of war, was that William would do his uncle's bidding, that he would sacrifice everything to his dynastic ambition and his desire to become master of the republic. What the French leaders utterly failed to anticipate was that William would strive to protect the sources of his *independent* power, if need be against his uncle. Indeed, it was the very war which France unleashed against the Netherlands which brought the prince the government of the United Provinces and destroyed thereby the regime of the "True Freedom." From the beginning, Louis XIV had asked Pomponne to observe "of what the prince is capable." Pomponne fundamentally erred not by misestimating William's character, but by failing to project into the near future the probable consequences of French action.

There was one last characteristic, though not necessary, miscalculation in the Dutch policy of France in this period. Louis XIV, under the dual influence of Colbert and Lionne, cast aside as of little value that long symbiotic relationship which had developed between France and the United Provinces in both politics and economics. Together they were masters of Europe; the cost to France of refusing to pay a reasonable price for the retention of Dutch amity was the creation of the Anglo-Dutch league which the French leaders so rightly feared. They were intent on punishing the United Provinces for preventing France from conquering the Spanish Low Countries in 1668. Yet France proved incapable of completing that conquest against the resistance of the States General. The lesson seems clear. Had Louis XIV recognized that he could not attempt to take the Low Countries without arousing the Dutch republic against him at once and the English realm sooner or later—a combination which he could not vanquish—, then he might have accepted a compromise over the fate of the Low Countries with the States General. But we find ourselves back at our earlier point. Louis XIV established his goals, then sought means to achieve them, confident that the immensity of French resources, his own competence, and the destiny of his house and his glory, would bring him victory.

Thus two fundamental judgments must be made about the French plans for war against the Dutch republic. First, they rested upon a narrow and undue emphasis upon the importance of the Low Countries, without adequate consideration of the repercussions of attempting their conquest. Second, the specific plans of political and military strategy rested upon confidence in the efficacy of a single campaign, with the expectation that although virtually every single factor would have to work in favor of France, they would not fail to do so. History reserves a special penalty for those who count too much upon her favors.

Had Lionne's war plans succeeded, this criticism might seem untenable. All historians, it may be, would then join in acclaiming them as a masterpiece. But their success depended on defiance of the probabilities: it is hard to say whether Lionne did not see the weaknesses of this grandiose scheme, or took an immense calculated risk. Pomponne, it may be safely maintained, would have stood down before such chances. If a great man in history must have in him at least a touch of the demoniac, as Louis XIV did, then Pomponne fell short of greatness. He lacked that combination of boldness and blindness which enables men to attempt what cannot, by any sober calculation, be done. It may be, however, that Pomponne was the kind of statesman who accomplishes more of the possible.

BIBLIOGRAPHICAL NOTE

The correspondence between Pomponne and the French court during the period of his Dutch embassy forms the principal source for this study. The original dispatches from the king and Lionne to Pomponne are preserved in MS 4712 of the Bibliothèque de l'Arsenal, Paris. The dispatches from Pomponne to the court are in the archives of the French foreign ministry, in volumes 89 through 91 of the *Correspondance de Hollande:* volume 88 of this series provided valuable letters from Abraham de Wicquefort to Lionne. Four other manuscripts in the collection of the Bibliothèque de l'Arsenal were used: MS 4713, dispatches from Grémonville, Des Arcis and Terlon to Pomponne; MS 4715, the relations of Pomponne's Dutch mission and his second Swedish mission (1671); MS 4586, Colbert's dispatches to Pomponne during his Dutch mission; MS 6037, Arnauld family correspondence (1666–71), used for unpublished letters from Pomponne to his father and father-in-law. All these materials were used on microfilm.

Pomponne's *Relation de son ambassade en Hollande, 1669–1671*, forming the first 137 folios of MS 4715 of the Bibliothèque de l'Arsenal, is cited in my edition published in the "Werken uitgegeven door het Historisch Genootschap" (series IV, no. 2) (Utrecht, 1955). F. A. Mignet's *Négociations relatives à la succession d'Espagne sous Louis XIV, ou Correspondances, mémoires, et actes diplomatiques concernant les prétentions et l'avènement de la maison de Bourbon au trône d'Espagne*, in the "Collection de documents inédits sur l'histoire de France" (Paris, 1835–42), form the indispensable printed source for the diplomatic history of France between 1659 and 1679; the third volume covers the period between the Triple Alliance of 1668 and the outbreak of war in 1672. The fundamental source for Dutch policy remains the various collections of John de Witt's correspondence: *Brieven geschreven ende gewisselt tusschen den Heer Johan de Witt, Raedt-pensionaris en Groot-Segelbewaerder van Hollant en West-Frieslandt; ende de Gevolmaghtigden van den Staedt der Vereenighde Nederlanden, so in Vranckryck, Engelandt, Sweden, Denemarcken, Poolen, enz.* (The Hague,

1723–25). This collection terminates with the year 1669, and though not absolutely correct in its transcriptions, is adequately reliable. Materials not included in this edition have been published from the notes of Robert Fruin in the "Werken uitgegeven door het Historisch Genootschap": *Brieven van Johan de Witt*, edited and amplified by G. W. Kernkamp and N. Japikse (series III, nos. 18, 25, 31, 33) (Amsterdam, 1906–13), and *Brieven aan Johan de Witt* (series III, nos. 42, 44) (Amsterdam, 1919–22), by Japikse. The *Correspondance française du Grand Pensionnaire Jean de Witt* was published by François Combes in the "Collection de documents inédits sur l'histoire de France, Mélanges historiques" (Paris, 1873). Abraham de Wicquefort, *Histoire des Provinces-Unies des Païs-Bas, depuis le parfait établissement de cet état par la paix de Munster*, ed. E. Lenting and C. A. Chais van Buren (Amsterdam, 1861–74), and F. Krämer, ed., *Lettres de Pierre de Groot à Abraham de Wicquefort*, in the "Werken uitgegeven door het Historisch Genootschap" (Series III, no. 5) (The Hague, 1894), are also essential. *The works of Sir William Temple Bar*t* (London, 1757) are equally useful.

Specialized studies of particular value are Pieter Geyl, *Oranje en Stuart* (Utrecht, 1939), N. Japikse, *Johan de Witt* (Amsterdam, 1915) and *Prins Willem III: De Stadhouder-Koning* (Amsterdam, 1930–33). A. Lefèvre-Pontalis, *Vingt années de république parlementaire au dix-septième siècle: Jean de Witt, grand pensionnaire de Hollande* (Paris, 1884), is inferior to Japikse's biography of De Witt. Johanna K. Oudendijk, *Willem III: Stadhouder van Holland, Koning van Engeland* (Amsterdam, 1954), which appeared after I had reached my own conclusions, gives a similar view of William to that adopted in this work. Simon Elzinga, *Het Voorspel van den Oorlog van 1672: De economisch-politieke betrekkingen tusschen Frankrijk en Nederland in de jaren 1660–1672* (Haarlem, 1926) is more valuable than the infrequency of references to it in the footnotes would indicate; because the thesis I adopted is at variance with Elzinga's, I re-examined and independently interpreted most of his material in this period.

Other works, primary and secondary in character, which are used only occasionally, are fully identified in the footnotes.

INDEX

Aire 69, 86.
Aix-la-Chapelle, treaty of, 1668 29, 34, 38, 39, 66, 69, 71, 79, 80, 95, 96, 99, 102, 108, 111, 112, 119, 120, 128, 131, 146, 148, 150, 161, 172, 173.
Algeria 11.
Alkmaar 182.
Alsace 12.
Amsterdam 1, 20, 21, 47, 53, 58, 89, 90, 97, 108, 137, 138, 150, 151, 161, 166, 182, 184, 187.
Andilly, Robert Arnauld, seigneur d' 4, 41.
Annat, François Canard, called Father 7.
Anne of Austria, queen-mother of France 5.
Antwerp 20, 42, 73, 85, 188.
Appelboom, Harald, Swedish diplomat 95, 101–106, 119.
Arlington, Henry Bennet, earl of 22, 23, 28, 29, 38, 81, 98, 124–129, 162.
Arnauld family 3, 7, 8.
Arnauld, Antoine, "*le grand*" 8, 40.
Arnauld, Antoine, abbé, Pomponne's brother 178.
Arnauld, Catherine Félicité 16, 41.
Arnauld, Simon Nicolas, see Pomponne.
Arundell, Henry Arundell, Baron Arundell of Wardour 127, 129.
Ath 131.
Aubéville, Nicolas de Sève d', French official 149.
Auersperg, Leopold count, Austrian official 110.
Austria 70, 112.
Austria, House of 99, 109.

Baltic region 186, 187.
Bargellini, Niccolò, papal nuncio 7.
Belt, the 7.
Bergen-op-Zoom 153, 172.
Bergues 38.
Bernarts, Pierre, French diplomat 43–46, 55, 56, 134, 141, 151, 170, 180, 182, 186.
Berni, Louis de Lionne, marquis de 10, 104, 126.
Beuningen, Coenraad van 21, 26–28, 31, 32, 34–37, 53–56, 59, 62, 64, 66, 70, 71, 89, 90, 110, 117, 124–126, 133, 134, 136, 137, 141, 143, 145, 147, 155, 158–160, 163, 164, 166, 185, 187–190, 194, 199.
Beverningk, Hieronymus van 53, 150, 155.
Biörnclou, Matthias, Swedish official 102.
Bonzy, Pierre de, archbishop of Toulouse, French diplomat 9, 32.
Boreel, Johan 111, 124, 125, 133, 141, 162–164, 166, 174.
Brabant 173.
Brandenburg 44, 108, 113, 119, 166, 200.
Breda 21, 123, 153.
Breda, treaty of, 1667 123, 127, 145, 181.
Bridgman, Sir Orlando 23, 123.
Britanny 174.
Brunswick-Lüneburg 91, 119, 166.
Brunswick-Lüneburg, ducal house of 44, 108, 113, 114, 169, 178.
Brussels 92, 99, 100, 102, 109, 173.
Bruynincx, Gerard Hamel 114.
Buckingham, George Villiers, duke of 127, 129, 132, 147, 159.
Burnet, bishop Gilbert 3, 50.

Cadzand 130, 132, 180.
Cambrai 69, 86, 92.
"Cantonment" of Spanish Netherlands 20, 60, 69, 70, 72, 74, 76–93, 139, 167.
Carlos II, king of Spain 21, 35, 64, 66, 72, 84–86, 90, 92, 93, 107, 132, 139, 149, 181, 183.
Casale 4.
Castel Rodrigo, Francisco de Moura, marquis of 27, 39, 61, 78.
Castille, Constable of, Don Iñigo Melchior Fernandez de Velasco y Tovar, duke of Frias 78–80, 87, 98–100, 109, 116.
Catalonia 5.
Catholicism, Roman 7, 8, 12, 33, 201.
Champagne 144.
Charente 174, 175.
Charles I, king of England 49.
Charles II, king of England 19, 22, 23, 32, 40, 54, 70, 81, 98, 111, 113, 122–126, 128–130, 133, 134, 136, 139, 141, 147–151, 153–156, 158, 159, 162, 164–166, 168–172, 174, 184, 198, 201.
Charles II, king of Spain, see Carlos II.
Charles III, duke of Mantua 5.
Charles IV, duke of Lorraine 39, 115–120, 144, 146, 149, 150, 154, 157.
Charles, prince of Lorraine 144, 157.
Choisy, Jean Paul de, French official 149.
Clarendon, Edward Hyde, earl of 201.
Clement IX, pope 7.
Colbert, Jean Baptiste 8, 9, 13, 14, 20, 27, 44, 104, 106, 131, 178, 185–196, 202.
Cologne 12, 113, 171.
Commons, House of 165.
Condé, town 38, 78, 80.
Condé, Louis II de Bourbon, prince de,

"le grand Condé" 27.
"Conseil d'en haut" 2, 10, 13, 16, 33.
Council of State, France 8.
Council of State, United Provinces 51, 57, 125, 136, 138, 171.
Courtin, Honoré 180.
Courtrai 42, 89, 126.
Créqui, François de Bonne, marquis de, French marshal 116, 144, 150.
Croissy, Charles Colbert, marquis de 9, 14–16, 32, 81, 88, 122, 123, 125, 128, 129, 134, 147, 158, 166.
Cromwell, Oliver 19.

Delft 138.
Denmark 106, 108, 119.
Deynze 42.
Dohna, Count Christopher von 24.
Dordrecht 47.
Dover 136, 148, 190.
Dover, treaty of, 1670 121–132, 134, 159, 162, 180, 190, 201.
Downing, Sir George 147.
Dunkirk 30, 38, 79, 166, 177, 178, 180, 182, 183.
Dutch war, see War of 1672.

East India Company, Dutch 141, 158, 189, 191.
East Indies 186, 189.
Empire, Holy Roman 113.
England 2, 21, 80, 83, 85, 88, 89, 91–93, 106, 121, 122, 153–156, 158–190, 198.
Estrades, Geffroi count d' 8, 20, 23, 24, 26, 28–30, 36, 44, 69, 79, 134, 135, 182, 183, 186.
"Eternal Edict", 1667 51, 54, 55.

Fagel, Caspar 28.
Feiling, Keith, English historian 3, 197.
Ferté-sous-Jouarre, La 6.
Feuquières, Isaac du Pas, marshal de 6.
Flanders, province of 9, 67, 69, 70, 72, 73, 77–79, 85, 88–90, 92, 106, 144, 148, 155, 158, 166, 177.
Flanders, French 41, 174.
Flanders, Spanish 92.
Flushing (Vlissingen) 52, 177, 180.
Fontainebleau, treaty of, France-United Provinces, 1662 20, 22, 31, 66, 98, 181, 193
Fouquet, Nicolas 5, 6
France, 2, 3, 7, 8 and *passim*.
Franche-Comté 14, 146.
Frederick Henry, prince of Orange 33, 49.
Frederick William II, elector of Brandenburg 2, 178, 179.
Friesland 43, 193.
Fronde 5.
Fürstenberg, Prince Wilhelm Egon von 21, 25, 107, 179.

Galen, Bernhard Christopher von, bishop of Münster 20, 86, 113, 169, 178.
Gamarra y Contreras, Don Estéban de, Spanish diplomat 66, 80, 97, 98, 104, 113, 116, 118, 119, 154.
Gardie, Magnus de la, Swedish official 96, 101, 102, 106.
Garonne 174.
"Gazette de Hollande" 9.
Gelderland 97, 193.
Gerbevillers, marquis de, Lorraine official 154.
Germany 12, 85, 89, 90, 100–121, 171, 179.
Geyl, Pieter, Dutch historian vii, 25.
Ghent 42, 62.
Goeree 132, 180.
Graeff, Andries de 53.
"Grand Alliance" 15.
Gravel, Robert de, French diplomat 62, 108, 114.
Grémonville, Jacques Bretel, chevalier de, French diplomat 46, 107, 109–114, 118, 200.
Groningen 138, 193.
Groot, Pieter de 30, 83, 90, 135, 141, 144, 145, 153, 154, 165, 170, 183, 191–194.

Haarlem 138.
Hague, The 1, 2, 8, 12, 22, 74, 76–78, 80, 89, 93, 94, 102, 105, 108, 113, 140, 150, 180, 181, 183, 193.
Hainaut 78.
Haine river 38.
Hamburg 10.
Hapsburg dynasty 33, 60.
Henrietta Maria, queen mother of England 138.
's-Hertogenbosch (Bois-le-Duc) 140, 153.
Holland, province 17, 47, 48, 54, 172, 182, 183, 192, 199.
Hooft, Cornelis 161, 162.
Höxter 169.
Huguenots 8, 33.
Huibert, Pieter de, Zeeland official 55.
Humières, Louis de Crévant, duke d', French marshal 79, 80.
Hungary 112.

Île de France 40.
Indies (see also East Indies and West Indies) 122, 124, 136, 147, 155, 191, 194.

James, duke of York (later James II) 8, 127, 129, 132, 169.
Jansenism 3, 4, 5, 7, 41.
Japikse, Nicolaas, Dutch historian 100, 136.
Jodoci, Johann Christoph, Mainz official 115.
"Joshua" medal 70, 72.

Königsmarck, Count Wilhelm Otto von, Swedish official 96, 102–105.
Kramprich, Daniel Johannes, imperial official 115.

Ladvocat, Charlotte 40, 42.
Ladvocat, Catherine 5.
La Fontaine, Jean de 160.
Lagny 6.
Leibniz, Baron Gottfried Wilhelm von 11.
Leopold I, emperor 27, 66, 68, 84, 107–109, 113, 156, 166, 171, 179.
Levant 186.
Liége, bishopric 117, 199
Liége, town 79.
Lille 38, 41, 42, 78, 79, 83, 89, 92, 93, 126, 131, 133, 153, 156, 161.
Linck 38.
Lionne, Hugues de 2, 6, 7, 9 and *passim*.
Lisola, François Paul baron de 33, 46, 62, 83, 99, 101, 108–115, 118, 119, 147, 148, 154, 156, 166.
Loire 174.
Lorraine 143–157.
Louis XIV, king of France 1, 2, 3, 6 and *passim*.
Louvestein castle 47.
Louvignies, Landat, baron de, Spanish general 116–119, 121, 146.
Louvois, François Michel le Tellier, marquis de 1, 10, 11–15, 27, 50, 79.
Low Countries, see Netherlands, Spanish.

Maastricht 89, 144, 145, 148, 153.
Madrid 79, 97, 173.
Madrid, council of 174.
Maintenon, Françoise d'Aubigné, marquise de 15.
Malagón, Don Balthazar de la Cueva y Henriquez, marquis of, Spanish diplomat 109.
Mantua 5.
Marie Thérèse, queen of France 21, 66, 84, 85, 87.
Mary, princess of Orange, wife of William II 49.
Maximilian Heinrich, archbishop of Cologne 171, 178.
Mazarin, Jules cardinal 5, 15, 16, 19, 44.
Marschalk, Jürgen, Swedish diplomat 96.
Medemblik 182, 183.
Meuse 118, 146.
Middelburg 52, 180.
Mocenigo, Pietro, Venetian diplomat 99, 124.
Monterey, Juan Domenic de Haro y Guzman, count of 173, 174
Münster 18, 169.
Muscovy 106.

Nantes 5.
Nassau, house of 49.
Netherlands, Spanish 8, 17–25, 66–68, 71, 77, 79, 83–85, 87, 89, 93, 95, 97, 99, 100, 107, 108, 128, 146, 149, 155, 161, 170, 183, 185, 188, 196, 199, 202.
Netherlands, United, see United Provinces.
Nieupoort 38.
Nijmegen (Nymwegen) 13, 14, 195.
Norway 199.

Oléron 174.
Orange, house of 19, 49.
Orange, principality 49.
Orangists 19, 21, 24, 53, 57, 90, 164, 183.
Orléans, Henriette-Marie, duchess of 125, 126, 128, 129, 133–136, 148, 159.
Orléans, Philip, duke of 14, 131.
Overijssel 172, 193.

Pagès, Georges, French historian 2, 200.
Paris 5, 6.
"Peace of the Church" 7.
Peletier, Claude le 6, 16.
Philip IV, king of Spain 19.
Picardy 41.
Poitou 174.
Poland 9, 121.
Pomponne, Simon Nicolas Arnauld, marquis de 2, 3, 4 and *passim*.
Port-Royal 5.
Portugal 199.
Protestantism 12, 169.
Pufendorf, Esaias von, Swedish diplomat 123.
Purmerend 182.
Pyrenees, treaty of, 1659 19, 150.

Quesnoy, Le 79.

Regensburg (Ratisbon) 62, 109.
Rhine 85, 107, 115, 118, 146.
Rhineland 12, 120, 170, 171, 199.
Richelieu, Armand du Plessis, cardinal de 4, 15, 45.
Rijswijk (Ryswick) 17.
Risaucourt, François de, Lorraine official 118–121, 146, 149, 154.
Rome 4.
Rotterdam 43, 182, 193.
Rousseau de Chamoy, Louis, French diplomat 96, 101–103, 106.
Rumpf, Christiaan, Dutch diplomat 192.
Ruvigny, Henri de Massue, marquis de 22, 28, 29, 122, 127.
Ruyter, Michiel de 149, 174, 175.

Saar 118, 146.
Saint-Albans, Henry Jermyn, earl of 129.
Saint-Cloud 135.
Saint-Germain 8, 10, 27, 30, 33, 102, 191.

Saint-Sébastien 144.
Saint-Nicolas, abbey of 61.
Saint-Omer 69, 86.
Saintonge 174.
Sambre 146.
Scheldt 20, 38, 42, 130.
Schönborn, Johann Philipp von, elector of Mainz 113–115, 118, 166, 200.
Scotland 79.
Sluis 130, 132, 180, 182.
Sound, The, straits 7, 199.
Sourches, Louis François de Bouchet, marquis de 17.
Spain 9, 12 and *passim*.
States General 8, 11, 19–22, 24, 26, 58, 71, 73, 88–143, 168, 173, 192.
States of Holland 24, 26, 48, 137, 150, 165, 187, 190, 192, 195.
States (republican) party 19, 47.
Stockholm 7, 9, 10, 81, 95, 102, 104–106, 178, 179, 184.
Strafford, Thomas Wentworth, earl of 201.
Stuart dynasty 19.
Sublime Porte 199.
Surinam 158.
Sweden, 2, 7, 8 and *passim*.
Switzerland 108.

Tarento, Henri Charles de la Trémoïlle, prince of 140, 143.
Tasso, Torquato 173, 174
Tellier, Michel le 4–8, 10, 104, 131, 178.
Temple, Sir William 21–24, 27, 46, 64, 80, 81, 100, 104, 105, 110, 111, 113, 119, 122–124, 126, 145, 147, 148, 153, 161.
Thames 175.
Thou, Jacques Auguste de, French diplomat 43.
Torcy, Jean Baptiste Colbert, marquis de 16, 17.
Tournai 131, 180.
Trier 115, 118, 166.
Triple Alliance, 1668 2, 8, 9, 18–29, 59, 61, 63, 69, 73, 74, 77–82, 85, 90, 92, 93, 95–98, 100–102, 107, 108, 110–112, 115, 116, 118, 120, 122–125, 128, 131, 140, 145, 146, 150, 153, 164, 165, 200.
Turenne, Henri de la Tour d'Auvergne, vicomte de 6, 8, 12, 27, 33, 35, 36, 38–40, 53, 123, 129, 131, 140.
Tuscany 121.

United Provinces 1, 2, 8, 11 and *passim*.
Utrecht 193.

Valckenier, Gillis 53, 54, 137, 161, 162.
Veere 52.
Verberie 144.
Verdun 6.
Versailles 13, 164.
Vienna 109, 111, 112.
Vlie 184.
Voorne 132, 180.

Walcheren 130, 132, 180.
War, first Anglo-Dutch 19.
War, second Anglo-Dutch 21, 35, 82, 130, 147.
West Friesland 47.
West Indies 186, 189.
Westphalia 119.
Wicquefort, Abraham de 31–34, 38, 43–47, 135, 192, 194.
William I, prince of Orange 49, 138.
William II, prince of Orange 19, 47, 49.
William III, prince of Orange 12, 14, 15, 22, 40, 49, 50, 82, 92, 125, 136–139, 151, 154, 158, 161–164, 168–171, 183, 201, 202.
Windisch-Grätz, Gottlieb count, imperial diplomat 154, 156, 157.
Witt, Cornelius de 12, 184.
Witt, Jacob de 47.
Witt, Johan de 12, 14, 19 and *passim*.
Wotton, Sir Henry, English diplomat 3.

Zeeland 21, 54, 56, 176, 183, 193, 199.
Zeeland, States of 52.
Zuyder Zee 47.